THE THIRTY-SIXTH WAY

THE THIRTY-SIXTH WAY

A PERSONAL ACCOUNT OF
IMPRISONMENT AND ESCAPE
FROM RED CHINA

BY LAI YING

TRANSLATED, ADAPTED AND EDITED BY

EDWARD BEHR AND SYDNEY LIU

GARDEN CITY, NEW YORK

DOUBLEDAY & COMPANY, INC.

1969

Library of Congress Catalog Card Number 75–78740

Copyright © 1969 by Lai Ying, Edward Behr, Sydney Liu

Printed in the United States of America

First Edition

THIS BOOK IS DEDICATED

TO THE MEMORY

OF ALL CHINA'S POLITICAL PRISONERS,

PAST AND PRESENT,

TO THOSE WHO MANAGED TO ESCAPE

AND TO ALL THOSE WHO ARE STILL CAUGHT.

CONTENTS

THE
THIRTY-
SIXTH
WAY

OF THE THIRTY-SIX WAYS

OF AVOIDING DISASTER,

RUNNING AWAY IS BEST.

(*old Chinese proverb*)

INTRODUCTION

by Edward Behr

EVERY TIME THE scheduled program of the French TV network breaks down, they bring out a hoary old thriller called *Macao, l'enfer du jeu* starring Erich Von Stroheim, which some assiduous TV viewers, in France, claim to have seen some twenty-eight times. Shot in French studios with wavering backdrops representing a curious "Chinese" background, the film contains nothing of any interest whatsoever except for one comic passage where the inimitable Von Stroheim, immaculate in white ducks, says in his heavy Prusso-New York accent: *"Vous avez pris livraison des mitrailleuses?"* (You have received the shipment of machine guns?)

I didn't expect to see Erich Von Stroheim on my first visit to Macao, but, conditioned by its reputation, I didn't, either, expect the gentle, Mediterranean seediness which pervades the minuscule Portuguese colony. A bored hydrofoil crew shuttles across the straits of the China Sea several times daily. The passengers are nondescript, respectable-looking Hongkong Chinese—or not so respectable-looking Hongkong bar girls off to gamble at the Macao casinos; the streets of Macao are sepia picture postcards of the French Riviera at the turn of the century. The streets are cobbled, the architecture rococo-flamboyant, the atmosphere sleepy and the whole place redolent of a forgotten colonial enclave. *"Noticias"* are in Portuguese, and a striking statue graced the main square in front of the post office—until the Macao Communists tore it down in a fit of collective rage and Maoist zeal in 1967. One couldn't really blame them: it was an unspeakable outrage, artistically speaking.

Most of the literature on Macao dates mainly from the immediate post-World War II years, when the whole place was, according to those who knew it then, a den of vice. But S. J. Perelman, writing in 1949, said after visiting the place that Macao was just about as exciting as Glasgow on a Sunday morning—and personally I have always felt that its sinister reputation must have been undeserved. After the Communist takeover of China in 1949, Macao lost whatever trappings of vice still clung to it.

Communist influence in Macao had been strong (today the Communists are the de facto rulers of the colony, the Portuguese governor merely the puppet ruler, left in place because it is more convenient to the Communists that way) and they did their best to clean it up. Gone are the brothels and opium dens; the gambling casinos have all the glamor of the Cedar Rapids YMCA; the Central Hotel (where once each floor was given over to girls of different nationalities and where, according to one veteran, they got younger and younger as you climbed from floor to floor) was closed in 1967 and only reopened in 1969. Fear of Communist demonstrations in Macao has sorely depleted its one resource —tourism. Hardy bands of Japanese still arrive for the day, however, bunched around their leader, clasping flags with the emblem of their particular group so that they will not get lost. Communist youths in Macao regard all tourists with cameras as potential spies. Their main purpose in life seems to be to bully travelers into surrendering their rolls of film—or at any rate, rolls of film impregnated with images, however innocent, of Communist posters or youth groups. Since both are constant features of Macao street scenes, the visitor is well advised not to take any pictures whatsoever.

But Macao is not just comic-opera Communism under the trappings of Portuguese rule. It is a neglected but fascinating twilight zone, and the closest most tourists of this decade will get to Communist China. For the Chinese, there is in fact no "iron curtain" between either Hongkong and Macao and the mainland. Every week, a battered passenger boat leaves Macao's shallow, colorful but dingy harbor for Canton, and daily there's a bus, crossing the frontier with all the routine of a well-worn public service. The driver and the ticket collector are middle-aged, uncommunicative, and uninterested. The passengers are, like all Chinese about to visit China, dressed with deliberate emphasis to look poor and to avoid ostentation. They carry bundles with them to give as gifts to relatives on the other side of the border— detergent powders, liquid soaps, T-shirts and assorted wonders of the capitalist world. They, too, are not communicative about life on the other side of the frontier. For the police on the Chinese side are thorough, and the amount of information collected by Communist sources about individuals living in Macao is prodigious.

Spy mania, on the Communist Chinese side, amounts to a collective, quasi-national obsession. Those crossing into China had better have a valid reason for going there—for one can be sure that each traveler is known to the authorities of the province of Kwangtung—and anyone pretending to visit his family and actually just wandering around the countryside would almost certainly be held for questioning on his return to Macao. Similarly, all Chinese nationals boarding the bus on the Chinese side of the frontier —Macao-bound—are carefully and thoroughly checked by the police. The Macao-based staff operating the bus are themselves vetted by the Communists and considered reliable enough not to attempt to smuggle either information or people out of China in their vehicle. Chinese police and militiamen closely guard the road it takes, and in more general terms, no one on the Chinese side of the border near Macao is allowed to live there unless he, too, is considered "reliable." Among the local villagers and fishermen, there is a high proportion of tough, indoctrinated ex-servicemen, who are daily reminded that their chief task is to keep a lookout for spies, defectors and illicit refugees. The capture of any such people leads to material rewards.

A privileged elite, however, still travels relatively freely between Macao and mainland China—though rarely by bus. These are the businessmen (some of them millionaires), the functionaries and the leaders of the Communist apparatus in Macao. Best known is a stocky, gold-toothed businessman called Ho Yin, who enjoys the best of both worlds. Ho Yin has both Portuguese and Chinese passports. He has all the trappings of the pre-Communist old-style Chinese patriarch—concubines, a large court of retainers and hangers-on, a smart "official" wife with a considerable reputation as a former opera singer, a large secluded house discreetly guarded by his own bodyguards, and a humble, self-deprecating manner. Several times a year, Ho Yin discards his Western dress and dons the high-collar cotton uniform of the Chinese Communist official. He sits, in Peking, in the People's Assembly—as the representative of overseas Chinese. He is entertained by leading members of the regime and has been granted frequent audience with Mao Tse-tung himself.

Ho Yin belongs to a species which has almost completely died out in today's China—though a few are allowed to survive and are produced periodically for propaganda purposes. (In Shanghai a capitalist "millionaire" lives in bourgeois splendor, with servants and even a Jaguar 2.4 limousine—and his sole purpose, one suspects, is to give interviews to Western journalists—or at any rate to that tiny handful of journalists occasionally allowed into China on rigidly guided tours. In 1965 and '66, several TV crews were allowed into China, and the Shanghai millionaire, complete with Jaguar, figured in all their documentaries.) In Macao the Communists find it convenient to run the place from within, using their own key men. Ho Yin is their number one man, and he is probably their most valuable representative there, for he owns much of Macao—and, as an honest broker for the Communist regime, he uses much of his wealth both to finance Communist activities in Macao itself and to remit hard currency to mainland China.

The list of Ho Yin's Macao holdings is almost endless; he owns nearly all the colony's hotels and restaurants, all the movie theaters, the local taxi company, a great many houses and apartment buildings, most of the big shops, and operates, though he does not wholly own, the main trading company importing cheap goods from China. He also controls building and dredging companies, and owns the leading bank in Macao. But his chief claim to fame is that he is the sole importer, licensed by the Portuguese Government, of gold.

Macao is, as far as gold is concerned, a free trading zone. The shipment of gold to Macao, through Hongkong, is in the hands of three old-established Hongkong bullion firms. Anyone may freely buy gold in Macao—but the re-export of gold from Macao is rigidly controlled. What happens to the tons of gold which come into Macao yearly is still something of a mystery: the bars are melted down and reshaped into tiny bite-sized slivers, easily transportable, and then smuggled out of Macao all over Southeast Asia, wherever currencies are shaky. This trade in gold—some of it, the importing part, legal—is largely under Ho Yin's supervision. He pays a huge yearly sum to the Portuguese Government for the importing franchise; he alone knows where the gold eventually ends up, and to what purpose. Variously, experts and investigators have concluded that the gold is shipped illicitly to mainland China, where it helps to strengthen Peking's gold reserves (a weak theory, this, for when the Chinese Government decides to buy gold, it does so openly on the London or Swiss markets); or that it's used to finance a world-wide drug traffic with the ultimate aim of turning all Americans into junkies, thus ensuring China's ultimate world victory (an attractive theory, but not taken seriously by China experts, though it would provide good raw material for an eventual thriller); or again that it's used to finance subversive activities all over Asia and Africa, which is possible. The more serious investigators, however, feel that the least spectacular explanation is the likeliest: the slivers of gold are sold to hoarders who, all over Asia, rightly distrust their paper monies—the profit on such deals going partly to Ho Yin and partly reverting to the Chinese Government.

Macao's other interest is as a vital, if minor, source of news about China. All "China-watchers," as they're called in the news business jargon, normally live in nearby Hongkong—apart from a handful of frustrated correspondents resident in Peking, who owe their permission to live inside China merely to the Chinese Government's need to maintain its own correspondents abroad. The system functions on a crude reciprocity basis. (Currently only a few Japanese correspondents and a skeleton staff of Soviets and East Europeans remain; the French correspondent of AFP, the French news agency, has been expelled and the British correspondent of Reuters is under house arrest.) The sources available to Hongkong-based China-watchers are, in descending order of usefulness, the mainland press, radio monitoring organizations and visitors or defectors leaving China. As Hongkong bureau chief of *Newsweek,* part of my job was to report on the convulsions rocking China from 1966 onwards. Like all Hongkong China-watchers I felt sometimes that trying to get at what was happening in China, to find a shaft of truth, was like looking for a needle, blindfolded and with both hands inside a paper bag, in a continent-sized haystack.

This is not the place to talk about the difficulties of reporting on Chinese affairs—and the handful of correspondents in Peking itself have an even more thankless task. The job has been a difficult one since 1956, and it has been getting more difficult every year. Only four years ago, it was possible, both in Peking and in Hongkong, to obtain a wide range of provincial and party papers, and careful reading of these apparently similar organs occasionally brought to light differences between them which, carefully analyzed, led to important discoveries. The method remains—more akin to cryptography than to straightforward journalism—but the tools of the China-watcher's trade have been restricted: first, by the Chinese ban on the export, or even the sale, of all but "authorized" papers, and especially by the spy mania, which, carried to its absurd conclusion, forbids journalists from even reading wall posters and threatens direst penalties for anyone volunteering information of any kind to strangers. The result is that wall posters, Red Guard newspapers and scraps of leaflets smuggled out of

China sell briskly in Hongkong at anything up to twenty-five dollars a page, and, naturally, unscrupulous dealers have been accused of fabricating them. Inevitably, too, the professional tipsters have come into their own, peddling information to please their prospective clients. The further away from the Chinese border, the more such snippets of fake news gather fake authenticity. I have seen a proven false rumor spread by a known, and mercenary, professional tipster headlined in Australian, New Zealand and, perhaps inevitably, Taiwan papers. This, then, is merely a parenthesis to say that experienced China-watchers are constantly aware that their legs are liable to be pulled, and are, consequently, suspicious of publicity-seeking "defectors."

Newsweek's expert on Chinese affairs, Sydney Liu, himself a veteran mainland editor, was the assorted China-watchers' best detective. Colleagues had a habit of referring all doubtful cases to him. With infinite patience, and drawing on his own immense fund of knowledge, Sydney Liu could, at the end of several hours grueling cross-examination, usually ascertain the value, and the reality, of alleged claims of those with sensational stories to tell. For the truth is that though a trickle of defectors still gets through, the really important ones have every reason to stay away from the press—usually because personalities remaining behind on the mainland could be compromised if they were to tell how they got away. Additionally, both the British and United States intelligence organizations shield the truly important defectors from contact with the press. An outstanding defector with a sensational story to tell can be "milked" for days or even weeks by an enterprising journalist. But afterwards, his usefulness over, he tends to be dropped by the wayside. In the hands of an intelligence agency, however, a valuable defector—i.e., one who can materially contribute through his experience and knowledge to the body of knowledge about China—can be of value for months if not years. Moreover, unlike the reporter or newspaper editor, who at best can offer only money as an incentive to talk, the intelligence agency can offer something far more valuable—political asylum, a passport and eventually a new nationality and even a new identity. Thus it is that of the handful of Chinese diplomats and officers who escaped in recent years, all chose to lose their old identities and acquire new ones. At least one is the prosperous owner of a successful Chinese restaurant in Manhattan—and he has become more American, in a few years, than most of his clients. He sleeps, however, with a revolver under his pillow.

So, by and large, the reporter can only hope to contact the defectors from China who are not considered sufficiently significant by either the British or United States intelligence organizations. Thus, the people who escape to Hongkong and to Macao from neighboring Kwangtung Province tend to tell the same story; they are almost always peasants from communal farms, with no knowledge of general conditions prevailing in China. They do provide a fascinating bird's-eye view of life in Kwangtung Province, but, inevitably, theirs is part of a repetitive story. Moreover, these are mostly simple people, often illiterate. They are not trained observers—why should they be?—and they themselves tend to confuse fact and rumor, what has happened to them and what they have been told about others.

This does not mean that their stories are valueless. But it does tend to mean that the grievances, the regimentation and general tedium of those subjected to collective life on communal farms in Kwangtung soon become well known. The interest of such defectors lies in the degree to which their stories can be cross-checked, and in the differing pictures given of the same area. A great deal of valuable information concerning the failures of the "Great Leap Forward" (1959–62) was accumulated thanks to the thousands of refugees who poured into Hongkong during that time. The gradually improving picture in China was also partly charted thanks to refugees in succeeding months and years—for people do not only pull up stakes and leave when conditions are at their worst. From them, for instance, one could learn that the policy—banned during the Great Leap Forward—of allowing farmers a proportion of private land for their own cultivation and private livestock as well—produce from both to be sold at "free" prices—was gradually back in operation; from them, too, it was established as an incontrovertible fact that peasants' money incomes, in Kwangtung Province and probably in the rest of the prosperous rural Chinese areas, were steadily increasing from 1963 onwards; and from them we learnt that "thought control" and regimentation were becoming, if anything, laxer from 1962 to the outbreak of the "Cultural Revolution" of 1966. Such trends were not precise studies, accomplished by sociologists with firsthand material. Rather, they were rough-and-ready estimates made on the basis of hundreds of questioning sessions with refugees. They all had their value—but few could be said to be of sensational character.

Then came the Cultural Revolution and the questioning of refugees took on a new and more urgent purpose. When the revolution began, the initial impression—and a correct one on the part of most China-watchers—was one of extreme confusion. At first, reports indicated that the Cultural Revolution was in essence a power struggle at the top, involving Liu Shao-chi, the Chairman; Peng Chen, the powerful mayor of Peking; and Mao himself. More about the Cultural Revolution later on; the important consequence—and the reason this book exists at all—lay in the impact of the Cultural Revolution on ordinary people—and the consequent new influx of refugees into Hongkong and Macao.

Traditionally, Hongkong and Macao have had basically different approaches in their attitudes towards refugees. The British one is perhaps rooted in the elemental, essentially British characteristic of viewing life, and all forms of physical endeavor, as a kind of game. In practical terms, the Hongkong Government's attitude towards refugees is as follows: all along the Hongkong-China border and in Hongkong waters, the apprehension of refugees is regarded as fair game—and such refugees are almost always returned to Chinese frontier authorities. (The exceptions are, of course, the "interesting" catches, who can look forward to almost automatic asylum.) But if the refugees manage to evade immediate capture, and successfully make their way into the New Territories and Kowloon, evading the police posts in the no man's land between China and the Hongkong enclave, they are almost certain to find some kind of haven. After a time, identity cards are issued, and the only danger facing them is extradition—used only as a last resort against proven Communist agitators.

The Portuguese attitude towards refugees was—until April 1967—a far more humane one. The Portuguese Government did not turn back refugees who managed to cross over into Portuguese territory—and after a routine fifteen days, refugees were granted temporary identity cards, which in time were exchanged for permanent ones. With such identity cards, refugees could proceed to Hongkong, but only for limited, three-weekly periods (no Macao refugees could settle permanently in Hongkong without proving either former residence or close family connections there). Unlike the British authorities, the Portuguese seldom, if ever, questioned refugees at length, but on the contrary affected a complete lack of curiosity as to their status or previous role in Chinese society. Unscrupulous smugglers quite frequently brought Macao refugees into Hongkong illegally, for fees varying, according to the season and the severity of customs guards, from $150 to

$250.* These "snakeboats," as they are called, were in the habit of dumping the would-be émigrés anywhere along the wharves of the Hongkong-Kowloon harbor during the night. If the landings were successful, the refugees just melted into the Hongkong ant hill, found jobs and settled down—taking care to stay out of trouble. The absence of jobs in Macao explained the eagerness of Macao refugees to make it as far as Hongkong. The worst that could happen to those apprehended in the act of trying to enter the colony illegally was deportation back to Macao.

But in December 1966, Macao itself was the scene of prolonged local Communist agitation which nearly put an end to the administration of the colony and left the Portuguese governor, as noted, a mere puppet in the hands of the powerful local Communist groups. Among other humiliating concessions made to the Macao Communists in March 1967 was the abrogation of previous rules concerning refugees. From March 1967 onwards, the governor pledged himself to turn over to Chinese border authorities all refugees entering Macao—and the Macao authorities have loyally fulfilled this dreadful condition. Understandably the influx of refugees into Macao has thinned to a tiny trickle as the news has spread, on the Chinese side of the border, of the new regulations in force there. But in September 1966—when I first met Lai Ying—the odds were more favorable for refugees attempting to flee China to Macao than to Hongkong. And it was with the vague intention of trying to make contact with recent refugees from mainland China that one Monday in September 1966 Sydney Liu and I found ourselves in Macao, shortly after the start of the Cultural Revolution.

On Monday morning, our local Macao correspondent told us that a batch of refugees was believed to have arrived that very day, or perhaps on the previous Sunday. He was not clear whether they had arrived by boat, but had heard that a small group of people had been picked up in an exhausted condition near one of the beaches. We immediately went round to the Casa Ricci, a Catholic organization set up to help refugees and destitute people in Macao, run by an admirable Jesuit priest, Father Ruiz.† The father confirmed that several refugees had arrived, and indeed had just reported to his headquarters after being questioned and proc-

---

* The amounts are expressed in Chinese (Jenminpao) dollars unless specifically referred to. One Chinese dollar (JMP) equals 47½ U.S. cents.
† Father Ruiz has since left Macao to take up an appointment in the Vatican.

essed by the local police. "You'll find them quite interesting," he said. "A rather unusual bunch—a cellist, a quack and a girl, a painter, I believe."

We drove to the refugee "village"—actually a converted playground in the center of town—and there Sydney Liu and I were introduced to Lai Ying and to three other people. It was lunchtime, and Father Ruiz had work to do back at the Casa Ricci. On my suggestion, the rest of us went off to lunch together.

In two taxis, we drove to a well-known Cantonese restaurant on Macao's main square and demanded a private room. (The restaurant, I discovered later, belonged to Ho Yin, the Communist millionaire businessman.) Sydney Liu ordered a succession of dishes. Soon, Lai Ying, obviously the spokesman of the group, began talking. She was, I remember, dressed in clothing provided by the Jesuits—dark blue cotton trousers, almost certainly from the Chinese "Communist store" (which undercuts every other shop in Macao), and a rather coarse white shirt. She was thin, with deep lines around her mouth, sunburnt and looked older than her twenty-eight years. Her forearms were bruised and scratched. Short, with broad shoulders and hair drawn back into a bun, she looked immensely tough, but when she smiled her face registered relief, tenderness and exhaustion. She frequently consulted the young man sitting next to her before answering our questions. She ate delicately, in contrast to the rest of the party. Everyone was quite obviously famished.

I was immediately struck by Lai Ying's powers of observation. Earlier, I had been intrigued by the descriptions we had heard in Hongkong of people forced to march through the streets of Canton with infamous painted slogans hung around their necks. Had Lai Ying seen any? She replied that one of her friends had been paraded through the Canton streets in this fashion. What did the boards look like? She took my pencil and neatly drew on the paper tablecloth to show how the slogans were painted on two boards, back and front, rather like those of a sandwich man but smaller, across one's chest and back.

It was during this lunch that we discovered just how unusual a bunch Lai Ying and her fellow refugees were. Lai Ying's own background—as a painter—immediately made her of more than routine interest. It was only later that we learned of her prison past and the real identities of her companions, for along with nearly all refugees, they had told the Portuguese police on arrival that they were "unemployed" or "peasants"—partly to conceal their real identities and partly to stay out of trouble by conforming to the norm, which becomes second nature to all Chinese nationals under the present regime.

After lunch Lai Ying and her three companions returned to the refugee center to rest (they explained that they hadn't had a real night's sleep since their escape began three weeks previously), but we saw them all again at length several times during the week. Lai Ying, who had an aunt in Macao, soon left the refugee center to live with this rather formidable, strait-laced old lady. In a week, Lai Ying was transformed from a tough, rather tomboyish figure into an attractive young woman. Her manner became easier: at our first meeting, in the restaurant, she had continuously looked over her shoulder to see whether she was being observed; after a week in Macao she was no longer afraid. But it was some time before she opened up to the extent of revealing crucial details about her own past. It was with considerable surprise that I learnt, a week or two after meeting her, that Lai Ying's own parents actually lived in Hongkong and were about to come over to see her. With the caution of someone who has been fighting a police state system all her adult life, Lai Ying had waited to see whether Macao was really "safe" before announcing her return to her parents. She was also concerned with the possibility of recapture. Macao, with its Communist bookshops and portraits of Mao, was a strange "colony" to come back to. Sydney Liu said she would be safe so long as she refrained from entering into argument with anyone, no matter how provoked, and so long as she stayed away from certain buildings, housing Communist officials and bodyguards.

In the next few weeks, Sydney Liu and I returned regularly to Macao to see Lai Ying. In the course of meetings with her (usually in a friend's house), we learnt that she had spent five years in jail and various "corrective" labor camps; and that she was married. Though Lai Ying never, in those first few weeks, complained that we were pestering her unnecessarily, she did seem puzzled, or at any rate amused, by some of our questions. To me the sessions were invaluable: I had done my stint of reporting on Chinese affairs, and had been to China for two months in 1964, but I had never, until then, realized what living in China meant for millions of ordinary people. It was not that Lai Ying was consumed with hatred at the extent of Chinese totalitarian control over her people. She was remarkably devoid of passion, and to a certain extent fatalistic, about her past. Above all, hers was the resignation and

patience of one who has been through the mill of Chinese bureaucracy and who knows that one's only chance of salvation is to
inhibit one's natural reactions and display immense self-control.

Lai Ying also exhibited a characteristic Chinese reserve: it was
a long time, for example, before she talked freely about her broken
marriage to the ambitious young doctor who, head over heels in
love, had expected that he would be able to "reform" her—
ideologically speaking; it was even longer before we realized that,
to escape, she had made the most hideous sacrifice any woman
can make—that of leaving a baby daughter behind. Many people
may criticize Lai Ying for this. It seems, on the face of it, an un-
natural and callous gesture. Yet it has to be seen in its context:
as Lai Ying told us much later, she knew that as far as she was
concerned, the Cultural Revolution meant her rearrest in a matter
of weeks or perhaps days and another spell in labor camps, from
which, this time, she might not emerge alive. In any case, she
argued, her daughter would not know a "normal" family existence, and would in all likelihood be placed in a home for orphans
if she were arrested, a home which would never open its doors to
the visits of a "counterrevolutionary" mother. And if this occurred, her daughter, in the monstrous Old Testament fashion
which is current in Communist China, would be branded all *her*
life as the daughter of a counterrevolutionary, just as Lai Ying
herself was branded, through no fault of her own, as the daughter of bourgeois landlords. (The fact that her family kept its head
above the poverty water line with great difficulty and through hard
manual work was of no concern to the Communist authorities,
and never is, for it is the "class origins" that count: no Calvinists
were ever more rigorous, intransigent or complacent about their
own "salvation.")

Lai Ying's reserve extended, also, to her relations with Hsu,
the young man who organized the escape, took part in it and
without whom Lai Ying would certainly not have left Canton.
Though Lai Ying claimed that Hsu meant nothing to her, it was
clear to me that they were lovers. And it is probable that they
began being lovers while both were still in the New Life labor
camp, as far back as 1963. Lai Ying was then a part of the
camp's entertainment troupe, and Hsu, also undergoing "reform,"
played the cello, violin and flute in the troupe's orchestra. Lai
Ying spells out in this book in some amused detail how the various
members of this somewhat privileged outfit within an immense
concentration camp managed to evade their guards' supervision

and have normal sex relations, despite the penalties involved if they were found out. But she remained mute about her own experiences and no amount of discreet probing enabled us to find out anything about her "private life" during the time she was in the New Life camp. This reserve, however natural under the circumstances, made the final editing of the book a long-drawn-out process.

To conclude, I should make it clear that Lai Ying was, at first, extremely unwilling to give a written account of her experiences in China. Like most refugees, all she wanted was a peaceful life in an atmosphere of freedom—"All I want," as she put it to me one day, "is to be forgotten." At first, it seemed as though she would never be won round. Then we put it to her that writing about her experiences would be a form of catharsis. She found she was brooding about her seven "wasted years," as she called them, and began, back in Hongkong, having nightmares, insomnia and quarrels with members of her family. All this, Sydney Liu suggested, might end if she wrote those wasted years out of her system. But having obtained Lai Ying's consent, we then had to obtain that of her family. Lai Ying's mother, like Lai Ying herself, a strong-willed, determined woman, was most unwilling to see her daughter make her experiences public. Her argument was that her own family unit, close-knit and resilient after decades of crisis, wars and finally the Communist takeover of 1949, would be threatened if her daughter revealed what had happened to her after her arrest. "There are many, many Communists in Hongkong," Lai Ying's mother said, "and we will no longer be safe." Finally, after much persuasion, her family agreed. The conditions made were reasonable, and have been strictly adhered to; they were that names should be changed so that nobody back in China should be easily identifiable, and that Lai Ying herself should approve of the final manuscript—which, since Lai Ying writes English with difficulty, but reads it fluently, was no problem.

—E.B.

CHAPTER I

STRANGERS ON A TRAIN

MY FOUR DAYS in Canton hadn't been very happy or satisfactory ones, and I was glad to be on the train again, on my way back to Hongkong, where I lived, and to my large, noisy and sometimes overprotective and over-affectionate family. Like all Chinese trains, this one was exceedingly slow, and since I was familiar with all the many stops along this five-hour journey (for I had been to Canton before), I spent most of my time on the hard bench daydreaming. I was twenty, and had discovered only recently that along with much enthusiasm for painting and drawing, I had a modicum of talent—enough, at any rate, to make recognizable portraits of friends and faithful reproductions of landscapes and *natures mortes*. Most of my spare time, when I was not teaching small children in a private school or studying, I spent painting and drawing, and I was grateful to my family for taking this passion seriously. I knew that I wanted to be an artist, and I had only recently discovered that people liked me, although I was not beautiful in a willowy, delicate way, as Hongkong's film stars are. I had always thought of myself as something of a tomboy; at sports, I had always outshone most boys of my own age, and staggered friends by my capacity for swimming for hours on end. Hongkong's swimming athletes are among the finest in the world, and I had been flattered by offers to join a swimming club and train seriously. Only an inherent laziness—and a general dislike of organized groups—had prevented me from doing so. Whatever thoughts I had on the train that day, politics were not among them. Of all the travelers, I was perhaps the most apolitical, the least involved in Communism or the Cold War. As I sat in the crowded train, without a care in the world, a large but efficient apparatus had me in its grip. Starting out of my daydream, and only half hearing my name being spoken, I looked up to see a large uniformed guard, impersonal yet authoritative, repeating in Cantonese a phrase: "The railroad superintendent," he repeated, "would like a word with you."

I stood up, uncertain whether to follow the beckoning guard or not. He pointed to the suitcase on the rack above me. "You'd better take it with you," he said. "The train's crowded and you might lose it." A sea of faces was obscuring the scene. Did anyone watching me realize what was taking place? The procedure, in retrospect, was undramatic, and accomplished without fuss, probably with a smoothness due to long practice. But my fellow travelers were perhaps more skilled at detecting hidden drama than I, the object of their attention. Expressions varied from hostility to intense covert curiosity, but in those few seconds, when we both stood, the guard and I, swaying as the train chugged along towards the border, I could see, with growing apprehension, that the dominant fear of the people around me was that they might be involved in something unpleasant themselves. A man whispered to his neighbor, and pointed. As if in a trance, I picked up my suitcase and followed the guard through the train.

At the very end of the train there was an empty compartment and from its vaguely official appearance—papers and forms on a small table, a spare uniform hanging on the wall—I realized it must be the office of the superintendent. The guard showed me in. I sat alone, expecting someone to come and look at my ticket, but no one did. Then, with a screech of brakes and a shudder, the train came to a sudden stop. The door opened, and someone in uniform shouted: "Off the train, quickly."

I should have realized at this stage that I was in real trouble, but still I believed that everything would sort itself out. "What's the matter? I have a ticket." No one answered. "It's perfectly in order. Look: it says April nine, nineteen fifty-eight. I have to be in Hongkong tonight because I have classes tomorrow."

A guard, as impersonal as the first one, had entered the compartment, picked up my suitcase and was taking it off the train. I followed him mainly because I didn't want to part with the suitcase. As he clambered down the steps he talked over his shoulder. "There are just a few questions we want you to answer. When everything has been cleared up, we'll give you a new ticket to Hongkong." Reassured in part by this, I got off the train. It was only then that I realized that we had halted between stations. I was standing on a culvert, near a road. All around were the lush green fields of Kwangtung Province. Standing beside the track was a reception committee of three: a stern-looking woman with spectacles and close-cropped hair, a typical party cadre; a pale, moon-faced middle-aged man in a creased yellow uniform; and a thin, austere-looking individual in a white sports shirt and gray slacks. The uniformed guard, still carrying my suitcase, was beckoning impatiently. "This way. There's a car. Get going," he said. The train creakily got under way. Could I have been the sole reason for its stopping in the first place? As in a dream I watched it gather speed.

All of a sudden I was very frightened, and felt my legs trembling. I nearly fell, but in a voice which I deliberately tried to keep as casual as possible, I heard myself ask: "What on earth is all this about? What do you want with me?" Nobody said anything, but one member of the group pointed to a car drawn up on the side of the road some twenty yards away. It was black, brand-new, with curtains of some thick blue material covering all the side and rear windows. They made me enter first. The woman cadre, the moon-faced man in uniform, the civilian and I all squeezed into the rear seat. The tall guard put my suitcase in the rear of the car and sat up front, along with the driver and one other person. Without a word, the driver started the car and drove off at high speed along the way I had come, back to Canton.

To this day I have not the slightest idea what prompted my arrest on the train. I had gone to Canton to attend the funeral of an elderly aunt who had begged me, in a series of letters, to visit her before, as she put it, "it is too late." But in the light of the charges against me made in repeated interrogations over the days and months that followed, I should at this point, to put this story in perspective, give the salient details of my life up to the day of my arrest, on April 9, 1958.

I was no newcomer to China. In fact, I was born in Canton in 1937, but my family, fearing the consequences of the Sino-Japanese War, moved to Macao when I was still a baby. It was in that tiny Portuguese enclave that I spent my childhood. We were singularly fortunate, for the Japanese respected Portugal's neutrality after their entry into the Second World War. Though my father, a former radio operator with a steamship company, was unable, because of the war, to find a job, he managed to earn a little money by running a tiny currency exchange booth in Macao's main thoroughfare. We were Catholics, and I attended Catholic schools in Macao, run by European nuns.

By Chinese standards, we were comfortably off: my family owned a twenty-room house in Canton, which had been divided up into four apartments, and the rentals from these apartments in normal times were a sizeable addition to the family income. In 1948, my father closed down his currency exchange booth, and we returned to Canton, occupying part of the family house but still renting out the upper floors. That year was probably the happiest of my childhood. Elsewhere in China, there was war, and it was apparent to almost everyone that the Kuomintang was bound to be defeated by the growing forces of Mao Tse-tung.

But, in common with most Chinese, we had lived with war on our doorstep for so long that we failed to take it seriously. Canton, in 1948, was so far south of the "front" that we felt ourselves to be relatively secure.

As the eldest of seven brothers and sisters, part of the burdens of running the household fell on my shoulders, especially since our two grandmothers lived with us and were too old to help much about the house. I was attending a junior high school for girls, and was regularly top of my class. Our problems were mainly down-to-earth budgetary ones: my father still had no regular job, and our tenants were only occasionally able to pay the rent. Food was expensive, and most of our savings had been wiped out by our stay in Macao. Still, in comparison with the lot of the majority of the Chinese people, or even that of the population of Canton, we were luckier than most.

On October 14, 1949, Canton was "liberated" by Mao's Communist armies. Looking back on this period, I can't remember that our lives were dramatically affected by the takeover. In public places, lists were posted up containing names of wanted people, and there were rumors of executions and large-scale arrests of known anti-Communists, who were sent to labor camps. Truckloads of prisoners were seen in the streets. A few of my father's friends disappeared. But our family had never been politically active. In the struggle for physical survival in post-war Canton, politics had always taken second place. In addition, there was no thorough attempt made either to indoctrinate the Cantonese population or to prevent those who feared for their lives from leaving town; for the first nine months after the Communist takeover of Canton, anyone who wanted to do so could openly and legally pull up stakes and settle in Hongkong, which was to treble its population in a short space of time.

Part of my immediate family circle did in fact leave for Hongkong a few months later, but the reasons were economic, not political: my father had found a job as radio operator aboard a ship belonging to a Hongkong-based company, and decided to move there with my mother and three of my brothers and sisters.

I was to remain in Canton to look after our house. In effect, with their departure, I became head of the household.

I was busier than ever, looking after my younger brothers and sisters, cooking for them and keeping the house in order. An aunt living with us did part of the work. (This was the aunt whose burial I had gone back to Canton to attend.)

If there was anything traditionally Chinese about our family, it had to do with our respect for education, and I never let household chores interfere with my school life. Here I should open a parenthesis and explain that during this period of my life (1950–54) I became, under the influence of teachers and youth leaders, an enthusiastic and, indeed, a fanatically keen member of the Young Vanguards, the junior branch of the Young Communist League.

Communist influence in Canton spread itself imperceptibly among adults, but the real targets—then as now—were the children and young people. I was among the first batch of Young Vanguards in my school, and proudly wore the red scarf. Some of our activities were harmless and even beneficial; it was our duty, we were told, to spearhead the movement for better health and hygiene in the city, and we went on rat hunts, campaigned for more sanitary garbage collection and helped townspeople to lead more sanitary lives. Our group went from street to street explaining that flies and mosquitoes spread diseases and should be destroyed. In simple terms, teachers and political instructors in charge of the Vanguards explained to us the elementary principles of Marxism-Leninism, and made them sound most attractive; indeed, I found a great deal in common with the principles of Christianity and regarded myself both as a young Communist and as a practicing Christian. Chinese Communism, in those days, was very different from what it is today: there was no personality cult; Mao Tse-tung was not worshiped as a supernatural being; and —as we could see with our own eyes—all religions were tolerated. People went to church, and priests, both foreign and Chinese, administered their parishes without immediate fear for their lives.

The Young Vanguard movement was essentially boy-scoutish, and, along with drill and the singing of patriotic songs (which were not, as they are now, songs of hate), it inculcated only the basic principles of Communism. Emphasis was on play and practical works more than on abstract theory. But we did, on occasion, call on local "capitalists" (designated by our instructors) and urge them to write "confessions." Again, such behavior—

absurd though it might appear to an outsider—was not accompanied by brutality; in our childish way, we really believed that reason and persuasion could make these capitalists into useful members of society, and, of course, we knew nothing of the repressive monolith then being set up by the Communists.

This was the period of the Korean War, and I remember in my own mind having no doubt whatsoever as to the validity of the Chinese attitude. I had been told, by instructors and teachers I respected, that America had committed aggression and had attacked first, and I had absolutely no reason to doubt them. So strongly did I feel about the Korean War that, along with a group of Young Vanguards, aged, like myself, around thirteen, I volunteered to join the People's Liberation Army to serve in Korea. I was turned down because of my age, but the keenness and zeal of my Vanguard unit (I was its junior leader) attracted the attention of the local press; we were photographed, and an article praised our unit as a "progressive model" and an example of what all such Young Vanguard groups should be. As a reward for our work, we were given a special red banner. For a long time, I treasured that Canton daily newspaper clipping. Having been turned down for the Army, our unit intensified its activities more in keeping with our age: we embarked on massive fly-killing operations; we taught Cantonese suburban dwellers the new Communist songs; and—again instigated by our instructors— urged everyone we came across to boycott the Hongkong dollar as a form of retaliation against "imperialist" Britain during the Korean War.

But despite my total involvement with the Young Vanguards, I was still tied to my family, and went to Hongkong at least once a year to visit them. In Hongkong I kept quiet about my activities in the Vanguards, and after such visits my instructors and my comrades half-mockingly criticized me for "hankering after the bourgeois life." So active was I in school, not only in the Young Vanguards but also in school dramatic, singing and painting groups, that I never took such criticism seriously, and despite the time devoted to extracurricular activities, I remained the outstanding pupil in my class.

There was another potential point of friction between me and the Communist Young Vanguards: my tendency to go to church on Sundays. In my family, we had been Catholics for four generations, and, along with some bigotry and narrow-mindedness, I had found much to respect in the nuns who had taught me in

Macao and in the priests I had met there and in Canton. In the early fifties, the Communist line in China was simply to deplore the fact that such old-fashioned customs still held sway. "We are in a new era, we should think of new things," was how one of our instructors put it.

Sometimes, I absented myself from Young Vanguard sessions to drop in on a couple of priests I knew, who lived in my district, Father Yip and Father Tan. Mostly I attempted to win them over to the Communist view of society, arguing that Christ himself had embodied a number of Communist ethics in his own preaching. We discussed dialectical materialism, the concept of the soul and immortal life, the Bible and the Darwinian theory of evolution. Occasionally, I even attended Mass at Canton's oldest and most famous church (Hsih Hsih, or Stonewall Church). I don't know whether I ever got the better of the priests in argument; without questioning the altruistic motives of China's Communist leaders, the two priests attempted to convince me that God's love and human love were more important than the class struggle, that spiritual matters were more important than political agitation, and that however scientific Darwin's writings were, the Holy Scriptures contained a higher form of truth. (As far as I know, Father Yip is still living in Canton. He is old now, and of course is no longer allowed to function as a priest. Father Tan, when last heard of, was in a labor camp in Manchuria.)

But it was certainly not because of my visits to the priests that, from 1953 onwards, my ardor as a young Communist gradually cooled. I realized, first of all, that if I devoted all my time to group activities, whatever their nature, my own grades would suffer, and I was determined to do well. Simply to keep up with my studies, I gradually cut down on my Young Vanguard activities. There was also a growing feeling on my part that our full-time instructors were, after all, on the mediocre side: they tended to repeat parrot-fashion what they themselves had learnt in their own study sessions. Free, wide-ranging discussion on the nature of Communist society, on the future of China and on our long-term goals had always been difficult, but became increasingly so. I had the impression that the adult Communist cadres with whom I came in contact had no real desire to discover the truth for themselves through the give and take of informal argument, and were constantly wary of being caught expounding unorthodox beliefs. And finally, I became somewhat bored with the activities of my Young Vanguard unit and looked back upon my time with them as an adolescent looks back to his or her scout days. Suddenly it all seemed rather childish to teach people Communist songs and to count up the number of flies one had killed during the day.

In 1954, I graduated from my senior high school with top marks, and was singled out for special congratulation by the principal. Still without knowing what I wanted to do in life, I decided to continue my studies at Canton University, then one of China's best. It was at this time that I came up against a hard fact of life in Communist China: I was, despite my grades, despite my record as a Young Vanguard, hopelessly handicapped owing to my "class origins"—about which I could do nothing. Having applied for entry to Canton University, I was notified that my application had been rejected. Other classmates, with school records and grades which did not compare with mine, had been accepted. Some of the successful applicants were friends I had coached and consistently helped in their exams. The teacher I went to for guidance was embarrassed. In the new era, she said, scholastic excellence was not the only criterion for university entry. My parents were in Hongkong, and I had gone there once a year at least; my father was known to have a house in Canton. He was a property-owner, and I, it stood to reason, was of "bourgeois origin." However hard I had worked, and whatever my record as a young Communist (and had I not largely given up my political activities in the last two years?), the government, in its sovereign way, had rightly decided that my class origins constituted a risk. "You might not," the teacher said, "serve the people with sufficient abnegation later on in life." The authorities were under no obligation to explain their decision, and I would do well not to complain or feel bitter about my rejection. This would only be a further black mark against me.

Mastering my disappointment, and determined to show that, bourgeois or not, I was patriotically inclined and not afraid of hard work, I applied to go and work in any capacity, as a "pioneer" in the remote Sinkiang desert, or as a "shock worker" in the new Lanchao oilfields. This was known to involve considerable physical hardship—and I wanted to prove how dedicated a young Communist I was. These areas were to China what Siberia was to the Soviet Union. To work there was an honor, but the party officials who recruited young people to go made no attempt to gloss over the physical discomforts which volunteers would experience. Most of those who volunteered for such work among my classmates were those who had failed their examinations. All were selected to become pioneers—all except me. Again no reason was given, but I understood only too well that the same reasons which had caused me to be rejected as a Canton University student had influenced the selection boards which selected the pioneer candidates.

I then tried to enter the Canton Artists School and was turned down. Discouraged, I decided I would not try again. I called on Bishop Teng* and without bitterness (but he must have sensed my disappointment) explained how my hopes had been dashed. He offered me a part-time job teaching the children of poor and destitute Catholics. In my spare time, and on my own, I learned to type, and tried my hand at commercial art. That same year, a friend of my mother's asked me to help her run her nursery school in Canton. All in all, I had quite a busy year.

Canton, in 1955–57 was not an unfriendly city and its cultural life was intense. Movie houses showed Chinese, but also Russian and even Western films (the Hollywood version of *David Copperfield* was especially popular). There were concerts, theater groups, foreign ballet companies and innumerable first-rate soccer teams, from the Soviet Union, Czechoslovakia and Yugoslavia— despite Tito's break with Stalin. Chinese plays and movies in these years were not the hideously boring didactic, doctrinaire paeans of praise for Mao they later became; some pre-1949 plays were still being performed, Cantonese opera was of course entirely traditional, and many plays and movies, including ones being produced under the new regime, were of some literary quality. Prices were stable, there was full employment, and a general new-found sense of security. Despite my own personal disappointment, I, along with the majority of the people of Canton, was the first to recognize the considerable benefits being wrought by the new regime. There was, especially in contrast to the following decade, an amazing sense of freedom. Tourists from Hongkong wore the daringly slit *cheongsams* without attracting anything more than mild stares. I saw some European girls, on a beach near Canton, wearing bikinis—the first I had ever seen. No police permits were needed to travel around China, and I visited friends in Peking and Tientsin, seeing something of my huge and beautiful country for the first time. People were not plagued by constant attempts at political indoctrination, and though the por-

* Bishop Teng was later sentenced to life imprisonment.—Author's note.

trait of Mao Tse-tung appeared increasingly in government offices, there was no Mao worship. If anything, it seemed to me, as a dispassionate onlooker, that not only in the political field but also in art, architecture and drama, China's intelligentsia, by accident or by design, was openly aping Soviet examples, occasionally with unfortunate results.

I would probably have stayed in Canton, a permanent resident of China, but I fell ill. A doctor advised me to go to Hongkong for treatment and to be with my family. Without difficulty, I obtained an exit visa, and after a short spell in Macao, visiting friends and relatives, I settled in Hongkong with my parents. My three brothers and sisters in school in Canton remained there, however, as did my aunt and our two grandmothers. They were too old, she said, to pull up stakes, and we would all come and see them regularly. In Hongkong my health improved and I soon got a job teaching small children in a Catholic school. I was exceedingly busy, for the school, though small, had few teachers and I taught everything—from English to mathematics, with varying degrees of success. In my spare time, I studied art.

Then in the spring of 1958, my aunt in Canton died. I had always been her favorite, and I felt ashamed that I had not been to see her. I decided to take a four-day trip to Canton to perform the traditional grave-sweeping ceremony. The Chinese tomb-sweeping festival and Good Friday happened to coincide that weekend, and the school where I worked was on holiday. My parents tried to persuade me not to go. Things had changed in Canton since I had left there a year before, they said. I didn't listen to them.

From the moment I crossed the frontier, I had a feeling of foreboding. Things first went wrong at Shumchun, the Chinese frontier post where one changes trains. Chinese customs officials were full of new-found zeal, and were making a determined attempt to crack down on the small-scale black-marketeering indulged in by many Chinese visitors from Hongkong. I had brought some fruit and candy for my friends in Canton, some new dresses, and I wore a new wristwatch. All these, I was told, would have to be left behind at the customs depot. I attempted to explain that they were gifts and that I didn't intend to sell my wristwatch. It was no use. The receipt given to me in return stipulated that "all items will be confiscated by the State if not collected within thirty days."

In Canton my grandmother was delighted to see me. She was

very old indeed, and recent events in China no longer mattered to her. We talked about my aunt, about my small circle of friends in Canton.

News of my arrival had spread; all day long, friends I had not seen for over a year called at our house. Most of the callers were from a small circle of Catholic acquaintances I had known over the years. All, without exception, were worried. They told me that a few weeks previously the Canton authorities had uncovered and "smashed" a "counterrevolutionary plot" said to have been organized by Catholics, and that a number of priests and Catholics had been jailed. "What on earth made you come to Canton at this particular time?" one asked me. "Aren't you afraid?" This was the first I had heard of a wave of arrests among Catholics in Canton—though I knew that the new regime was treating practicing Catholics with a certain amount of suspicion—the matter had, I was told, been reported in Hongkong newspapers. I said that I had nothing to fear. I had been a none too active member of a church choir, but had never done anything which might be construed as plotting against the state. Besides, though I now lived in Hongkong, I still felt that the Communist Government of China was, on the whole, a good thing.

My friends naturally inquired after mutual acquaintances now in Hongkong, including a number of priests, some of whom had been expelled by the Cantonese authorities. Among them was a Jesuit priest who had been most popular in Canton until his expulsion. "How is Father O'Mara?" was a question I had to answer several times. I told them he was well, but worried about the fate of Catholics who remained behind in Canton. My visitors all asked to be remembered to him. How changed my friends were; furtive, apprehensive, occasionally speaking in whispers, they behaved as though they feared that anything they said would later on be used against them. Personally, I felt that their fears were exaggerated. Yet, when the time came for me to take the train back to Hongkong, and as I said good-by to my friends on the platform, I realized that I didn't intend to return—not, at any rate, for some time. Things had changed in the town I loved so much. Some of the fears of my friends had rubbed off on me.

CHAPTER II

PRELUDE TO PRISON

ONE HOUR LATER, I was to know how well founded my friends' fears had been. But as I sat squeezed in the car, surrounded by party policemen and officials, I still didn't realize the full implications of what had just happened, not even when the car drew up in front of a large secluded house guarded by a uniformed soldier. Still without speaking, the woman cadre motioned me to get out and led me to a bare room. Then she ordered me to undress. I stood naked while she meticulously examined every piece of my clothing, attentively fingering the lining. Then, after allowing me to dress again, she began searching my suitcase with equal thoroughness. A man entered with a paper for me to sign— an acknowledgement that I was being held for questioning. Such was my bewilderment that I didn't even bother to read most of it, but obediently signed. Then another man appeared with a camera and took several photographs of me.

When all this was over, the woman cadre opened another door and ushered me into a long, narrow room with double windows and thick curtains. The walls, it occurred to me, were soundproof. On the long table were stacks of papers, files, pencils and, disposed at every seat except mine, steaming glasses of tea and packs of cigarettes. Seven men were seated at the table. They watched intently as I entered the room and sat down at the end of the table. There was a short pause while they sipped their tea, fiddled with their pencils and cigarettes and, lighting up, blew smoke in my direction. Their faces were grim. One of them, in a soft voice, began asking me routine questions: name, age, birthplace, family background and, inevitably, my class origin.

Between replies I kept saying: "Who are you? Why am I here?"

"So you don't know why you are here? You don't know what this place is? You'll find out, sooner or later. In the meantime it is best that you tell us everything you know, and everything you've done."

"But what can I say?"

"That's for you to decide. You know best. Let's start at the beginning. Who sent you to Canton? What kind of mischief were you up to? Who are your contacts in Canton and in Hongkong? Tell us the whole story."

I explained how, after my aunt's death, I had traveled to Canton for the tomb-sweeping ceremonies. "I don't know what you suspect," I said, "but I have done nothing wrong." Several men banged the table with their fists and gave other signs of impatience and indignation. "Liar!" one of them shouted. Another said: "You will be sorry. We have proof." Their apparent leader, the soft-spoken man who had opened the proceedings, motioned to the others to be silent. Then, in a conversational tone, but speaking slowly, he said: "It's useless for you to deny things. We have full information about everything you said and did since you arrived in Canton four days ago. Now, listen to me carefully: it is the government's policy to be lenient to those who make a full and complete confession of their own accord, and to be strict towards those who refuse to co-operate. Those who make a clean breast of things are well treated, and, if their confessions are important, they may even be rewarded. The bigger the contribution, the bigger the reward. If you speak up and confess everything, we will treat you leniently. We may even give you some kind of reward if what you tell us is of real value. But if you obstinately refuse to confess, you are throwing yourself into a bottomless pit." He paused, and then added, in a louder voice: "Now do you understand?"

I began again, telling them in greater detail the true, and innocent, reason for my trip to Canton. I was not allowed to continue. One elderly man cut me short. "Look," he said. "We have all the time in the world. You'd better make a full confession. If you don't make that confession today, you can make it tomorrow. Or in a month's time. Or a year from now. We're in no hurry. We can hear it in eight or ten years' time, if you like. It's up to you. And it's all right with us, too, if you never make a confession. We have sufficient information to sentence you in any case. The only reason we ask you to confess is that you're young and have been used by others, and we feel sorry for you and don't want you to go to jail for the rest of your life. So the sooner you stop acting tough and get down to business, the better." The casual way he talked scared me more than anything else. He wasn't talking like a policeman, or like a judge, but like someone explaining elementary facts of life to a particularly stupid child.

He paused to allow all this to sink in. Then he went on,

persuasively, in a more kindly voice: "Think of your parents, your family, your brothers and sisters. Think about the future. The imperialists got you into this mess. Do you want to sacrifice your life for them? It's not worth it, is it? You're only twenty years old. Do you want to spend the best years of your life in a labor camp?" He paused. "We are trying to save you. Think it over."

I felt like bursting into tears, but didn't want to give them that satisfaction. As I listened, I remembered my parents urging me not to go to Canton, then the conversation with my friends that very day. They had said that simply practicing religion had become a crime, that people had been punished for being Catholics and had been arrested and deported on trumped-up charges. What were my interrogators trying to get at? Dimly at this stage, I understood that these men were accusing me of taking part in some vast Catholic plot, about which I knew nothing. The inference was that they wanted me to denounce as "plotters" the friends I had seen during those four days in Canton. Although I was dreadfully scared by their threats, I determined then and there that I would implicate nobody. The sugary words of the men around the table were forced, and I could not hope for release. I made up my mind that if some sacrifice were needed, I would be the victim. But under no circumstances could I be a party to the arrest of my friends. Curiously, as I thought about all this, I felt calmer and more collected.

The questioning was going on. As I remained silent, others around the table who had not yet spoken opened fire. "Well, if you won't speak up, let us do the talking for you," said one young man. "On April seventh, two days ago, a person called Chang came to see you. And someone called Kuang. What did you talk about? What information did you pass on to them? What reports did they make to you?"

Another one thumbed through papers in front of him. "You passed on messages from a counterrevolutionary agent, one Father O'Mara. And didn't you arrange for him to correspond through you with his agents in Canton? Under the guise of informing his 'parishioners' about his 'health'?"

"You prayed for the health of these counterrevolutionaries when you were in Hongkong, didn't you?"

"O'Mara is a Vatican agent. The facts are well known. He was expelled by the People's Republic. You collaborated with this agent against your own government, didn't you? Yet you regularly went to see him and even dared to act as courier for him. What other activities did you come to Canton for? What undercover plans were you making in connection with these counterrevolutionaries? How much money did you receive from the imperialists for acting as their agent?"

With the mention of Father O'Mara's name, I realized that I had been followed since my arrival, and that those questioning me must have received reports of my conversations with my friends. For the first time, it crossed my mind that conceivably, one of these friends, probably under a similar form of duress, had been persuaded or compelled to inform the police about our innocent conversations under my grandmother's roof. Which person could it be? The prospect was so horrible that I didn't want to think about it. It seemed only too obvious that someone in my small circle of acquaintances had betrayed me and invented the story of my being a counterrevolutionary courier in order to escape arrest. Had anyone else been arrested during my Canton stay?

I decided to admit what was public knowledge: that I was a practicing Catholic. I explained that the emphasis in the Catholic religion was on good deeds and prayer, that such activities were strictly religious and that I had never been involved in any plot of any kind. I told them that I had engaged in no political activities whatsoever while in Hongkong. I said that I had known Father O'Mara in Canton, and that I had come across him again in Hongkong, and that I had attended religious services there conducted by him. Though Father O'Mara had been deported from China, he was still a priest in the eyes of Catholic believers, I said. Father O'Mara had indeed asked me to convey his greetings to his former parishioners in Canton, but had given me no sinister message or made any anti-government or anti-Communist pronouncements of any kind. Under law in the People's Republic, freedom of worship was guaranteed. Was it a crime to attend Mass? I said that I had heard stories that in recent months Catholics in China had been questioned by the government, but that personally I had not believed these stories. If I had thought they were true, I would certainly not have returned to Canton, even for a short visit. I was getting excited, and was determined to express my point of view. All the interrogators wanted to interrupt me, but I didn't let them. When I finished, there were wry smiles and sneers.

My statement, said one official, was "further evidence of my reactionary obstinacy."

"You have your freedom of belief," said another, "but we have something much better—freedom of anti-religious belief." And he sat back as though he had said something profound. A third official asked me whether, since I was a believer, I thought that an angel would appear to carry me off to the safety of Hongkong. I couldn't help answering that Jesus Christ himself had been crucified, and that I certainly expected no supernatural help. All the time, I was praying silently for strength to see this thing through.

Then the whole routine began all over again, with slight modifications. It must have been late, and in groups of twos and threes, my interrogators left the room, leaving a smaller quorum to continue the questioning.

The others returned, chewing toothpicks. I felt hungry, not having eaten anything since morning. "Gentlemen," I said, "you have filled your bellies, apparently, but I have no right to eat." One of them, who ordered me to call him "judge," asked me whether I had had anything to eat that day. I said I had had breakfast, but was one supposed to eat only once a day?

One of them left, returning with a large bowl of rice with some pieces of pork on top. "Food for criminals," he said, was no longer available. "This is cadres' food." I ate a little at the table, but suddenly the sensation of hunger left me as I reflected on my predicament. I put the bowl of food aside.

"Food is precious. You must not waste it," one of the "judges" said sententiously. And the questioning resumed.

By now they had, I think, given up trying to make me confess membership in an international espionage gang, and, instead, were telling me what they obviously had learnt themselves before becoming investigators. It was common knowledge, I was told, that the Vatican was a political and ideological arm of American imperialism. All priests sent abroad by the Vatican were special agents cloaking their activities as spies under the guise of religious or missionary work. They were all, without exception, "anti-Communist, anti-People and anti-China." Religion could not be separated from politics, and insofar as religion was to be permitted in China at all, it was to be organized and carried out by the Chinese themselves.

The interrogation had degenerated into a debate on the nature of religion and by this time there were only two, and then only one judge left. I was dead tired: I had been sitting at the table without a break for fifteen hours or more. The strong light in the room made it difficult to fall asleep, but occasionally I slumped forward. Without thinking of the possible consequences, I got up from time to time to stretch my legs and walk up and down. It was now dawn.

At last the one remaining judge rang a bell and someone came with a bunch of keys. I followed him down a long corridor with locked doors on either side. He stopped in front of number twenty-one, unlocked the door and escorted me in. Then he locked the door behind me. I just had time to grope for a wooden plank bed, and fell asleep. I had never been so tired in my life.

Soon after, it seemed to me, a voice was shouting, "Mealtime." A panel in the heavy wooden door of my cell was opened, and a hand placed a bowl of rice on the floor and withdrew, closing the panel. Looking around for chopsticks, I took stock of my cell. It was tiny—about seven feet long and perhaps four to five feet wide, with a small barred window high up near the ceiling, so high I couldn't even touch the window sill. There was a grass mat on the bed, a small wooden table with chopsticks and a glass of water, and a washbasin. In the corner was a portable toilet, and above the door, a small loudspeaker blaring out military music, which began at about the same time as breakfast came. It was tuned in to Canton radio and, as I discovered later, broadcast the news as well as music. The walls of the cell were damp, and there were traces of dried blood on the wall above the bed. I was relieved to discover that the blood was that of squashed mosquitoes, of which there were an enormous number. I tried to eat the coarse brown rice and salted vegetables, but everything stuck in my throat.

All of a sudden the door slammed open and an official shouted: "To the court!" I was escorted out the way I had come a few hours earlier, and noticed that there were, on two floors, long lines of cells similar to mine. A clock showed that it was 10 A.M.

I was back in the same room with the long table. But there was only one official there—the one who had been the last to remain with me the night before. He seemed cordial. He lit a cigarette, and offered one. I refused. "My name is Tseng," he said. "I am the chief judge investigating your case. Any questions you have can be addressed to me."

"In the first place," I said, "will you please tell me where I am, and what kind of a place this is? Then I would like to write to my parents to explain why I did not return to Hongkong on time. I would also like to have my wristwatch and other personal belongings, which I left at the Shumchun customs office. And I would also like to have some sheets and some spare clothing. My grandmother in Canton will make up a parcel for me if I am allowed to tell her where I am." I knew by this time that there was no hope of early release, so was determined to be as comfortable as possible.

Tseng burst out laughing. "You really are much too demanding and much too naïve," he said. "I don't want to hear any more requests until you've made a full confession. I will, however, get you a bedding roll, towels and so on. But you must be a good girl and confess your crimes in a proper way and not waste everybody's time as you did yesterday. Now, where were we? The Vatican as an arm of American imperialism . . ." And he began lecturing me in exactly the same way as the night before.

The idea that priests I had known in Canton and Hongkong could be spies and "imperialist agents" was so ludicrous that I was unable to restrain myself. I smiled and shook my head. "All right," he said, sensing that he was making no headway. "Tell me about Hongkong and what you did there." I found myself telling him about church activities in Hongkong, about bazaars, choir practice, Christmas tea parties and so on. From time to time he would question me about a certain priest or prominent Hongkong layman. He would make notes. "Obviously members of an intelligence network," he said. "Go on." Tseng was now joined by three or four others. Like a recurring theme in a piece of music, there was the insistence on the part of the "judges" that I had been sent to Canton by Father O'Mara to collect information on behalf of an imperialist organization. In between such accusations, made sometimes bluntly and occasionally indirectly, I was asked irrelevant but detailed questions affecting my personal life. Who had obtained a teacher's job for me in Hongkong? What "favors" or "rewards" had I obtained from Father O'Mara for my work? The second day's questioning differed only slightly from the first, and lasted until midnight.

Returning to my cell, I found a thin bedding roll on the bed, two suits of prison clothing, a toothbrush and some toilet paper. Mosquitoes began harassing me more brutally than my interrogators, and, bitten all over, I attempted to sleep rolled up in a towel. That week was a repetition of the first day, with daily sessions from 10 A.M. to midnight, and a short break while "prisoners' food" was brought to me—which I had to eat under the gaze of my judges. Later—I lost count of the actual days—

I was left alone in my cell all day, the monotony only being broken by food—at seven in the morning and then again at 5 P.M. At lunchtime I felt hungry, and tried to forget both the gnawing hunger and my troubles by sleeping.

The times of the questioning sessions changed. Now I was awakened at midnight, to find some or all of the judges sitting at the long table. There began to be a kind of dreadful familiarity between us, for they knew a great deal about my earlier life. From their questions in those nighttime sessions, it was obvious that they had investigated; they knew about my record as a Young Vanguard—which they interpreted, of course, as an attempt on my part to infiltrate the Communist Party; they knew about my school grades, and my disappointment at failing to enroll at Canton University. They knew, too, about my applying for pioneer work in Sinkiang and my baffled surprise at being once more rejected. All this, presumably, they obtained by questioning my former schoolmates. I admitted the facts but refuted their fabrications and innuendoes—that out of bitterness at being turned down as a student I had deliberately enrolled in an "imperialist espionage organization" based in Hongkong.

I lost track of time almost completely. They began questioning me once every second day, then several days went by without a session in the long room. But by now they were well on the way to achieving their goal—which was to obtain from me a written confession that I had indeed engaged in "espionage activities under the cloak of religion." After what may have been three weeks or a month, or a little longer, they gave me paper and pen and ink and asked me to put down my confession in black and white. It was obvious to me by this time that I could not hold out indefinitely. Anything was better than endless solitary confinement. So, while still holding out and refusing to admit my crime, I began, as they had instructed, writing out the story of my life as I had told it to the investigators.

It was a long process, and my "confession" failed to satisfy them. I rewrote it, not once, but many times. The stumbling block invariably came when I refused to invent details of a Vatican-staffed espionage organization in Hongkong, of which I had, so they said, been a part. I thought of the innocent church activities I had taken part in and didn't know whether to laugh or cry. Writing the confession must have taken another two months at least, and during this period—as prisoners do the world over—I got to know the place I was locked up in, despite the fact that I was still in solitary confinement.

I was moved three times—each time to a similar cell but on a different corridor. From these moves, I noticed that the house— a suburban villa in appearance, as I had briefly seen it—held at least a hundred detainees, and perhaps more. Several were, like myself, from Hongkong. Although I never saw any of the other inmates, we would whistle tunes which only Hongkong residents could have known. At night I heard the sounds of men and women shouting, and occasionally crying and hammering on their cell doors. I became desperately eager for the daily news bulletin, my only link with the outside world. I prayed and sang, and to keep from falling ill I did physical exercises early in the morning. My only trip outside my cell came in the morning when, under escort, I went to fetch some water for my wash-basin and emptied out—in a communal toilet—the slops of the previous day. Several times I toyed with the idea of committing suicide, but dismissed it, partly because I had been brought up to view killing oneself as a sin, partly because my interrogators would certainly congratulate themselves and point to this as an additional proof of my guilt. I would not give them this satisfaction.

One night, my cell door was opened by Tseng himself, who told me to come with him. Expecting a further midnight session, I followed him down the familiar corridors, but instead of enter-ing the long room, he went past it, and instead ushered me into a smaller room, which may have been his office, with armchairs, a desk and filing cabinets. He gestured to me to sit in an armchair, and sat down himself, very close. There were two mugs of steaming tea and he gave me one. "Let's have a talk," he said. "This is not an official investigation session. I just . . . want to get to know you better."

It was still summer, and dreadfully hot. The blouse I was wearing was worn to a frazzle by my frequent attempts to wash it with coarse soap. It was sleeveless and torn. Tseng laid his arm across the back of the armchair, and I felt his sleeve pressing against the back of my neck. Ostentatiously, I sat up so as to avoid physical contact with him. Tseng was young, with strong features, a dark complexion, and always wore a military-type olive-green uniform without badges of rank. "Sit back and relax," he said. "Isn't it a pity that a pretty young girl like you should end up here just because you got entangled with the imperialists in

Hongkong and ended up as one of their running dogs? Why be obstinate? Why keep holding out? Look"—and he brushed my face and neck gently with his fingertips—"you're covered with mosquito bites."

Tseng, in the past, had in turn been threatening, bullying, impersonal or sarcastic, but he had rarely been human, and never gentle or considerate. He obviously enjoyed his work too much, and had implicit faith in the validity of his own beliefs. At first, I was moved by his words. He went on, speaking almost in a whisper, and occasionally touched my arm and shoulder. "Your confession's not at all adequate, you know. It's quite clear that you refuse to make a straightforward, full confession to the people owing to your backward ideology. But it's apparent to me at least"—more stroking of arm and shoulder—"that you have been thoroughly cheated by the people who sent you to Canton. Compared to other agents we have questioned, you are both candid and naïve, and not as guilty as they. We feel there's hope for you, in spite of what you've done. I personally have gone out of my way to argue with the others in your favor, and believe that you are capable of reform and that in the long run you could even contribute to the people and to our nation. What do you think? Do you agree?" His arm was around my shoulders now, and he was whispering, his face to mine.

Looking down, I noticed that the fierce, incorruptible Judge Tseng was having an erection. I moved away, abruptly, and recalled his past sarcasms, his endless probing and sudden real or simulated fits of anger. I became angry too, but decided to conceal my real feelings. "All I really want," I said wearily, "is to go home."

He smiled, puffed on his cigarette. "So," he said softly, "we plead guilty then?"

I lost my composure and swore and ranted at him. I was *innocent,* and the only charge against me—if it was a charge—was that I was a Christian. "The charges are entirely fabricated—and you know it!" I almost screamed.

This didn't seem to bother him. Like the other judges, he had to a quite incredible degree the capacity for ignoring, or just not hearing, those facts which did not fit in with his theories. "Look," he said, still in a conversational, intimate tone, "you're not so badly off here. You did something wrong, and you deserve some form of punishment. When I took part in the revolution, I was much younger than you are now. I had two uniforms, free

towels, laundry and soap, and about two dollars [eighty U.S. cents]
pocket money a month—not enough for a haircut or cigarettes.
You shouldn't grumble about this place. It's for political prisoners and is several cuts above the average prison—as you'll find
out later on." He paused, lit another cigarette. "I am going on
leave in a few days," he said. "You can talk about your problems
with Judge Li." I sat back in the armchair, yawning. He patted
my shoulder again. "Now, get back to your cell," he said gently.
He escorted me downstairs, and stood outside as the door was
locked. For some time, as I knew from the slight noise coming
from the other side of the cell door, he remained there, staring
at me through the peephole. I ignored him and curled up on the
bed. Eventually, he went away.

CHAPTER III

"NUMBER 2675"

IT WAS MID-JULY before I was moved out of the interrogation center. Like all my moves as a prisoner, this one came as a complete surprise, for I had expected to stay in the center at least until I had been formally sentenced. But it was as an accused person that I was transferred.

One morning, a warder opened my cell door and told me to hurry and pack up my things. Since I had practically no personal belongings, I was ready almost immediately. He opened the cell door, and escorted me to the top of the stairs. There, lying against the wall, was my suitcase. For one wonderful moment, the thought came to me that perhaps, after all, the absurd charges had been dropped. I would now be taken to Canton railroad station to be escorted out of the country. It seemed too good to be true, and when I saw the warder returning with a bulky file (presumably my dossier), my hopes were dashed. "Oh no. You're not going to Hongkong," he said contemptuously in reply to my timid question. "Pick up your suitcase and follow me."

I tried to lift it and discovered that I could hardly do so. I realized, for the first time, how weak and wan I had become during three and a half months of solitary confinement. As I stepped into the open air I became dizzy and blinded by the unaccustomed light of day. Outside the villa the same soldier still mounted guard. Everything was as I remembered it when we first drove up there in the packed police limousine. In the light of day, I looked at my hands and forearms—white and thin. I thought: I must look awful.

The warder said something to the sentry about our "going across the road," and he nodded. Half carrying, half dragging my suitcase, I followed the warder. Outside the villa was a stretch of open ground, a kind of miniature, unkempt park, with tea stalls. Beyond a line of dwarf banian trees there was a huge building, surrounded like a medieval castle with walls topped by spikes. And barbed wire. We paused before what must have been one of several entrances, guarded by two soldiers with fixed bayonets. They were scrutinizing the passes of all those entering and leaving the building, but they must have been forewarned about my arrival, for the warder and I walked inside without being stopped.

While the warder was reporting to an official, I had time to have a quick look round, and caught a glimpse of an inner courtyard filled with people. Squatting down on their haunches, their heads shaved, their hands tied behind their backs, were prisoners. They were dressed in rags, and must have been peasants, for they were barefoot and their toenails were brown—the distinguishing mark of all those who work long hours in paddy fields. Some of them were crying silently. I wondered what they had done to be here and what fate was in store for them. I never saw them again, for then I was called away and told to report upstairs. The warder led me up the stairs and left to return to the villa.

I found myself in a small office, taking orders from a young woman, aged about twenty-five. She had an ugly yet placid face, giving her a strangely equine countenance—it was no surprise to learn later that prisoners referred to her as "Horseface." She spoke impersonally but not harshly. "Take some clothes out of your suitcase but the rest must stay in custody with us," she said. "Any cash?" I had a little money in the suitcase and with it she offered to buy me soap, toothpaste and toilet paper. She gave me two strips of paper to paste over the closed suitcase, which I signed and dated. Then she led me to my new cell, the second on the right of the main staircase. I remember its number still—thirty-five.

I had hoped, after the long spell alone, to be put in a cell with other people, but the cell she showed me into was empty—though it was much larger than anything I had known so far, with three bunks disposed in a U-shape around the room. Otherwise, its furniture and other characteristics were about the same. "Your number is twenty-six seventy-five," she said. "Here we don't use names, only numbers. Remember that. You must address other prisoners by numbers too. It is strictly forbidden to reveal one's name or the nature of one's crime. Understood?"

I nodded. "My name is Sun," she said, "and everyone calls me Keeper Sun. [She thought.] Here you call the prison officials keepers. You may summon a keeper by knocking on your cell door but you're not to do so unless it's absolutely necessary." Sun pointed to a set of instructions pinned to the cell door. "Read these carefully and memorize them," she said. "We'll ask you to recite them by heart in a day or two."

I had nothing to do but read and learn them by heart, which was easy. All prisoners were to obey all orders given by the keepers. Smoking, possession of sharp or pointed instruments were forbidden; the timetable must be rigidly adhered to and everything should be done with the minimum of noise; prisoners must refer to themselves and to others by their numbers only and discussion of one's personal affairs and of one's case was prohibited; prisoners must neither join in "secret societies" nor gamble; passing messages in any form, even through gestures, was likewise forbidden; and prisoners were urged to "seriously concern themselves" with current news events and participate in all activities sponsored by the authorities.

The regulations cheered me up a little. Obviously, there was still room for some communication in prison, since the authorities themselves prohibited so many things. Perhaps I would, after all, receive news from the outside world in this way. I even looked forward to prison work after my months of idleness. But these feelings didn't last long. As the day went by, I became even more depressed than before. I thought about my family in Hongkong, and in Canton, and wondered whether I would ever see them again. The sight of the shackled prisoners in the courtyard had come as a terrible shock. I had never seen anything like this before, and this spectacle, like so many other things I was to witness later on, made me realize the extent to which people living in Canton had been unaware of the government's discreet but brutal use of force and of the implacable nature of the Communist regime.

Looking back, my months in Canton's Number One Prison, as I discovered it was called, were among the most tolerable ones in captivity. As the warders often remarked, this was a showcase prison, often visited by foreigners. It was clean, they said, and the food, they claimed, was better than in any other prison in China. I learnt something about its history from casual remarks dropped by keepers and, eventually, from other prisoners. It had been a prison in Kuomintang days and, as the keepers were never tired of pointing out, in the "bad old days" many good Communists had been held here, in unspeakable conditions, and some of them had been tortured to death.

Some of the keepers, I discovered, had in fact been prison warders in pre-Communist days, and those who had aided Communist prisoners then, or shown particular care for them, had been singled out to continue serving on the prison staff. This in itself was a good thing, for it meant that among the more elderly staff warders, there were some "professionals" not over-concerned with politics, trained in their job and with a past record of humane behavior.

The majority of prison warders, however, were of post-Kuomintang vintage, and they, quite obviously, had been given such jobs because, through stupidity or lack of education, they were unfit for anything else. They all had an elementary grounding in Communist ideology, which they repeated parrot-fashion, and came from "correct" working-class backgrounds—which was the *sine qua non* for their obtaining such a post in the first place. Only once did I come across a prison staff officer of any real quality. Mostly the warders were fairly despicable people—prompt to take advantage of the prisoners, sexually or otherwise, with a high proportion of voyeurs among them. Yet the Number One Canton Prison was, in retrospect, the least brutally run establishment I was to experience in China, partly because the warders were corrupt, weak and as bored as the prisoners themselves, and partly because it was so large, with such a huge reserve of prisoners who could be drawn upon to perform a wide range of duties. The prisoners came from a cross section of Chinese society and were there for a wide assortment of reasons. Perhaps the best way of telling something about my life in the new surroundings of Number One is through a series of portraits of prisoners and warders alike, and sketches of unrelated incidents of note which occurred during my time there. These incidents happened, of course, in the terrible void of prison life, marked only by the sameness of daily routine: reveille at six, breakfast at seven, physical exercise in the courtyard, a ten-minute spell in the showers to wash oneself and one's clothes, the cleaning session of one's cell with a borrowed broom, indifferent food again at 5 P.M. and lights out at nine.

As it turned out, I was alone for the first month, and this further spell of solitary confinement was, I discovered, deliberately ordered by the judges handling my case. My first cell-mate was a well-dressed young woman in her late twenties, of unabashed bourgeois and urban origin. Her name, she said, was Yen Shiao-ching, and her ladylike refinement contrasted with her conversation, often brutally frank and deliberately scatological. I remember marveling at her spirit, quite unbroken despite her twenty-year sentence on an espionage charge almost as baseless as my own.

"How are you, fellow prisoner?" she said, dumping her belongings on a bunk and sitting next to me after Horseface Sun had shown her in. "You must be lonesome here. I'll keep you company for a while." Her boisterous cheerfulness made me suspect, at first, that she might in fact be a police informer, specially sent to worm more "secrets" out of me, but I was so longing for company that I would have welcomed a spy.

"My, but you're pale," she said. "You can't have seen the sun for months." She patted my head. "Afraid? Silly girl. I really am glad to be here with you. You should have seen what it was like in the cells attached to the People's Court. There must have been twenty people in a cell meant for four." I lent her a towel, and she washed herself. Point-blank she asked, "Are you a political prisoner?"

I was still completely under the spell of the horse-faced keeper who had lectured me about the rules and regulations in force, and I pointed to the set of regulations pinned to the cell door. "You know you shouldn't ask such questions," I said, "and you shouldn't say things like that out loud."

Yen laughed. "Damn the regulations. They can't shoot us for talking, can they? We're in jail already. In any case, I'd prefer to be shot than to spend the next twenty years in this place."

She told me all about herself. She and her husband, both primary school teachers, had gone to Hongkong some six years previously to visit relatives there. They had gone on a spending spree, and an acquaintance, whom they hardly knew, had lent them some money, which they had never bothered to repay. Carelessly, they had forgotten about the debt, returned to Canton and continued with their teaching.

Then, five years later, out of the blue, a stranger turned up at their home, reminded them of the debt and tried to blackmail them into joining a pro-Kuomintang espionage organization. They refused, knowing that the penalty, if found out, was death. But, unwilling to reveal the incident to the local authorities for fear of getting into trouble themselves, they had done nothing. The stranger was arrested shortly afterwards and had implicated them in his confession. She and her husband had been arrested one night and, after a summary trial, found guilty. Her husband got life imprisonment, and Yen herself, twenty years.

Though she had been in custody for about the same time as I, Yen knew the tricks of prison life far better and initiated me in all sorts of prison lore. She explained that there was no sense in arguing with one's judges, who were out to impose a sentence in any case, and would never be swayed by rational argument, however convincing. "One's sentence, and one's actual time in prison, is related to one's attitude," she said. "Above all, pretend at least to be 'progressive' and admit everything. It's easier that way, for all concerned, and one's chances of remission and of an easier time are far greater." She gave me a complete rundown on the warders and trusties operating the prison, warning me against some and reporting favorably on others.

I began following her instructions, and discovered how right she had been. It was not hard for me to take an interest in political indoctrination, which took the form of reading the *Nanfang Jih Peo,* the official paper of the Kwangtung Provincial Committee of the Communist Party. In fact I read everything in it so attentively that I became the object of mild mockery. All news, of course, concerned achievements in the political and economic fields, but one item, one day, particularly attracted my attention. It was a report of a Chinese Foreign Ministry warning to the United States following the intrusion, over Chinese air space, of an American plane. I imagined what would happen if war broke out between the United States and China, and the U.S.A. won. The political prisoners, I supposed, would be released immediately. This frequently recurring daydream was, I found, shared by almost all political prisoners I later came across.

One day, reading the paper, I discovered it was my birthday. Yen said, "How would you like to celebrate by having some chicken for dinner?" She searched her luggage, and pulled out a can of cooked chicken—a present from her family which she had somehow managed to smuggle into the cell. "We'll get Chou Teh to heat it up for us," she said. "He's a good man, and someone we can trust." She explained that Chou Teh, who distributed food occasionally, was a former official sentenced for "corruption." "Whatever you do, don't have anything to do with Chen" [another trusty, a woman, who also was in charge of food distribution]. Chen, she said, was in jail for smuggling watches from Hongkong, and was very greedy. "I know, because I shared a cell with her once."

That night we had a splendid feast, and Yen, generous as ever, insisted that I eat most of the chicken. She did her best to cheer me up. "Don't worry," she said. "Once you've actually been sentenced you'll be able to write to your folks and even get occasional food parcels. They even say that if you're sent to a labor camp, members of your family are allowed to visit you there."

While I was still sharing a cell with Yen (who was removed after some ten days), a third prisoner joined our cell. She was an old, old lady, wearing the typical black pajama suit of Kwang-tung Province peasant women. Yen and I were friends by now, and for some time the old lady remained aloof. Finally, as we were discussing our cases, she interrupted us. "You know nothing about the real nature of Communism," she said. "You have no idea of its ferocity or viciousness. Look at me. I'm fifty-six. I look seventy at least. For the last fifteen years I've been in and out of jail." The old lady explained she was a Taoist preacher, a member of the Ikuantao sect, which had been repressed by the Communist authorities because of the importance which it gave to individual human values. "Just for being a member of the Taoist movement," she said, "I received a twelve-year sentence. They put me to work in a labor camp. I can't tell you what it was like. I almost died and they released me. Then, for no apparent reason, they arrested me again. This time they gave me fifteen years. Don't ask me why. I haven't done anything. I don't think I'll last much longer. They know this, but it means nothing to them."

Yet the old lady, whose name was Ping Chi-wei, was, like Yen, full of spirit. She taught us how to read the stars, and palmistry, and told us that an Ikuantao priest of high repute had predicted that "the red sun will fall, the white sun will fall, and the five stars will not last long." The red sun, she said, symbolized the Japanese, and the white sun the Kuomintang Government. The five stars—the emblem of the Chinese People's Republic, would, she said, follow in due course. Her belief in this kind of superstition helped her to maintain her morale.

Not all cell-mates were like Yen and Ping Chi-wei, whom I still remember with affection. There was Ah Hsiu, a convicted smuggler, a thin, intent woman of about thirty, who was a self-confessed lesbian and insisted on combing and brushing my hair, washing my clothes and one night made more direct advances, which I had to repel with force. Luckily, she only stayed two days. For her, as she admitted, prison was no hardship as long as she was with other women, "not old and ugly women, of course, but fresh young girls like you." She talked uninhibitedly about lesbian love affairs in prison, and said that despite the prison regulations and the constant surveillance, such love affairs went on. Several girls in the prison, she said, were in love with her, and some of the women keepers, she said, were lesbians too.

As time went on, our cell became increasingly crowded. This was the beginning of the Great Leap Forward, and the paper we were allowed to read was full of stories about fantastic production gains. At the present rate, I remember reading, China would overtake the Western world in sixteen years' time. "Progress in one day equals that of twenty years elsewhere" was one headline. For us, the Great Leap Forward's most immediate consequence was to cram the Number One Canton Prison beyond capacity. At times, there were not three, but six people in my cell at the same time. We devised a rotation system for sharing out the bed space adequately. The turnover of cell-mates was high, and most of those arrested were there in connection with alleged failings under the aegis of the Leap Forward, conveniently labeled as "sabotage." As the days turned into weeks, and then months, I became something of an old-timer myself, and explained the ways of the prison to new arrivals. I was myself beginning to feel somewhat hard-hearted too. But the fate of some of the ignorant peasant women, picked up and taken to jail without any explanation, was always saddening. They would cry and cry, and there was nothing one could do. Some were undernourished, and others were seriously ill. I remember one woman bleeding profusely all over a mattress and lying there groaning with pain.

The Great Leap Forward also had a dramatic effect on our food supplies. According to the paper, food production was going up in leaps and bounds. An acre of land, one story said, now produced thirty tons of rice. But the food declined in quantity and quality in inverse proportion to the Leap. Our two meals had been, at best, inadequate, but as time went on they became worse and worse. For days at a time there would be no rice at all, only watery soup, which in ordinary times would have been used as pig swill. Rice, when it came, was watery. After my sentence, I occasionally received food parcels from my family but these were few and far between, and it was impossible not to share these luxuries with my cell-mates. The food situation must have been bad for everyone, keepers as well as prisoners, from hints dropped by a few warders. But there were occasional exceptions: the senior officials of the province, we were told, got special food. And in the cell next to mine, a confessed Kuomintang agent got three steaming-hot meals a day, including rice, pork and even chicken. This, a warder said, was because she was "fully cooperating" with the investigating authorities, who wanted to keep her in good health to extract as much information as they could from her.

When her usefulness was exhausted, she was taken out and shot.

As I gradually discovered, a large proportion of prisoners in Number One were Catholics, and on Sundays, when most of the keepers were on holiday, and only a skeleton staff was maintained in the huge jail, there would be loud community singing of hymns and Catholic songs. Just how many Catholics were held there I never discovered, but from glimpses of prisoners, and from occasional notes passed by trusties, I discovered that I knew at least a dozen from my own school days in Canton. There was Belinda Wong. I had last seen her during those fateful four days in Canton just prior to my own arrest. She had come to my grandmother's house, and we had talked of trivial, girlish things. There was Wei Mo-ching, the leading soprano in our choir, whose relatives in Hongkong I knew well. There was an elderly priest who had worked with a French Catholic mission in pre-Communist days and given me occasional French lessons. And many, many others. While I never managed to get near enough to these Catholic friends to talk to them, just the knowledge of their presence around me was good for morale, though I often wondered whether they in turn had been arrested because the authorities had discovered they knew me. In my occasional, silent prayers, I had the feeling that I was not alone, and that a group of us was in fact praying—and hoping—together.

I was still not free of Judge Tseng, who still came to see me on various pretexts. The first time was when I filled in a form required for some kind of census. Under the blank space for "crime," I wrote "Catholic." Tseng summoned me to a small investigation room that afternoon. "You really are most unreasonable," he said. "An educated girl like you should know that 'Catholic' is the name of an organization, not the correct designation for your crime. No, I won't argue with you. The months we've spent together hoping that you'd recognize your mistakes and come round to the right path eventually, so that you can serve your country and the people, have obviously been in vain." I remembered Yen, my first cell-mate, and her words of caution. I said I was only too willing to co-operate. Tseng then asked me a number of questions, all of them trivial. Did I discuss with Father O'Mara my impressions of Peking after my visit there a few years previously? Did I admit that I had told some classmates how bitter I was at not entering Canton University? Had I, in Hongkong, prayed for Catholics I knew who had either been arrested or deported? I answered "yes" to all these questions, simply to get everything over with. He then drafted a confession embodying these statements, and I signed it. "Now you must make a serious effort to reform," he said. "We have a library here, and I will see that you get some books." He pressed a bell, and a warder took me back to my cell.

In due course I received a pencil, some paper for making notes and three books. I remember their titles well. They were: *The Nation and the Law* (a handbook of rules and regulations in the People's Republic), *Marxist-Leninist Views concerning Religion* (a précis of quotations about religion from Marx and Lenin and other, lesser-known Communist theorists), and *Religion—the Anti-Science* (a refutation, from a scientific point of view, of Biblical theories concerning the creation of the universe). I read them all, greedily. Shortly afterwards, I was allowed to write my first letter to my grandmother in Canton. It was in the form of a stereotyped note. Horseface Sun warned, as she helped me fill it in, that it should contain "nothing about your case or your troubles, whatever they may be. Just send greetings and say you're fine. Don't ask for lots of luxuries, which would only give your family an additional financial burden." I nevertheless asked my grandmother for money, some canned food and some toilet articles. I knew that she would write my parents in Hongkong and they would manage to send her some money. Letters, I knew, went out on the fifteenth of each month, and replies—and parcels—were distributed the same day a month later. As the next fifteenth of the month drew near, I became terribly excited. And, sure enough, Horseface appeared that day with a parcel, and a letter. All it said was: "All the family is well. Don't worry. Be sure to reform yourself and unite with the family as soon as you can." It was in my younger brother's handwriting, and showed he was still in Canton, and unharmed. I cried.

The stilted language, I knew, was not his fault. It was the only form of communication acceptable to the prison authorities. The parcel contained clothes, sugar, cakes, canned food, sandals and a fountain pen and ink. Each month that followed, for as long as I was in the Canton jail, I received a parcel of some kind. I knew how difficult it must have been for my family, in times of famine, to send me food, and my pleasure at getting such parcels was a little marred by remorse at the thought of the trouble I was causing.

I connected the privilege of receiving parcels to my new "co-operative" attitude towards Judge Tseng, for I was not sentenced for several more months. Again, the court appearance came as a complete surprise. One morning I was whisked away to a room in the prison. There were six judges behind a table—none of them members of the earlier investigating team—and two bored "witnesses," presumably prison officials, to serve as audience and comply with the legal pretense that such trials were public. There was no court case as such, no summing up of evidence, favorable and otherwise. It was all over in a few minutes, almost as soon as I had entered the room. I remember the sequence of events well. The court clerk (recognizable because a small signboard was on his desk) said: "Stand up. The sentence will now be read out." Everyone stood. I was trembling and as scared as I have ever been. The chief judge mumbled something—a garbled account of my supposed confession—and then paused, cleared his throat and said: "Sentence is: five years' imprisonment followed by three years' deprivation of political rights. Any questions?"

"What difference does it make?" I said. "It's what you have said that counts." The judge handed me the paper he had just read, and said that if I wished, I could appeal to the Higher People's Court within three days. Afterwards it would be too late. Nobody else said a word. I was marched out. Other prisoners were waiting. I memorized the preamble to the sentence and can still recite it word for word:

"The offender reported to the counterrevolutionary former Bishop Teng on the condition of Catholic churches in Peking after a visit there in 1955. She spoke disparagingly of the People's Government after failing to pass an entry exam to Canton University, smearing and libeling the People's Government and alleging that her failure was due to her family background and to her Catholic religion. While in Hongkong she was an active participant in so-called "fellowship" work organized by one Father O'Mara, an imperialist element previously deported from China. She also prayed for Bishop Teng, a counterrevolutionary who is now under arrest. The offender also went on a special mission to Canton, to pass on reactionary instructions from Father O'Mara, including the treasonable instruction that Catholics "should continue to do their duty" and that Catholics in Canton should help each other.

"She has been a counterrevolutionary actively taking part in treasonable activities under the cloak of religion, including liaison missions and correspondence on behalf of reactionary plotters. The offender shall receive five years' imprisonment and three years' deprivation of political rights according to the regulations contained in the Seventh Code of the Constitution of the People's Republic of China. Signed: The Second People's Court of the Canton Municipal Government."

By now I was sufficiently versed in the ways of Chinese People's Courts not to appeal. I knew, from other prisoners' experiences, that there was not the slightest hope of obtaining a reduction of one's sentence and that the only effect of an appeal was to delay the proceedings and, occasionally, to increase the length of the sentence. But when I returned to my cell I sobbed for hours, despite the admonition from Horseface that I had no right to cry; such noise, she said, was contrary to regulations.

CHAPTER IV

PRISON GAMES AND PURGES

THE MONTHS IN CANTON PRISON went by slowly; we were crammed into our cells (six or eight in space meant for three) as more and more prisoners turned up. At first, I was solicitous and sorry for the new arrivals. Eventually, as a prison veteran, having seen scores of cell-mates come and go, I became hardened and almost indifferent to their fate. Most of the new arrivals had been arrested for technical black market offenses such as running a "free market" (which had been quite legal until the Leap Forward) or for smuggling food or goods into China from Hongkong. Others had been picked up for "speaking out against the government." A minority consisted of criminals, mostly convicted thieves. There was a steady deterioration in food, which from insufficient and bad, became abominable—a starvation diet that reduced all of us to various kinds of ill health, indifference and lethargy.

I didn't entirely escape from the general rule of the place, which was that any prisoners with special skills should take part in the running of the prison establishment. My first job came when one of the keepers ordered me out of my cell one day and told me that, since I could write well, I was needed to help write down the confession of one of the prisoners under interrogation. It was no use protesting that I didn't want any part in the sentencing of another person. I was led into a room where I had on occasion been interrogated, prior to sentence. The keeper made me sit at the desk where the investigating judge usually sat. In front of me there was a young, sweet-looking girl of perhaps eighteen or nineteen. She was dressed in bright, tight-fitting clothes, obviously from Hongkong. She was crying bitterly. "Here," the keeper said, "is someone who will help you write your confession, since you can't do it on your own." And he left us alone, closing the door.

By this time I was sufficiently aware of prison methods to know that I shouldn't show any outward sympathy towards the girl. I was convinced that I was being observed, or that the room was wired for sound. So I spoke to her gruffly, and she responded with more tears and pleas of innocence, as though I myself were the judge. This made me somewhat ashamed. "You don't think I'm really a judge, do you?" I said. "I'm a prisoner, like you. I'm just here to help you write things down. Are you sure you can't write yourself?" The girl explained that she had had no formal education, and had married at seventeen. Her case was a banal one of smuggling contraband into China from Hongkong, and she eventually told me about it, sniffing and sobbing occasionally. "I didn't want to do it," she said. "Daddy made me. He said nobody would spot my small parcel of powdered pearls and that all I had to do was to hand it over to some cousins of his when I reached Canton." (Powdered pearls are highly prized in China, among people who don't believe in Western medicine, for their health-giving and aphrodisiac qualities.) I put down her confession bit by bit, putting the blame on her father, who was responsible for getting his daughter arrested, and cursing his greed. Throughout the interview I was sympathetic but impersonal. Obscurely, I knew that here was a test of my own prison behavior.

I never found out what happened to the girl. But this first job led to others; subsequently, whenever I was called out of my cell to act as scribe for illiterate prisoners, I was careful to put on my one and only cheongsam, the tight-fitting dress slit down the side at the hem, to show that I, too, was from Hongkong, and a prisoner, not a judge. But I had realized, as I helped my pretty little smuggler write her confession, how easy it was to slip into the jargon of the interrogating judge, how tempting, too, it was to browbeat and bully someone into making a full confession.

On occasion, I was shocked by the hardened attitude of the women prisoners charged with various criminal offenses whose "confessions" I was made to write. One in particular had the jauntiness of the tough gangster woman. She was twenty-eight, and pretty in a hard sort of way. "All right, take it down, I know it all by heart," she said, having taken in at a glance that I was not a real judge, but a prisoner, and a Hongkong resident at that. "My name's Li Shih, born in Nanhai, married briefly and divorced. I shared a room with three men in a boarding house and we all made a living forging rice ration tickets. We managed to buy seven thousand pounds of rice that way and sold them at a vast profit. We spent the money on wine and splurged on banquets. I don't know where the men are. I don't remember their names even. There's no money left. Got it?" I wrote everything down, and when I had finished, the pockmarked keeper Ah Wu came to take her away. As he led her out he pinched her bottom. She laughed. Later I learnt that she had been put in a single cell, and was visited not only by Ah Wu but by other keepers. Many prostitutes in fact managed to keep up their trade in prison, obtaining special food in return from the keepers' canteen, and whatever "luxuries" were available on Canton's open market.

Inexplicably, I was taken off the job of writing confessions one day and was never called upon to do so again. Instead, I was assigned to washing clothes belonging to the prison staff—which gave me some exercise and allowed me out into one of the prison courtyards, where the washing sessions took place. Even this I welcomed, despite the appalling filth of the clothes handed to us, since it involved at least a trip out of my cell. Somehow, the prison authorities also found out that I could draw, and I was one day led into an office and told to copy some propaganda posters, to be hung up on the walls of the prison canteen for cadres. The posters showed factory workers and peasants, scrubbed and cheerful, working hard to fulfill their part in the Great Leap Forward. They were not difficult to copy. By late afternoon I had reproduced a number of them. A keeper called Liu, a fierce, unsmiling young man, looked at them carefully. "This one's no good," he said. "Look, you've made the worker look like a hunchback. This," he said sententiously, "is obviously a consequence of your reactionary state of mind." I pointed to the original, which I had duplicated to the best of my ability. "Granted, the original drawing is poor, but you should improve on them," he said grudgingly. "You know how to draw, don't you? Can't you understand that this is not what the glorious workers look like?" I eyed him covertly. Could he, after all, be blessed with a sense of humor? No, Keeper Liu was dead serious. I had to tear up the offending poster and set to work again. This time I made the worker into a Hercules. Keeper Liu was satisfied.

My cell-mates, too, learnt that I could draw, and pestered me to draw their portraits on whatever paper was available. I drew them, to their delight, mostly on lavatory paper, which was all that was available. I even made a complete mah-jong set out of an old cardboard box, and as counters we used some dusty, wafer-thin dry biscuits which I had obtained from one of the keepers. The 136 mah-jong cards soon became dog-eared, but I was particularly proud of the four jokers. Their faces were in the unmistakable likenesses of Judge Tseng, who had supervised my interrogation, Horseface Sun, pockmarked Ah Wu and another, particularly ugly keeper called Liao. One of my cell-mates would keep watch by the door to warn us of approaching footsteps. We played for hours. But one day, during a clothes washing session, I was fool enough to tell another woman prisoner about our mahjong sessions. The next day the cell was searched and the set found. Sun put on a convincing act. She stormed, she raved, she screamed. Fortunately she didn't look too closely at the faces on the jokers, and there was little disciplinary action she could take; the prison was too full to allow for spells of solitary confinement, and the food already so meager that to reduce rations would be to cause us to starve to death. Eventually, since I accepted full responsibility for making the mah-jong game in the first place, I was ordered to write a full confession, which I did, in suitably abject terms. The set was, of course, confiscated.

By this time my awe of the prison staff had largely disappeared, for over the months I had realized that beneath the formal sternness of the prison authorities, their parrotlike quotation of Marxist slogans and their apparent eagerness to "serve the people" by appearing to be model prison warders, there was a very real odor of favoritism and corruption. Perhaps inevitably, the bored and frustrated male keepers—and the male trusties—constantly tried to take advantage of the women prisoners. And my eventual departure from Canton Prison was the result of an upheaval and full-scale purge among the prison staff when such laxity was eventually discovered by senior officials. I am not too proud of my own conduct in this connection—insofar as I, too, took advantage of the keepers' weaknesses. In my own case, however, I was not only eager for special treatment and better food—to avoid outright physical collapse. I needed sympathy, and above all I needed to feel that I wasn't completely alone. The monthly, stereotyped notes from my family provided the only link with the outside world, and apart from a few cell-mates, who never stayed long, I found I had little in common with the run-of-the-mill prisoners who came to my cell and left it after a few days. That is how I came to develop a feeling of friendship, which grew into something more, for Yu Ching-lung, the prison doctor, who was so very different from all the other keepers and trusties. Ironically, I was eventually responsible for doing him considerable harm —for the doctor was himself a trusty and his sentence was prolonged largely as a result of what I was compelled to write about him in my last confession before my own transfer. Here, as far as I remember it, is the full story of Yu, who was eventually responsible for the bulk of the prison warders in the women's section of Canton Prison being purged.

I first met the prison doctor during the hideously hot Canton summer, after I had begged Horseface Sun to get me some treatment for a bad rash of prickly heat which had turned septic and was causing me much pain. For days I had hoped that the prickly heat would go away—our cells were unbelievably hot—but persistent scratching had made it worse. The cell itself was dirty and my nails, however much I attempted to keep them clean, were always black. Finally, a series of large boils erupted all over my shoulders, my back and my thighs, and all I could do was lie face down on my bunk, crying with pain and exhaustion. I no longer cared whether the keepers, Peeping Toms almost to a man, saw me naked or not. I couldn't bear my back coming into contact with anything. In the past, I had spent hours squatting by the cell door, simply in order to take advantage of the slight breeze from the corridor outside (my cell faced West and caught the sun most of the time), dressed only in my underclothes; on one occasion the pockmarked keeper Ah Wu had grabbed me through the cell door aperture and I had had to struggle to get free. But in my present state I could not have aroused anything but repulsion, for I sensed—though I couldn't actually see it, for I had no mirror—that my entire back was a mass of boils and sores.

Eventually the doctor came, accompanied by Horseface. He looked at my boils carefully, without saying a word, and left. A short time later he was back at the cell door. Opening the small window in it, he called me over: "Here's your medicine, twenty-six seventy-five," he said. "Take these pills. Put the liquid on your boils and above all, leave them alone." He paused, and winked. "I've heard about you already. In fact I've seen you several times, but you haven't seen me." I realized he must be alone, and the thought dawned that perhaps he was a prisoner too. In Mandarin (which most of the Cantonese staff couldn't understand) he said softly: "Take it easy. It'll soon be over."

"Where's Keeper Sun?" I asked.

"Don't worry about her. She relies on me for certain things. I'm not afraid of her. See you tomorrow."

I was puzzled and intrigued by the doctor, even that first day, when I was in pain. He talked as though we were old friends. His concern seemed genuine and his cheerful manner was a boost to morale. He was a striking-looking man, in his early thirties perhaps, and I learnt later what I had suspected from the first: he was of mixed blood with fair hair, light brown eyes and regular features. His mother was a Russian refugee; his father, Chinese, from Shanghai. My other hunch proved correct: he was himself a prisoner, although an exceedingly privileged one. By his own admission, he had been sentenced for smuggling medicine into China from Hongkong. Only later did I find out that there were other charges as well.

The following day, he came to see me, again accompanied by Sun. I explained that I had had difficulty in applying the medicine to my back. He asked me to lie down on my bunk. He was gentle and efficient. "Don't stand up," he said. "Stay as you are until the liquid has dried." In the next few days, he often came my way, opened the window in my cell door and waved. "How are you? Better? That's good." It was the first time since my arrest that I had been shown any kindness, and my heart went out to him. Gradually, my back healed. The rains came, and the temperatures dropped. I didn't see the doctor often, but I thought about him. There wasn't much else to do.

Some time later, the Moon Festival occurred and this turned out to be an occasion for the prison staff to make money out of those eager to get some kind of special food, however rotten, to celebrate what is China's most important traditional holiday. The Moon Festival is above all the occasion for large family gatherings, and we felt particularly homesick. In Hongkong my own family would be together. In China, I gathered, the Moon Festival had lost some of its importance, and in any case food shortages caused by the Great Leap Forward precluded any feasting. But Chou Teh, one of the trusties responsible for meal distribution, opened my cell door window that morning and said: "Hey, you have money? Extra dishes today if you can pay."

"How much?" I asked.

"You can have some boiled chicken at eighty cents a catty" (about 1.1 pound). I gave him eighty cents. "You'll be able to eat all that all by yourself?" I assured him that I was so hungry that he need not worry on my account. That evening, he brought me the chicken. It was dark brown in color, and the taste was vinegary, with a great deal of ginger. I suspected that the spices might have been added to conceal the original taste of the chicken, and other prisoners who had bought some agreed that the chickens used for this special dish had either died of illness or of old age.

I had just finished the chicken when Keeper Liao opened my cell door and said that the time had come for another investigation. I couldn't believe him, for my case had been finally settled, but followed him through the deserted prison corridors. Liao was an exceedingly ugly man, almost a hunchback, but he was among the least unpleasant of the warders; obscurely, I felt he liked me. Often, when no other keepers were around, he would open my door panel and chat. Tonight he was silent and I wondered what it was all about. There seemed to be no judges on duty, and keepers were not authorized, or competent, to carry out investigations of their own. I cast my mind back on the past few days and wondered whether I had unwittingly broken any of the prison rules.

At last we came to an empty office. Liao ushered me in, shut the door and went over to the window. "Look," he said. "There's the moon. I knew you couldn't catch a glimpse of it from your cell, so I brought you here so you could see it." I was touched and thanked him. He responded by taking me in his arms and kissing me, holding me close to his barrel-like chest. I struggled to get free. "Leave me alone, you fool," I said. "Do you want me to scream for help?" He let go of me, looked miserable and said: "Please don't do that. Sit down. I want to tell you something."

"I won't sit down and I won't stay," I said. "Take me back to my cell."

Liao sat down himself. "Please don't be angry," he said. "I shan't take advantage of you. I'm in love with you and want to marry you." He went on to say that he had spotted me ever since I had come to Canton Prison. Of all the women prisoners he had seen, I was the nicest, he said. My sentence wouldn't last long. He was convinced that I would be set free soon "because you are so different from the others." This being so, Liao said, he was prepared to wait until I left the prison and would marry me immediately afterwards. Would I agree to this?

I shall never know to what extent Liao was sincere; in his conversations with prisoners, he was always referring to the fact that throughout his life, both as a guerrilla fighter and thereafter, he had never had time to find a wife. The thought of marrying this grotesque figure was so absurd that I wanted to burst out laughing. At the same time that part of me which had become wary as a result of my prison experience dictated that I should take advantage of Liao's indiscretion to extract some benefit from it. So I quietly told Liao that he was out of his mind to talk this way to a prisoner, and that he was probably aware that if this became known he himself would lose his job and be put in jail himself. Liao became agitated, and begged me not to tell anyone. "If I were free, I'd help you to find a wife," I said. "Now, take me back to my cell." I knew that from then onwards I had some hold over Liao, and I must confess that I took advantage of this to get additional food and other minor privileges.

Later I found out that Liao proposed to all the likely girl prisoners.

That night, I was violently ill; so were other prisoners who had eaten the special dish of chicken and I again asked Horseface Sun to get Doctor Yu. He gave me an injection and said he would be back with pills. He appeared at the cell door and spoke to me in a low voice. "Here are the pills," he said. "There's a note inside. Read it carefully."

It was a brief, affectionate note—not a real love letter. Doctor Yu said he "preciously cherished" the memory of our first meeting and wanted to be "your faithful friend." "If you need anything, I will always be at your service," it said.

Coming after Liao's clumsy declaration the doctor's note impressed me. He had also written that he himself had been brought up a Catholic, and always tried to do his best to help the Catholic prisoners. He came to visit me several times from then on, pretending that my general condition needed looking into.

I found him an amusing, attractive person—and he was a mine of information about Canton Prison. He told me about the various keepers, how they were all, in some way or another, in his debt for services rendered by him. Even the chief warden, he said, regarded him as a specially valuable prisoner because he had treated and cured his two sons when they had been near death. He managed to supply the prison staff with medicine from the prison stores at a time when any form of medicine was in short supply in Canton. Even the uncompromising Horseface Sun was using him to get medicine for her sick husband, he said. In return, he was allowed more or less to do as he pleased inside the jail. He had the free run of the place, and used the meal distributors, trusties and even some of the keepers virtually as errand boys. It was my first insight into the unofficial workings of the prison.

Doctor Yu was as good as his word, and thanks to him I started getting slightly better food. On several occasions, instead of watery soup, I got a bowl of rice with slivers of pork concealed in it—an unheard-of luxury. He also gave me cod-liver oil and vitamin pills, which I badly needed, for my joints were swollen and my hair was starting to fall out. Horseface scolded me when— as often happened—I used to ask her to get Doctor Yu for me, but now I no longer feared her. She was quite obviously furious at the preferential treatment I was getting, but unable—or un- willing—to complain about the doctor. As for poor Keeper Liao, I treated him more like a messenger boy than anything else. But he never thought of objecting to this.

Throughout the autumn, I continued to see the doctor often, though usually only for a few minutes at a time. It was probably being in prison that focused my thoughts on him. He wrote me short notes, and they varied from the jocular to the sentimental. I remember one of them well, because it would not have been out of place in a cheap novelette: "I have constantly observed you these past few days," he wrote. "I have the greatest admiration for you. It's as though you were specially sent here to give me comfort and encouragement.

"I don't think I could live without being assured of a glimpse of you every day. Would it be possible for you to love me? Could you envisage sharing your life with me?"

The question seemed academic, for we were both sentenced to years of imprisonment. I never gave him a definite answer. Though I liked him, I felt that it was absurd to get engaged under such circumstances. But I was flattered by his interest in me. One has to bear in mind the grinding monotony of prison life to understand the importance of my mild love affair with Doctor Yu.

Then, as autumn became winter, I saw less and less of him. On a rare visit, speaking through the window of my cell door with a docile guard by his side, he said that Keeper Sun had a grudge against him, and had warned him against showing too much con- cern for the women prisoners. In fact, without my realizing it, the scene was set for a widespread change.

The doctor's assistant was a rather unpleasant young man called Li Wei. It was Li Wei who first hinted that Doctor Yu was in trouble. Li Wei was perhaps jealous of the doctor's success with women. In any case, one day he asked me to draw some- thing for him. I didn't particularly like Li Wei, so I refused. "You draw for all the others," he said. "Why don't you want to draw for me? If Doctor Yu asked you, you'd do it like a shot." I didn't say anything. "Of course you know the doctor isn't in- terested in you any more. He's found another girl—she's a Catho- lic too, by the way. In cell number twenty-eight. She's called Li

Jen-kuan and she looks a bit like you. If you don't believe me, just keep your eyes and ears open."

The news didn't really bother me. Doctor Yu, I thought, was entitled to his own private life. I told Li Wei that he was mistaken if he thought that there was anything unusual about my relations with Doctor Yu. "I like him and respect him," I said, "because he was very kind to me when I was ill last summer. I know Li Jen-kuan," I added. "She's a friend of mine. We used to meet after church on Sundays in Canton. Be sure and give her my love." Deep down, I was a little jealous. But again, one must remember that in jail the smallest things take on an exaggerated importance.

Shortly afterwards, a keeper ordered me to change my cell, and I was moved from number thirty-five to number thirty-eight. That evening, when the time came for the evening meal, it was handed out by three unfamiliar little women wearing face masks against germs. The following morning the usual meal distributor was missing again. The prison corridor buzzed with rumors. Usually at mealtimes one exchanged a few words with whoever was handling the food. The new people refused to talk and moved hurriedly away. The keepers had vanished, too, and a new batch took their place. I had the feeling that Doctor Yu might be involved and sent out a written note asking for the doctor to visit me, on the pretext of a stomach ache. The man who came to see me was not Yu, but a new doctor, also a prisoner, very formal and very impersonal.

Finally, two days later, I was summoned for questioning. This time I was taken to a part of the prison I had never been in before, and the man whose office I entered seemed to be of high rank. The prison staff addressed him as "comrade section chief." He was a wizened, middle-aged man, forthright, direct and with an air of authority about him. He reminded me of some of the veteran Communist cadres I had met in the early days of the Communist regime. He was neither fanatical nor of the bullying kind, yet one felt that he deeply believed in his job and in the party. He came straight to the point.

"There have been some changes in the prison," he said, "and you may believe with some degree of accuracy that these changes are in part connected with your own behavior in jail. Certain charges have been laid against a number of the prison staff. We want to get to the bottom of this. You can help us." He reminded me that it was my duty to speak up, and that it could be held to be proof that I was undergoing satisfactory reform. He even said there was nothing personal about it. "It's rather like confessing to one's priest if one is a Catholic." He paused. "Now," he said, "will you help us?"

I was at a loss to answer. My immediate reaction was to remember all that had happened to me in the nine preceding months since my arrest. Why should I co-operate with such people? I hated them for depriving me of my freedom, for the mental and physical sufferings they had occasioned. My instinct was to challenge all the rules I was subjected to. I decided to say nothing. Besides, it seemed to me that there was little to confess. Yes, I had had a platonic flirtation with Doctor Yu. Yes, I had used Keeper Liao to gain a few minor advantages. What right did the prison authorities have to pester me in this way? I mumbled that I had nothing to say.

Section Chief Chen shook his head sadly. "I am sorry for you," he said. "You are missing the chance of confessing your faults. You should be frank with the government. I had hoped it would be possible to find a way of reducing your sentence if you had exposed the mistakes of others and your own shortcomings in prison. You don't want a lengthier prison sentence, do you?"

I kept silent.

"I will give you more time," he went on. "You are a highly intelligent person. I don't think you like the idea of confession. You regard yourself as above that sort of thing. But you must trust the government and the party. It's the only way."

The next day I was back in the section chief's office.

"If you won't talk, there are others who will," he said quietly.

"Here, for instance, is part of a confession from a prisoner you may know—Wei Mo-ching." Indeed I knew her well. She was a Catholic, sentenced to fifteen years imprisonment on a charge as trumped-up as mine, and—according to the gossip of the prison —suffering from acute tuberculosis.

"You may even be familiar with her handwriting. Read what she has to say." And he handed over the stapled sheets of paper.

I read: "Doctor Yu took great care of me. He was most kind and gentle, and professed his sincere love for me. I fell in love with him. He made me promise that I would marry him after I finished my jail sentence. He asked me to write to my fiancé— he is also in jail—to break off my engagement, which I did. Doctor Yu would come and talk to me through the cell door. We would hold hands and he would say how much difference I had made to his life. . . ."

There was more of the same.

I said: "This has nothing to do with me."

Section Chief Chen handed me another batch of papers.

"Here's another confession," he said. "Please read it."

This one was from Li Jen-kuan, the girl mentioned by Doctor Yu's assistant. I read only a few lines. "The doctor said that all the prison inmates are in love with him. But he said that I was much the best-looking of all, and that he cared only for me. He wrote me little notes daily. He helped me with small favors whenever I asked him. We used to talk, through the cell door, and sometimes he would take my hand and kiss it."

"Now," said Section Chief Chen, "do you see what kind of a person Doctor Yu is? Do you still have nothing to say?"

He could see me wavering. "If you don't want to set everything down straight away, that's perfectly all right," he said courteously. "But the government wants to get to the bottom of things, no matter how long it takes. You may go now."

I went back to my cell, but not for long. The new keeper ordered me to pack again. We crossed the street. I found myself back in the detention center where I had first been interrogated.

This frightened me very much. I was in solitary confinement, and the reason for my going back to this place might well be that I would be sentenced all over again. I was distraught with anxiety, and there was no one I could turn to. I no longer trusted anyone. The following day, Section Chief Chen came to see me. I asked him why I had been moved. "It's very simple," he said. "We thought it would be easier for you to make up your mind here, away from the other inmates, the keepers and so on."

He said he gave me his word that my confession would not lead to any new charges against me, and that it would not lengthen my present sentence. "I think you are not really at fault. The others have taken advantage of your youth and innocence." He said that to prove his trust in me he would show me documents which he was not supposed to show to prisoners. "This," he said, "is part of Doctor Yu's record. You will see he is not quite the person he has made himself out to be."

The record was a full one. It contained photographs of him with his wife and two children, a small son and an even smaller daughter. Why had he told me that he was unmarried? The record was more revealing. It showed that he had only partly told the truth when he had said that he was in jail for smuggling medicine from Hongkong into China. According to the charge sheet, he had used the money to lure young women away from their families, and the main charge, in fact, was one of rape, substantiated by formal accusations of eight young girls under sixteen. In his defense, the doctor had claimed that all of them had been willing, and his seven-year sentence—a lenient one in view of the seriousness of the charges—had taken this into account. There was even a letter from the doctor's wife, asking for a divorce but making no financial claims on him. The letter was a dignified, restrained one, probably written under duress. But it revealed Doctor Yu as a completely unstable personality, forever running after women, and I felt, there and then, that he was mentally ill. For in jail, his pursuit of eligible young women was pathetic and fruitless. Why compel someone who is in any case serving a fifteen-year sentence to break off her engagement? There seemed to be a streak of madness here.

I therefore decided that I would be wrong to keep silent. In any case, Doctor Yu was in sufficient trouble already. But if I were to write about his conduct in jail, I would have to bring all the others into it as well—and the over-all result would be to harm the keepers more than Yu himself. Quite frankly, I didn't mind what the consequences would be.

So in the long run I wrote a confession, telling everything about my life in jail—or almost. I gave a fairly full account of Doctor Yu's flirtation, his interest in me, his frequent notes and sentimental love letters; but I also explained how the lax mechanism of the jail had allowed all this to occur, and how Doctor Yu benefited from the complicity of keepers and prison staff. I was not particularly proud of myself when I finished.

As it turned out, my confession was only a drop in the ocean. By the time Section Chief Chen had finished, almost everyone on the staff of the jail was in trouble. Later on, I got to hear the result of his investigations: Doctor Yu had his sentence prolonged by another ten years; Horseface Sun was sacked. She confessed to having slept with the insatiable Doctor Yu after he had promised to teach her how to play the mouth organ! Pockmarked Ah Wu, the most notorious Peeping Tom in the prison, was sent to a labor camp. It was established that he, too, had slept with women prisoners. Keeper Liao, who had proposed marriage to me, was also dismissed. I was in fact able to do him a good turn after all: I did not mention in my confession his extraordinary proposal of marriage made on the night of the Moon Festival. But another keeper, who had been even more of a Don Juan than Doctor Yu, was sentenced to fifteen years in jail. Even today, I find it difficult to write about Yu, his charm and his way with women. For even outside of a jail, he would probably have had considerable success as a ladies' man.

For the rest of my time in Canton Prison (for I was moved back again), we settled down to dull routine, under the strict, impersonal supervision of a stern set of keepers who stuck completely to the prison rules. With nothing to do, I found the routine hideously boring. Part of the time I was in a near coma as a result of constant pangs of hunger. It was with relief, three months later, that I packed my few belongings after being told that I was definitely being moved—probably to a labor camp.

CHAPTER V

FULL HOUSE

I WAS TAKEN not to a labor camp, as I had expected, but to a place I recognized immediately—and with dread, as one of the worst jails in China. Those familiar with Canton know all about Tsang Pien Mansions. People don't linger in the street outside but walk past it as quickly as they can, avoiding the entire street when possible. The entrance is usually cluttered up with trucks full of handcuffed prisoners, of people being brought there under police escort by Jeep and even by pedicab. It is the jail nearest Canton's main courthouse, and a common form of insult in Cantonese is to say: "Why don't you go to Tsang Pien Mansions for a rest?"

Roughly, this is the equivalent of saying: "Why don't you go to hell?"

A taste of the hell came while I was being "processed" once more before being assigned to a cell. Someone screamed, "Squat down!"

I said I couldn't. "My legs go numb. I'm sick." I was polite, but defiant. Giving a short grunt, the tough female warder tripped me up, expertly, and pushed me to the floor. She looked at me with the eyes of a dead fish, and silently, with a gesture born of long experience, tipped the entire contents of my suitcase onto the filthy floor.

"Hongkong identity card, eh?" She picked it up and looked at it. "Well, you won't be needing that any more." She tore it up.

I shouted. "But the judge said . . ."

"Shut up. So you still think you'll be going back. You must be dreaming."

She went back to the torn ID card and deliberately tore it into smaller pieces. "Now you may take this"—pointing to a few clothes—"but all the rest is confiscated. Books, private possessions. Not allowed here."

I stared past her, ignoring her. She shook me roughly. "Mind how you behave. I'll see to it that if you get any funny ideas, I'll knock them out of you. Come on. Up. Move!"

I was carrying my bundle, cowed and speechless. We were

walking along a corridor. The cell doors were not solid, but were openwork iron gates. One could see through them into the packed crowds inside. Suddenly she opened a gate, pushed me inside, slammed the gate shut behind me and left.

The smell of excrement and urine hit me first and I thought I would faint. The cell, as I remember it, must have been about twelve feet square, with two double tiers of bunks on either side, a narrow passage in between and a toilet at one end. Inside this small area there were between thirty and forty women lying packed together on the bunks and squatting on the floor. There just didn't seem to be any room for an additional person and I just stood where I was, with people squatting around my feet. A stern, hollow-eyed old hag pulled me inside. "Here's your place," she said, pointing to a few available inches next to the toilet. "You should have come earlier if you wanted a place on a bunk." She noticed me holding my nose, and said: "If it's luxury you want, you should go to a hotel." She walked back to her own assigned place, and I noticed that she had more space on her bunk than the others. As she moved, the women got out of her way. I concluded she was an old-timer, an unofficial cell leader and the local bully.

Someone shouted my name. Looking up, I discovered that I knew one of the inmates. She was an elderly lady of a respectable family and had shared my cell in Canton's Number One Prison a few months after my arrest. She had been sentenced to a long prison term for having counterfeit money in her possession—the money had been given to her by a relative from Hongkong and she had not known it was worthless.

We talked about old times and about our cell-mates. "Watch out for the cell leader," she whispered. "She's a real dragon. She used to be a Buddhist nun, but it hasn't improved her temper any. She takes a positive pleasure in getting the other prisoners into trouble, and reports everything people say to the authorities. Be careful. They don't just shout here. They hit you."

A bell rang for lights out. Everyone slept where they were. The lucky ones could actually lie down on their bunks. The rest half sat, half propped themselves against each other. I tried to keep away from the toilet. But if I was to avoid it, I had to get uncomfortably close to my neighbor. She immediately pinched me, hard, in the leg.

I shouted: "Hey! What did you do that for? That hurt."

My neighbor, whom I could hardly distinguish in the dark, said:

"That's what you get for pressing against me." She turned her back.

Other voices were raised now. "Shut up!"

"Damn her, she's waking everyone up!"

"Give her a damn good kick."

A warder appeared in the passage outside. "Quiet everybody! Anyone making a sound will have to stand till morning." Everyone kept quiet.

There was still no way for me to lie down. I got up and squatted in the passage between the bunks. I fell asleep in a sitting position.

At daybreak we were let out in two groups to wash. There was a tiny bathroom, with a tap and two basins—and twenty people all fighting for them. Knowing that I didn't stand a chance, I just wiped my face on a damp, dirty towel, and waited until the others had finished. One of the prisoners was drying herself and getting dressed. Another prisoner splashed her accidentally. Furious, she picked up a basin of soapy water and threw it over the other woman's clothes, then grabbed her by the hair and scratched her face. They fought, using terrible language. The ex-nun heard the commotion and rushed up. "Keeper, keeper, Chang and Li are fighting again!" she shouted with obvious relish. They were made to empty the toilet as punishment.

There was constant bullying here, and the prisoners were as nasty to each other as the warders were to them. The appalling conditions of the jail seemed to have turned them into animals. They vented all their anger and their frustrations on each other. And in this lot there was a high proportion of hardened criminals, including murderers.

Apart from a daily visit to the bathroom, where I finally learnt to grab the tin basin and fend for myself, I only explored the prison corridors once—and that was on my third day, when I was ordered by the ex-nun to empty the brimful toilet bucket. It was too heavy for me to lift alone, and the old lady I had known in Canton Prison offered to help.

We had to carry the bucket step by step downstairs, and on the floor below I could see there were cells for men, just as crowded as ours. There was a great deal of activity, prisoners coming and going, some of them clutching pieces of paper. There was random shouting, which an armed guard seemed not to mind—or perhaps (he looked like a Northerner) he couldn't understand what they were saying.

Prisoners had put their heads through the bars of their cell doors.

"Got your diploma?"

"Right. Ten years."

"Well, now you know where your meals will be coming from."

"I got more than that. Twenty."

"Do you know, the judges are working overtime. They're lining up to be sentenced."

"Business is booming all right."

An old man stood leaning against one of the cell gates. He said: "You know, in all my sixty years, I've never seen people standing in line to be sentenced. That's socialism for you."

"Yes, socialism is good."

A few of them broke into the then popular song, "Socialism is Good," to the bewilderment of the sentry.

I could hardly believe the men. Yet I, too, saw a long line of prisoners, shepherded by harassed guards, lining up outside an improvised court near where we emptied the toilet bucket. Every few seconds, it seemed, prisoners would emerge with their slips of paper—the record of their sentence. They seemed quite unmoved. Many of them, from the banter which they exchanged with the waiting prisoners, had received ten- or twenty-year sentences. I remembered how I had cried all night, and was ashamed. I wondered how many of those now emerging from the court had been arrested on trumped-up charges. The courtyard inside the jail was packed with handcuffed prisoners of both sexes. Some were crying, others were almost jaunty. My companion told me that there was literally no room any more for prisoners, now that the Great Leap Forward had got into its stride. Anyone who spoke up, in however moderate terms, against present-day hardships was liable to arrest. "Soon," the old lady said, "there'll be more people inside jail than there are outside."

When we got back to our cell there were seven new women prisoners, and they could now scarcely sit. We had difficulty in putting the toilet bucket back in its accustomed place. I thought to myself: "I can't stand it here; I'd rather die. At that moment, a warder came up to our cell door. From the outside, she shouted out a list of names. Mine was among them. "All right," she said. "You'll be moving off. Get your things and assemble in the corridor." I thought: I don't care where they take me now. Anything is better than this.

If I had known what was in store, I wouldn't have been so pleased.

CHAPTER VI

STONES

THE GOOD PEOPLE OF Canton going about their business in the early morning paid no attention to the truck which drove out of Tsang Pien Jail and through the streets. If they had looked closely, they could have seen that inside it were some thirty prisoners handcuffed to each other. I was relatively privileged, sitting up front with the driver and one of the guards, and without handcuffs. The truck lumbered through Canton center with agonizing slowness. We did not know where we were going, and I thought that this time we might be due for a long trip north.

A town takes on a new and mysterious quality when seen through a prisoner's eyes. This is his sole glimpse of people leading a normal existence. I felt understandably sad as the truck turned down streets I knew well, crossing the Liu Hua Bridge, past the Sun Yat-sen Memorial Hall and out into the dingy suburbs. It was obvious we were heading for the countryside, but I knew better by now than to ask the driver where we were bound. After little more than half an hour, the truck turned off a main road and down a dirt track, through paddy fields and into a large enclosure.

It seemed to be neither a prison nor a labor camp but a mixture of the two. There were soldiers standing around, by large barnlike buildings which were set down in a kind of wasteland. The buildings were in a hollow, and all around were some gray-looking hills. Dotting the landscape were huge piles of stones, and a small-gauge railroad track ran through the camp. We saw one inmate who might have been a man or a woman, for his features were so haggard as to be sexless. He was in rags, a skeleton, as filthy as a beggar, and obviously in the last stages of exhaustion. Yet he was squatting on a small stool, chipping at a large stone with a hammer as though his life depended on it. As we got out of the truck, we saw that there were several such groups, gathered in a rough circle, all breaking stones with their hammers. They looked as if they were at death's door, and I was speechless with terror at the idea that this was how we would look in a few weeks' time. Above the sound of the hammers chipping away, a raucous woman's voice

could be heard booming out through a megaphone, encouraging
the inmates on to further efforts. "Use your strength, work hard,
fight for better production and show that you're eager to repent
. . . no slackening off. Keep it up. Show your love for the people
by hard work." We were, I learned, at Niu Tou K'eng Reform
Camp for political prisoners and hardened criminals, one of several
camps in Canton's suburbs. Compared to other such camps, it was
small, with about 130 women and five hundred to six hundred
men, a few dozen cadres and about thirty soldiers to guard the
premises. In a sense, it could be described as an open prison, for
there were no walls, no barbed wire and no visible signs of confinement. But for all practical purposes it was a slave camp, and
its staff drove the inmates so hard that, for most of us, utter
exhaustion would preclude any chance of escape. Moreover, as I
learnt, the farmers in the neighboring paddy fields would have
reported escapees, for they were terrorized by the proximity of the
guards and never came near our camp. The men assembled and,
still handcuffed to one another, were marched away. A woman
cadre came and looked me over. I was ordered to follow her and
she led the way into one of the barns. It contained four rows of
double-deckered bunks. I was allotted an upper berth. There was
of course no mattress, just bare boards and a couple of moth-eaten,
dirty blankets. "You needn't start work till tomorrow," she said
as though doing me an immense favor. "But in the meantime
you'll write out a report about yourself—family background,
personal history, the nature of your crime and so on." I stared
at my new surroundings. The walls were made of bamboo and
mud, the floor was beaten black dirt and the entire place stank
of sweat, dirt and dust, I tried to sweep my own bedboards
clean and spread some of my clothes out. I made a bundle with
the rest to serve as pillow and lay down.

I wasn't alone long. A clutter of people came into the barn for
the noon recess. Some of these people I had already caught a
glimpse of at work. They were covered in dust and grime and it
was still impossible to tell by their faces who was young and who
was old. They moved like sleepwalkers. Each carried a hammer, a
small wooden stool, a carrying pole, two wicker baskets and a
hoe. Sheer physical exhaustion was written on each face. But one
woman came up with a broad smile and clasped my hands. I felt
the hardness of her calloused palms. "Don't you recognize me?
I'm Wei Mo-ching. From Hongkong. Remember? I was in the cell
opposite yours in Canton Prison. I used to visit your home in

Hongkong. You haven't forgotten me, have you?" I knew only her voice. I didn't dare say: "I don't recognize you. You look at least fifty years old" (she was my age), but burst into tears. Wei Mo-ching was a sweet, gentle girl I had known slightly in Hongkong, but to tell the truth I was crying not only because I felt sorry for her but also because I knew that this was how I would look after a year in this place. "Don't cry, it's forbidden to cry here. It's a bourgeois stigma to be afraid of hardship, that's what they say here. Oh, they're very orthodox in this place, I can tell you. Don't ever express your true feelings, or you'll get into fearful trouble. Obedience, diligence and repentance. That's the way to survive here," Wei Mo-ching said, and she attempted to comfort me by brushing my tears away. Her fingers were like sandpaper.

An orderly had brought a basin of vegetable soup into the barn and the women lined up for it. I did not get any. The food had been calculated on the basis of one small bowl each, and the staff had obviously not been informed of my coming. After draining the soup, the women all stretched out in their bunks and were soon fast asleep. At one-thirty, the bell rang for the afternoon shift, and a woman cadre yelled at them to get out fast and start work again. I sat on the boards of my bunk and for the umpteenth time wrote out my family history and my confession.

It was pitch-dark the next day when the bell sounded, summoning us to work. The 130 women in the four big barns immediately got out of bed and folded their blankets army-fashion. I did the same, more clumsily. Following the others, I went outside to a crude latrine in the open air. All the women except me had small buckets with water, and they washed and brushed their teeth in the open air. I had no bucket, and no idea where to draw some water from, and spent precious minutes wandering around the camp, too shy to ask. The result was that I was late for parade.

One of the section leaders saw me and hustled me over to a waiting squad. "Everyone's late because of you!" she said and shook me by the shoulder. "This is our unit, Number Two Squad, and we're assigned to stone breaking. Everyone has a quota here, and even the oldest, slowest inmate is expected to get through thirty to forty baskets a day. You're new, so I won't expect more than ten baskets from you this first day." She spoke with the clipped tones of a drill instructor. I learnt with some surprise later on that she herself was a convict, but a trusty whose zeal and brutality provided her with a privileged position in the camp, including special rations.

Each squad was assigned on a rotating basis to a special task in what was in fact a huge quarry. One squad was responsible for removing the earth from the rock face; another squad moved the huge chunks of rock down the hill to the plain below once the rock surface had been blasted; others carried the chunks of rock out to the various squads engaged in stone breaking; and others collected the stones, broken down to a few inches across, loaded them into small rail carts and pushed them through the camp on the small-gauge railroad to a point where they were taken out of the camp on trucks. The stones were used both for building and road making.

We moved off to a clearing, where huge pieces of rock were lying about. The section leader gave me a small stool and a hammer with a bamboo handle. Looking up to the hills beyond, I could see armed sentries silhouetted against the sky. The megaphones started blaring and we started hammering.

An inmate working nearby took time off to show me how to work. "You hold the large stone in your left hand—so. You should break it by hammering at the grain, and try for a natural break in the stone. You'll get used to it after a while. The thing to remember is to make them neither too big nor too small. Three inches across is ideal." I hammered away, and as the sun became hotter, I was drenched in sweat. We were working in an exposed clearing, with no shade and no hats.

One of the girls on my left gave a sharp cry as a small piece of stone flew up and hit her in the forehead. She started to bleed quite heavily and the section leader came over. "Well, what are you stopping work for? It's only a small cut. Afraid of a little blood? It'll heal." I noticed that everyone around me was accumulating large heaps of cut stones. For all my hammering, I had only a few.

At eight-thirty, after we had been at work for two hours, there was a break for a meal. An orderly came round with a tin tray. There was a small bowl of rice each, and a basin of vegetables, into which we all dipped. The rice tasted good. We had all eaten in five minutes, and set to work again. My right hand was blistered and painful, and my back was sore with squatting down on the low stool. I was unused to exercise, having been cooped up for almost a year in a prison cell, and felt that this probably explained my poor performance. I had to grit my teeth to keep at it.

The noon bell rang. We marched back to our barn, swallowed some kind of bitter mixture of rice and bran mash and lay down on our bunks. Like everyone else, I fell asleep, awoke with a jolt when the bell rang again and mustered outside with the others for the afternoon shift.

That first afternoon, the blisters on my right hand burst and I could hardly hold the hammer. I twisted a rag round my palm, but every stroke of the hammer was painful. The afternoon dragged on, endlessly.

At last it was time to stop work and another unit took over, whose task was to weigh and check everybody's work and load the stones onto the miniature railroad. But first, we had to carry our stones ourselves to a central point where the supervisors checked them. This was what the carrying pole and the wicker baskets were for. I noticed that most women in my squad had broken between thirty and forty baskets of stones, and some had worked even harder, and had sixty baskets to show for their day's work. I had a miserable three and a half baskets of stones, and even then I made a mess of it, tripping over and spilling my first basketful, which I had to kneel down and collect all over again.

"Is that all? You mean to say"—pause—"you've only done *three and a half basketfuls?*" It was difficult to tell whether the incredulous anger was real or simulated. "Didn't you hear me say that ten baskets was an *absolute minimum* on the *first day?*" I was like a child at fault and looked down at the ground in front of me. The section leader was beside herself with rage. "Now, you go straight back and break some more stones. No rest for idle people like you."

Alone, I continued hammering away and would have been at it all night, such was my fear of the section leader, had another inmate not summoned me to the barn an hour later. "It's bath time now," she told me. "The section leader says you can have a bath with the others. What we do is we go to a well and get some water, and wash there. Then we keep some more water for the following morning. There are special times for going to the well. We're only allowed there after work." I said I didn't have a bucket. "You can share mine for the time being," she said. "Next time you write home, ask for one and have it sent out."

As we walked in a group to the well, I was trembling all over with fatigue and could scarcely lift the bucket of water I had been lent. Vaguely, I had expected the bathing session to mark the end of the day. It was dark by now and all I wanted to do was to crawl into my bunk and sleep. Our activities for the day had not, however, been completed. Around 8 P.M., a woman cadre ordered us out again and marched us to another barn, which was used as a lecture room. There were no bunks and no seats. Everyone sat on the small wooden stool which they had brought with them. There were some five hundred men already squatting inside the barn. We women filled the last few rows. At the end of the barn there was a raised stage, and several cadres were sitting there behind desks.

One of them, the camp director maybe, was making a speech. We were subjected to an endless string of platitudes about proving one's ability and willingness to work, improving one's quotas and so on. This was followed by another speech by a cadre which made no references to our work—or to our plight—but extolled the "glorious revolution" and the improvements which had been the people's lot since 1949. Then some inmates were called up onto the platform. These were people who, owing to their work record and their proven docility, were being promoted to be section leaders. The camp director got to his feet and explained that their promotion was all part of a new scheme. In future, there would be competitions between the various squads to show which could do best. Obediently, the newly promoted section leaders echoed their master's concern, and themselves called for more and harder work from all of us, pledging themselves to emulate those who were indulging in the Great Leap Forward in other fields.

Finally the meeting ended, but not before the camp director had announced that our political session the following night would be devoted to a general discussion, amongst ourselves, of what we had just heard. I had dozed off several times during the meeting, which must have lasted almost three hours, and fell into a sound sleep as soon as I got into my bunk. But in the middle of the night, I woke up, remembered where I was, and felt depressed. I remembered the speeches. Doubtless there had been exploitation and cruelty in the "bad old days" before the revolution, I thought, but surely our present predicament was worse then exploitation— with its hypocritical emphasis on achievements of the "Socialist Society" and "reformation through labor." Our present masters not only compelled us to submit to their inhuman program, but also required us to endorse it and sing its praises. I wondered how many people inside China realized what really went on in "labor reformation camps." Suddenly, I began itching all over, and scrabbling about in my bunk, I spotted a dozen or more bedbugs, in single file, crawling out of a gap in one of the planks of my bed. I killed them all, wrapped myself in a blanket and fell asleep.

After a week, I felt as though I had been there for years. My skill improved rapidly. The second day I was out stone breaking, I managed to fill nine baskets; the day after, I had fulfilled my quota of thirty baskets; and after that, I managed to produce more, certainly never producing less than thirty baskets a day. Perhaps because the discipline of the camp was so severe, I hardly spoke to the other inmates. My prime concern was to survive. Here, I was no longer a refined little lady from Hongkong, but had better keep silent and only speak when spoken to. From the cadres' contempt for the sick, and the casual way people were carted off to die when they were too weak to work, I knew that we could not expect any kind of mercy or humane treatment from anyone in authority. And I knew that the camp was riddled with informers, for to gain a few extra privileges, many of the inmates would literally do anything to curry favor with those who ran the camp. In this respect, the trusties were worst of all. They reported to the cadres any suspicious behavior of their fellow convicts, and were constantly on the lookout for subversive talk. Yet somehow we managed to keep up a steam of comment, under our breath.

When it rained, as it did frequently, we were soaked through, yet had to go on with our work, in the full knowledge that we would remain in our soaked clothes all day. Quite often, our other change of clothing was soaked too, so that alternately we shivered and sweated in the sun. We had nothing to look forward to but the end of the day—even then we often were kept awake by political sessions until late at night. We felt so murderously inclined that I wonder if the cadres realized how close they were to being hit over the head with the hammers we had in our hands. Even the sight of armed soldiers patrolling on the skyline was not really a deterrent, for I often reached the stage where death appeared as a pleasanter alternative to the life I was leading. Our special hatred, on these occasions, was mutely directed towards the families of the cadres, who lived in relatively comfortable brick houses and had plenty to eat. Wives and children of cadres would make a show of joining us in fine weather and breaking stones themselves, at ten cents a basketful. (Later the incentive was reduced to the equivalent of five U.S. cents a basket, and their zeal decreased.) As soon as it started to rain, the cadres would scuttle over from their offices with umbrellas in their hands and solicitously escort their families back home while we, of course, went on working in the wet open air.

During one spell of wet weather, we worked under pouring rain for three consecutive days. The camp was a muddy swamp. Perhaps worst off were the women who had to drag the large chunks of rock down the hill to where we broke them up. I remember, as a young girl in Canton, having seen a photograph of a young coal miner, naked except for a loincloth, harnessed to a pit truck. It was often printed in Communist books and periodicals as an example of inhuman exploitation under the old society. Apart from the fact that we were clothed, after a fashion, our plight was similar, if not worse. And in addition to the brutally hard work, we had to acquiesce in the cruel joke of praising the system which had been responsible for incarcerating us.

From time to time we were allowed a respite. Our precious holiday was known as Big Sunday, and it was called this way to differentiate it from other Sundays, when we worked as usual. On the average, we enjoyed one Big Sunday every three weeks, although occasionally they would come once a fortnight and at other times only once a month, according to our own "productivity" and the cadres' whim. On such days, not only did we do no stone breaking or rock hauling, but we were delivered from the drudgery of lectures and spent all day either resting on our bunks or washing our clothes. In the mornings, for a precious fifteen minutes, those with relatives in Canton were allowed to see them. The way such meetings were arranged was a monument to practical good sense.

We were allowed to write and receive one letter a week each. Needless to say, all our letters were handed in for posting unsealed, and the letters we received had been opened and carefully scrutinized by the camp guards. Such letters usually contained phrases such as: "When can we come and see you?" We knew when a Big Sunday was coming up because the guard would say, handing over an opened letter: "You can tell your folks to come next Sunday"—or in two weeks' time, whenever the next holiday was decreed. Sometimes, after having written to our relatives to tell them to come, we had to write a second letter telling them to postpone their trip. Invariably, we knew in advance when they were coming—and, of course, the guards knew all about our various family circumstances.

There was something terribly pathetic about these brief meetings. We would be kept in our barn until the visitors were announced. Then we would be led out and made to squat on the ground. Our visitors would remain standing, if they wished, or they could squat too. But we had to sit on our haunches, and remain in one spot. We were not allowed to walk up and down with our visitors, and of course there was no real conversation. All the cadres turned out for such an occasion, and watched us like hawks. Perhaps the saddest thing about such meetings were the sounds of inmates gobbling down food brought to them by visitors. We ate with the single-minded intensity of hungry animals. Indeed, for those who had been in the camp a long time, this was the one real purpose of such visits; in the fifteen minutes allocated to them, they put away as much cold fried rice and pork as they could manage to eat, without bothering to exchange more than a few words or grunts with those who had brought them food. For no one was allowed to take extra food back into the prisoners' quarters, and after a time our sole preoccupation was with food.

One of the women in my barn had her own name for such visits. She called them "tomb sweeping days," after that ceremony for the dead, when relatives visit a cemetery, tend graves and plant flowers, even leaving food offerings behind if they are devout. She said there was not much to choose between the two functions: relatives were not allowed any real conversation with the inmates, and left their offerings with us with heavy hearts, as though we were already dead. There was usually a great deal of crying too.

I was briefed by a fellow prisoner the day before my first Big Sunday came round. "Whatever you do, don't complain," she said, "or you'll never be allowed another visit again. On the contrary, you must speak up and say that the government is taking good care of you, that you enjoy the work and that you realize it's for your own good. It doesn't matter," she went on. "They'll understand how things really are, just by looking at you. But you must make a good impression on the guards. Don't be afraid of laying it on thick."

That first visit was tremendously exciting, for I had seen none of my family for nearly a year. My younger brother, then still living in Canton, came with a friend. He was carrying food, a plastic bucket and toilet paper. My brother looked over his shoulder and whispered: "You look *awful*. Things must be hard here." I spoke out as I had been advised, but managed to make a face—there were cadres all around us. He nodded. "Don't let grandmother know what's happened," he said. "She thinks you're back in Hongkong. She knows nothing about what really happened. It would kill her." We looked at each other. He had grown, and was obviously burdened by new family responsibilities. "How long are you here for?"

"Five years."

"Why? Whatever did you do?"

I shrugged, and started eating some cake he'd brought me. All around us prisoners were eating. "Can't explain," I said with my mouth full. "Not my fault. Nothing bad really. All a mistake." I didn't dare discuss my case with him, for any recrimination on my part could have led to retrial, and I knew the cadres were watching every gesture. Yet somehow I couldn't bring myself to blurt out that I had been sentenced for "espionage under the cloak of religion." For one thing, I was afraid that he would burst out laughing, for the whole thing was absurd. A bell rang and the guards shooed the visitors away. I picked up my plastic bucket and my toilet paper and went back to my bunk.

CHAPTER VII

IMPACT ON FOUR LIVES

I HAD ALREADY DISCOVERED, during my earlier months in prison, that I possessed unsuspected reserves of strength. Perhaps my Catholic upbringing was a help. In any event, I managed to keep my sanity perhaps better than most of the inmates in the labor camp, and though I was sometimes very close to letting myself die, I never allowed myself to become, as some did, a mere animal, guzzling food once a fortnight on visitors' day under the gaze of pitying relatives.

But I can never forget the fate of some of my fellow prisoners. Even in the darkest moods, I never wholly despaired of seeing my family once more. Though at times my five-year sentence might as well have been a hundred years, I knew that if I survived the labor camp, I would at least get out alive, and live to plan my escape from China. If I were caught, then I would surely kill myself, for the alternative was too hideous to contemplate. But I had a sporting chance, I felt, and would worry about recapture later. Others, whom I got to know well in the labor camp, had no such hopes. Their tragedy resolved itself in different ways. But no one at the time expressed any surprise at what happened, and there was precious little awareness of the gratuitous suffering involved. We were all too busy surviving ourselves.

I got to know a prisoner called Li Sheng slightly when I was transferred from my stone breaking job to carrying trays of earth from the top of the quarry to the area below. This switch in jobs was exceedingly painful. I had just about gotten used to breaking my quota of stones, but, unlike some of the tough peasant women in the camp, I had never carried heavy loads on my shoulders before. Even after one of the women prisoners had made a cotton pad for my shoulder I would sometimes drop everything, squat down and cry with sheer exhaustion, tears dripping onto my bare knees. My sub-unit leader, whom we called The Tiger, would stand behind me, nagging and ranting. "You think this is hard work? Why, your load's no heavier than the rice you ate this morning, you good-for-nothing little shirker." And when I slipped and fell, which occurred often in the mud and rain, she would yell: "You did that on purpose. Now you go straight back and get another load." Among the prisoners shoveling the earth onto my trays were some who were illiterate, and whom I regularly helped write letters home. They did their best to put the smallest possible amounts of earth onto my trays, but they, too, had to watch out, for everyone was scared of The Tiger. Some women prisoners, infuriated by her vicious tongue, sometimes answered back, and on several occasions one of them tried to kill her, pushing her down onto the ground and attempting to push her over the cliff. But The Tiger invariably got the better of such encounters. She was very strong, and ate real food, not the bran and sour rice we were given. The prisoners who assaulted her were all severely punished.

Li Sheng didn't need any help from me to write letters home. He never wrote any, and gradually, as time went on, I understood why. I never did gather why he was a prisoner, but since he had been a government clerk in pre-Communist days, he may simply have been held on suspicion of anti-Communism, as a former official, however lowly, of the Kuomintang regime.

Li Sheng was one of the few inmates in the camp to have made an earlier escape, and little by little he told me about it. He had been loading large stones onto trucks which were driven to Canton construction sites. He knew the truckdrivers would usually, before starting back into town, go and drink tea in the cadres' canteen. Usually there were three laborers assigned to each truck. Li Sheng told his teammates that he had a bad stomach ache and would try to get some medicine for it. He walked away, holding his stomach. He hid nearby, and when everyone's back was turned, he leapt under one of the loaded trucks, wedged himself under it, perching on part of the axle and clinging to the chassis. Eventually the truck drove off. Somehow, Li Sheng managed to stay put all the way, and found himself, still clinging to the underside of the truck, at a construction site in the center of Canton. He had the presence of mind to wait until complete darkness. Then he crawled out from under the truck, found his bearings and an hour later was knocking on the door of his own home.

He told me that he had vaguely hoped that once home he would be able to lie low and get new papers under a false name to start life afresh. He was prepared for anything—except for the reception he got from his wife. She opened the door, took one look at him and said: "What the hell do you think you're doing here? Go and give yourself up immediately, you fool, or I'll report you to the police." Li Sheng was staggered by the change in his wife, for before his arrest they had been very close.

"You can't do that," he said. "At least give me something to eat."

His wife turned on him again. "You don't know what trouble we've been in since you were taken away," she said. "Sneered at and bullied in the factory. I was branded as a reactionary element. The children were expelled from school. I've had to sell practically everything we had just to get food to eat. And you with your letters asking me to come and bring you biscuits and sugar. We've been eating banana peel. How do you like that? The police have been here already. They told me I was to report to them as soon as you showed up, or I'll be in trouble too." Then Li Sheng's wife broke down and she cried, hugging him and hysterically holding onto him. "You can't stay here. Can't you understand that? I can't see you any more."

Li Sheng realized it was hopeless. "I won't give myself up," he said. "I *won't* go back to the quarry. You can't imagine what things are like there. I'd sooner die. You must have some money somewhere. Just help me get to Hongkong, if you can't let me into my own home." Still crying, she gave him a crumpled bill. She looked at him, tears still streaming down her face. Then his wife slammed the door.

Li Sheng realized that even if he had money, he couldn't get food in any restaurant or food stall without a ration card. He thought of a friend, a former internee at the quarry who had recently been released. In the middle of the night, he walked straight over to see him. But his luck was no better there. A woman, hard-faced and haggard, opened the door. "I'm looking for my friend Lao Ming," he said.

She gave him a long glance, taking in his soiled clothes, his thinness, his desperate hunted look. "That'll be difficult. He's dead."

"How did he die?"

"The fool died of indigestion. He was so hungry he ate too much at one go, complained of a stomach ache and died."

Li Sheng left hurriedly. He knew then that he was all alone in the world. He was arrested a few minutes later, in the street. As he was being taken by a policeman to a station, in a pedicab, he saw Lao Ming's widow talking to a small group of people in the street. "She's the one who turned me in," he told me. "I know it was her. It couldn't have been my wife." But he severed all connections with his family just the same.

One night a few weeks after he told me the story, Li Sheng, in a fit of depression, threw down his shovel and made a run for it, and a sentry shot him through the foot. What exactly made him try again, I'll never know. Perhaps he just wanted to see his wife and children once more. Perhaps he just couldn't stand the idea of remaining a slave worker for another ten years at least (for after his first attempt, another five years were added onto his original sentence). Before taking him to the hospital to have his wound dressed, the soldiers beat him. A cadre looked at his leg and said, sneering, to no one in particular, but loud enough for Li Sheng to hear: "He'll never walk again, that's for sure." That night, after his wound had been attended to, he was taken to a cell and locked up. There he tore his trousers into strips, made a rope with them, and garrotted himself to death.

Li Sheng ended his predicament. Others went mad. There was Yi Chung, for instance, a Christian woman, middle-aged and of a poor family, who was convinced that she had been taken to the labor camp because of her Christian upbringing. At first she behaved normally, breaking stones with the rest of us, attracting no attention. Then, gradually, she slackened off. She would sit, her eyes wide open, staring into space. Her food ration was reduced, but she seemed not to care. She no longer washed. Nothing any of the guards or trusties did appeared to have any effect on her. When relatives came to see her, she crammed in the food they brought her, but no longer spoke to them.

Then she started preaching, in a loud voice. Nothing could stop her. Her ravings were a strange mixture of Christian and pagan exhortations, interspersed with cries of self-pity. "Oh my Heavenly Father," she would scream over and over again as we sat breaking stones or lay at rest on our bunks, "please have mercy on your Sacred Son. I am persecuted because I preach the truth. Have mercy on me. It's so wretched here." At first, the guards would slap and beat her, trying to keep her quiet. Occasionally, when her shouting spell occurred during working hours, they tied her to a tree. Finally no one bothered any more, and her cries punctuated our lives for twenty-four hours a day. "Repent, repent, all ye sinners," she would shout. "The end of the world has come. Your souls will burn for evermore. Ghosts will come and haunt you. Take care." She would also keep up a running commentary on whatever was going on around her. "Look, a bad woman," she would say, pointing to The Tiger. "She will be punished by hellfire. The sun is hot today. Cool, cool, the mountain streams I know."

Yi Chung's breakdown may have been contagious. One day we were given a "shock assignment." A blast had blown up part of the quarry, and trucks were waiting to take the large stones to a construction site in Canton. We were told we would have to work all through the day to get the stones taken down the hillside and loaded. It was an impossible order. A job like that usually took two days at least, and we were tottering from lack of food. The order came at noon, and one of the workers in my team, a middle-aged woman called Chen, flung down her carrying pole with its trays and screamed at The Tiger: "What have we done in our past lives to deserve this hell? May you suffer, you devil, what we're suffering now." She was ordered back to work, but seemed consumed by some kind of frenzy. All of a sudden she fell to the ground in a fit. She clawed the ground, saliva dribbling from her mouth. She banged her head against a rock, and had to be forcibly restrained, or she would have killed herself. The work on the site was interrupted while she was carted away, back to her bunk in the barn, where she was allowed to rest. Here she lay for days in a catatonic trance. Occasionally a warder would come and visit her, shake his head and go away. Then one day, returning from work one evening, we found Chen eating her own refuse. She had urinated into her rice bowl and poured it over her head. She fingered her excrement lovingly, rubbing it over her face and hair. As she did this she sang a traditional Cantonese love song:

> *When I have combed my hair,*
> *And rubbed myself with fragrant oil,*
> *And sipped my tea at leisure,*
> *I'll return home for a languorous sleep*
> *And dreams of love.*

So hardened were the inmates of the camp that Chen's behavior was regarded as a comical diversion. Some women crowded round to have a good look. Some even laughed. Others complained of the smell, and she was removed to the camp clinic.

Chen, like many others in the camp, had been sent there after being convicted of "deliberately sabotaging the Great Leap Forward." What she had actually done was this: when police came to take away the iron gate to her small house and removed the steel window frames to make use of them for industrial purposes, she had protested loudly and attempted to prevent them, hitting them with her fists. She was a simple soul, and kept saying to herself as she worked in the quarry: "They were my windows. It was my gate. They had no right! They had no right!" The injustice of it all had turned into an obsession.

Perhaps the most dramatic case of all was that of a young woman, Hua Yu-wang. She was the only inmate ever to arrive in a chauffeur-driven limousine. I happened to be near the camp entrance when she arrived, and at first I thought: here are two visiting dignitaries. What an ill-matched pair! He was old and fat, in a smart, well-tailored tunic. She was in her early twenties, in red checkered blouse and tight-fitting slacks. She was also exceptionally beautiful. Yi Chung, in one of her spells, was watching too. "Nice-looking, isn't she?" she said. She approached the young woman in red. "Miss, with your pretty looks and your city manners, why are you coming here to suffer?" The newcomer turned away, horrified.

Shortly afterwards, I saw the car drive away. The fat old man was sitting in the back, alone. From camp gossip, and the events that followed, we got to know the circumstances of Hua Yu-wang's arrival. For Hua Yu-wang was the fat old man's wife, and he had just dumped her at the labor camp for an unspecified time, thus ridding himself of his young wife in a manner ironically reminiscent of old China, when unsatisfactory wives were sold by their husbands. The only difference was that Hua's husband, instead of being a feudal lord, was an important official in the Public Security Bureau of Canton, a veteran of the "Long March" and a prominent party member.

As Hua later told us, her troubles began when, as a young clerk in the Public Security Bureau, she attracted the attention of the elderly department head. One day the local party secretary summoned her to his office. What did she think of her boss, Comrade Liu? Hua was nonplused. She said she had respect for him as a Long Marcher, that he was efficient, methodical and hard-working, and kind to his subordinates. The party secretary nodded approvingly. "Tell me, comrade, we have an important task for you. Do you think you can carry it out?"

Hua answered in the official jargon of Communist China. "I shall be pleased to oblige, if it benefits our work and proves helpful to my colleagues." The secretary looked down at his desk, gave an embarrassing little cough and plunged into the subject.

"Our chief," he said, "as you say, is a Long Marcher, with a war record and many wounds as a guerrilla veteran. He lost his wife a long time ago. She was killed by the Japanese. Now he needs help and care and the presence of a companion. To cut a long story short, he has watched you at work, and feels you would be the most suitable one to carry out this role. The Party Committee has approved his request. You are a member of the Youth Corps and you must take guidance from the Party. However, you need not give your answer straight away. The end of the week will do."

Hua knew she was in a terrible fix: she didn't want to marry someone at least thirty-five years older than she was. She had planned to marry Chang, a young fellow worker. To prevent the party secretary from carrying out his designs, she decided to marry Chang immediately. The party officials may have been expecting such a reaction. They refused to issue a marriage license. Hua then defied her party superiors. She and Chang began openly living together, and she avoided her boss whenever she could. But this lasted only a short time. Chang was arrested one day and sent to a labor camp in the North, charged with "violating the marriage laws." Hua was given the alternative either of marrying Liu, her boss, or of going to another reform camp. Meanwhile, her party superiors and the members of her youth group begged her to be sensible and marry the department chief. They said she was throwing away an opportunity. She should be proud of being the wife of such an important man. Eventually, she agreed, but not because she had warmed toward him. Her indifference had turned to loathing, for she rightly assumed that her boss had been responsible for sending the man she loved away. And she vowed to have her revenge.

In the months that followed, she slept with her new husband and with every man who took her fancy. Eventually her husband found out, and got rid of her by taking her to the nearest labor camp. Overnight, she had gone from living in a large house with servants and a car at her disposal to the same barn as the rest of us, eating the same appalling food. Her husband did not, of course, come and visit her. Her relatives stayed away. Night after night she would shriek and sob.

Hua Yu-wang was even more unprepared for the back-breaking routine of the quarry than I was. Try as she might, she never managed to break more than a few basketfuls of stones a day.

The Tiger constantly taunted her. "What are you crying about, you unspeakably lazy thing? You should be glad that your husband didn't make things far worse for you. You must have driven him to desperation for him to send you here. And you'll never leave, never, do you hear me, unless you improve." But Hua Yu-wang would just cry and cry over her basket of stones. Her work-mates talked about the case quite openly in her presence. "Think of it. He was forty years older if he was a day." "I hear he couldn't do it at all." "That's why she did it with others." "Having the best of both worlds, I call it." "You don't think she wanted to marry him, do you? She was forced."

At first Hua Yu-wang wouldn't eat any of the camp food. When she saw the bran mash, the cabbage and the occasional dark brown rice, she would start crying again. But the others didn't care. They pushed her aside. "You don't want any, do you? Not what you're used to, I expect. Here, let me have it." And several women started quarreling over her share.

But soon Hua Yu-wang was as ravenous as the rest of us, and prepared to wolf down the kind of food she had first rejected. Because she could never fulfill her "production quota" of stones, her ration was reduced, and since no one ever came to visit her, she got no extra food. She started stealing food, and was beaten up by the inmates of the barn. Gradually, she lapsed into madness. She would go up to a male trusty, put her arms round his neck, and softly, as though talking to her lover, she would whisper: "Please let me go home. I don't like it here. I don't want to live here. Take me with you." The men would usually push her away, or let her embrace them, laughing and making coarse jokes. When caught doing this by the guards, she was severely punished. She stared at her pile of stones, motionless, and spent long afternoons, handcuffed, on her bunk. The camp cadres gradually came to regard her as being incurable. The idea that she had gone out of her mind as a result of her experiences at their party's hands did not seem to occur to them. This was brought home to them, however, when she wandered over to the men's dormitory, stripped herself naked and waited for the men to return from work. When they appeared, she rushed up to the unit leader, hugged him and said in his ear: "You must let me go. I'll do anything, but I must get out of here. You must understand. None of the others do. Please," smothering his face with kisses, dragging him down onto the nearest bunk. She was eventually overpowered by soldiers, taken back to our barn, forcibly dressed and handcuffed. Four separate huts were built, about the size of pillboxes. Here Yi Chung, Chen, Hua Yu-wang and a woman trusty who had started having visions and fits were locked up. There were small windows for food, but no furniture and no light. From then on we saw no more of them, but interminably we heard their screams, shouts, curses and demented singing. Inmates in the barn called the noise from these four cells The Mad Women's Symphony.

Finally, I must talk about Ching. He was a tall, well-built young man, one of the camp's champion stone breakers. When he swung his heavy hammer his muscles rippled and he looked like a professional strong man. At one point during my spell in the quarry, I was assigned to the relatively easy job of weighing stones which other prisoners had broken. Ching would bring his basket to me. When the trusties were not around we talked, in the few brief moments of respite from work. Ching, it turned out, was an overseas Chinese, from the Philippines, who had voluntarily returned to China as a student, full of hopes for his country's future. Before he left the Philippines, his father had had a dragon tattooed on his right forearm, an age-old ritual among the Chinese community there. Ching showed me the tattoo. "Look, it hasn't brought me very much luck, has it?" He laughed. Ching had splendid teeth, and nothing, it seemed, could depress him for long.

"During the beginning of the Great Leap Forward, students no longer went to classes. Instead, we either had to go and work in the fields or 'make steel.' I was 'making steel.' It was crazy! They'd take all this stuff, iron gates, brass bedsteads, anything with hard metal in it, and toss it into a furnace. It was quite obvious to anyone with a little technical knowledge that the steel produced in this way would be useless for anything. It was then that I started having real doubts about the whole thing. I wanted to return to the Philippines. My faith had been shaken. Besides, I hated the bullying, the thought-control, the joyless, senseless discipline. I wrote home along those lines. My letters were opened, of course. What a fool I was! They accused me of "subversive plotting against the state" and gave me fifteen years. My own fault, really. No one had compelled me to return to China."

All this he told me at intervals, over a period of days. Ching also taught me an important lesson. One day, I expressed surprise at his cheerfulness. He was working industriously, for the camp authorities had announced a pardon, in anticipation of Na-

tional Day on October 1, for the very best workers in the camp.*
"You've got to show them they can't break your spirit," he said.
He quoted a Chinese saying: "A scholar can be killed, but he can't
be humiliated."

Shortly afterwards, I was taken off the stone weighing detail,
and did not see Ching again—until one time a few months later.

I was back on stone breaking and we were once more in the
middle of a desperate "production overfulfillment" campaign—
though since we were all getting weaker and weaker, we were in
fact producing less and less. One morning, the whistle blew. It
meant: everyone stop work and parade for a special announcement.
We were marched to an open-air enclosure, with a platform on a
raised dais. A banner had been erected. It said: *Meeting for the
Carrying Out of the Sentence by the Provincial People's Court.*
The camp's leading officials were sitting at a table on the dais,
along with some outsiders. These must be the judges. They came
from time to time to pass sentences on prisoners accused of
serious crimes, but never before had there been a parade like this.

The camp director stood up. "You have been brought here
today," he said, "to witness the carrying out of a sentence on a
counterrevolutionary element." There was a ripple of uneasy whispering among the 800 men and women squatting on their wooden
stools. "Let this be a lesson to you all," the camp director went
on sententiously. "Remember that prisoners who fail to repent
and are determined to remain enemies of the people cannot possibly escape harsh punishment. Repent, stand on the side of the
government, and redeem your crimes by working hard and admitting your past crimes, and you will, eventually, live to be born
again to a new life." Soldiers appeared. Struggling in their midst,
dirty, haggard and long-haired, his hands tied behind his back,
was Ching. I was overcome with horror. One soldier tried to
force Ching to bow his head, thrusting it down with both hands.
But Ching resisted, and looked straight ahead, defiantly. He was
led in front of the platform. An official read through the charges
at great speed (I was reminded of my own appearance in front
of a court). Ching, twenty-six, former student, who had been
convicted for attempting to contact imperialists overseas, had been

* This, we discovered later, was just another way of egging the slave
laborers on to further efforts under completely false pretenses. For when
October 1 came, only a handful of people were released, and all of these
were trusties and unit leaders subservient to the camp authorities, and
even they were chosen among those who had only a few more weeks of
their sentences to run.

sentenced to fifteen years' hard labor. He had always refused to admit his guilt. While in the camp, he had conspired with a small group of prisoners to escape, with the aid of counterrevolutionaries abroad.

"Ching is a diehard counterrevolutionary. He is incapable of reform. Consequently he is sentenced to death—the sentence to be carried out immediately."

I watched my friend, tears streaming down my face. He looked up at his judges. Then he shouted: "Down with the Communists! Long live freedom!" And again a ripple of uneasy whispering broke out among the assembled prisoners. It was unheard of to do what Ching had done. Then I realized he was going to be shot before our eyes. I couldn't look. Time was frozen. There was scuffling, more shouting and then a volley of shots. Ching was dead. All day his body was left exposed inside the camp, by the main path, so that all of us were compelled to look at it. I collapsed when I saw his body, vomited and dragged myself away. Later I fainted, and some of my teammates had to carry me back to the barn.

I thought of the famous saying by Mao Tse-tung which had been drilled into everyone in China: "The old society turned human beings into demons. The new society turns demons into human beings." It also made them mad, and occasionally made them die. Ching, I learnt later, had been betrayed by one of a small escaping group, who was publicly praised by the camp leader for his beneficial action. Ching's death taught me that open defiance of the system was not possible. I also learnt a lesson which, to most Chinese, had become second nature: never trust anyone. Never open your mouth. Mouth platitudes. Praise the government. Praise Mao. Praise your jailers. Never, never let anyone know what's in your heart. Otherwise, you'll end up in front of a firing squad, like the poor, cheerful, tough, resilient young man called Ching.

CHAPTER VIII

FIGHT FOR SURVIVAL

AFTER SEVERAL MONTHS in the stone quarry, we were taken one day to another camp. The exact date is unknown to me—I had lost count—but it must have been early in 1960. The second camp was only a few miles distant from the first, and rigorously similar in aspect. The work was no different, either. Here, too, was a huge quarry, and the same set routines of blasting, digging for rock and stone breaking. The only possible difference was that, if possible, conditions were even worse—though whether this was due to the over-all worsening situation in China or not, we were unable to tell. Even the hardened cadres and soldiers who ran the camp seemed on occasion somewhat embarrassed by our plight. They were, as they admitted on the rare occasions when they spoke to us informally, as much prisoners of the system as we were. They were responsible for seeing that the camp's production quotas were fulfilled—and they had no responsibility for determining what was possible and what was downright inhuman. Higher authority, we were left to suppose, didn't care what methods were used to keep production going.

Meanwhile, rations were cut again and again, in quantity as well as in quality, until one almost began to feel sorry for the camp cadres; they were trying to fulfill production targets with a crowd of sick, often half-demented prisoners, whose hunger and ill health led to a serious drop in productivity. Neither threats nor punishments nor even inducements could be of much use in getting us to work harder. We were all, except for those who had taken refuge in madness, working as hard as we could already—often up to sixteen hours a day. But as conditions deteriorated, we were slower and slower on the job. Inducements to work harder were no longer taken seriously: what could the camp authorities offer? The old promises of a reduced sentence were sneered at. The camp inmates had been duped too often.

Nevertheless, material inducements still led to small positive responses. Nobody believed, after October 1, that people would actually be released on evidence of hard work, however many "merit points" were accumulated (the accumulation of such points, and their recording in a camp ledger kept in the commandant's office was the subject of much gossip, and I sometimes wondered whether I was not back in some ineffably terrible school), but there were certain small benefits to be doled out, even in the present famine. For an outstanding piece of work, inmates would be surreptitiously slipped a bowl of soup, or allowed to draw a small towel from the camp stores, or even get a shirt or a set of coarse but new underwear. There was little sadism among the cadres—far less than among the trusties, who were compelled to act tough in order to prove to the camp staff that they were worthy of trust—and, perhaps, of premature release. The cadres offered what material inducements they could with pitiful supplies. But the inhuman pace of work turned the whole camp, especially after October 1, 1959, into one which would not have disgraced Himmler. Alone of the inmates in the quarry, I had read about the existence of such places in Germany. I also thought that we looked very much like Victor Hugo's description of the Cour des Miracles.

From Autumn 1959 onwards, until the first camp was finally closed down, our staple food was bran, sometimes boiled in soup, sometimes baked like bread. It was bran mixed with sawdust, added to which was some coarse, pulpous, fibrous mess which we eventually identified as the crushed stalks of already pressed sugarcane and rice stalks. That was our diet, and it was almost inedible, even to hungry, desperate people. In addition, we got two bowls of watered rice soup daily. The rice was devoured in a couple of spoonfuls. The rest was mostly water. Sometimes, when we were lucky, the water had a cabbage leaf or two floating in it. Once a week, we would draw our weekly ration of what the camp authorities euphemistically described as "fresh vegetables" —a clove of garlic, occasionally some yellowed, hardened onion leaves or, if one was particularly fortunate, some pickled vegetables preserved in salt. Prisoners were allowed to buy salt, a pound at a time, and it was necessary to mix the salt in one's food, which was completely unsalted. The cadres urged us to eat plenty of salt, to prevent heat exhaustion. They sold it at an inflated price: thirty U.S. cents a pound.

Such a diet contained practically no real nutritive substances and scarcely any vitamins or calories. Some prisoners managed to gorge themselves on bran, either because they fought the weaker prisoners for it or because the more delicate prisoners simply couldn't touch the stuff. They became no stronger than the rest.

Fights over food were common. Our new camp, fortunately, was only a few miles away from the old one, and most of us had relatives who continued to bring us food. Without such visits, many more of us would have died. We knew that conditions were bad all over China, and were constantly lectured, with supreme irrelevance, both on the achievements in the agricultural field of the Leap Forward and on the heinous crime of saboteurs who interfered with its progress and were responsible for temporary food shortages. Our visitors dropped small hints of the difficulties they had in obtaining food for us. My family sent money from Hongkong, and relatives brought me biscuits, sugar and, occasionally, canned pork. But from October 1 onwards, visits slackened off, for the camp authorities were increasingly reluctant to allow our families to see us. A system of food parcels had been instituted, but such parcels, too, became rare. From visitors who whispered to inmates when the cadres were not listening, we gathered that many food parcels had been sent and had never reached their destination. They may have been stopped at the source, by postal workers. But the general concensus among the inmates was that the cadres opened such parcels themselves. They also stopped all letters referring to the dispatch of such parcels from reaching their destination. We wondered whether the occasional bowl of soup or small plate of meat given to outstanding workers did not come from a store of food parcels set aside for this purpose. The cadres continued to look well fed.

Another serious shortage after October 1 was that of water. Prolonged drought had dried up a number of wells. We were rationed to half a basin of water a day, in which to wash ourselves and our clothes. The cadres held handkerchiefs over their noses whenever they entered our barnlike barracks. For a time, we were taken to a stagnant pool to wash ourselves, but emerged covered in slimy green ooze. After this unsuccessful experiment, water carts appeared, and were replenished from a nearby commune.

It would be no exaggeration to say that, with the exception of the camp cadres, everyone working at the quarry was to some extent seriously ill. First of all, there was a hepatitis epidemic; hepatitis was not considered to be a serious disease, and the sick inmates, dizzy and nauseous, would carry on with their stone breaking and load hauling regardless of their condition. Such prisoners could only be distinguished from the rest by their yellowed eyeballs and their own discovery that their urine had become dark brown. At one point, almost everyone in the camp was "pissing dark," as they put it, and some prisoners worked till they dropped, then died quietly at night, for hepatitis, under such conditions, can become a killing disease.

Another common complaint among all prisoners, but especially women and older men, was what we called dropsy (and what was, though I only discovered it later, a disease called beriberi, caused by malnutrition). Inmates afflicted in this way waddled grotesquely on swollen legs, occasionally supporting themselves on sticks they had managed to cut from tree branches. Their sole dispensation was that they were exclusively assigned to stone breaking, and not made to haul carts or carry rocks. It was a common sight to see older men and women massaging their swollen knees and crying silently with pain at intervals of breaking stones. When I was hauling carts full of rock, I would make a point of giving those with the worst cases the easiest pieces of rock to break.

Other common ailments were rheumatism and arthritis—I still feel occasional twinges in my right arm—and among women inmates, a particularly frightening collapse of the womb (prolapse) with the appearance of a large red external growth. Even young women developed this condition, which left them disfigured for life. There was no proper treatment for any of these "occupational" diseases, caused by malnutrition and physical exhaustion, though people with beriberi, as a special favor, were allowed to purchase a bit of brown sugar daily—if they could afford it. Often sugar supplies simply ran out, and then there was nothing at all to be done.

Among the prisoners, but this time rigidly segregated in the men's wing, was my old acquaintance Doctor Yu, the Don Juan of the Canton Prison, who had somehow learnt from the men prisoners that I was an inmate too. He told whoever would listen that his troubles were all my fault, and spent the rest of his time trying to make contact with what women were available. He was, the men prisoners said, still his cheerful, carefree self, and even in camp he flourished. He had the almost hypnotic gift of gab of the traditional Chinese herbalist and fortuneteller, and impressed the wives of the camp cadres, who came to him for treatment. He wore a white doctor's coat, looked neat and well fed, and was rumored to have accumulated considerable savings through treating prison guards and their families. He even managed to get a prisoner to pass on a message to me. He said he bore me no grudge, and would always do what he could to help. Money, medicine, anything he could provide was at my disposal. By now I had learnt my lesson. "Just tell him," I said, "to leave me alone." The amorous doctor seems to me in retrospect to have been a born survivor. Nothing apparently got him down—not even his sentence, now increased to seventeen years—and he remained as interested in women as ever, despite the possible penalties. He acquired a radio set which one of the cadres had given to him to mend and listened to Voice of America newscasts on it, relaying the news to other prisoners until he was caught. Even then, he must have talked his way out of serious punishment, for this was an almost capital crime and all he got was an additional six-month sentence.

To try and improve prisoners' morale, the camp authorities tried to get a song-and-dance team organized, to put on shows for the prisoners. I was selected to be part of it, but we gave up after a few performances. We were too exhausted to sing. The experience was most useful later.

Apart from an occasional free Sunday, the holiday I remember best was our one outing, accorded at the height of the famine. Ironically, it was a visit to the Canton Agricultural Exhibition, designed to prove to bewildered peasants from all over Kwangtung Province that in other parts of China, at least, the Great Leap Forward had meant a miraculous increase in agricultural productivity. To this day, I remain baffled at the thought that I—along with some thirty other prisoners, both men and women—was selected out of more than eight hundred inmates to go along with the party. We were told a few days in advance that a big treat was in store for us, and given time off to wash our least shabby set of clothes. We then climbed onto trucks under heavy but discreet guard (for nearly all the camp cadres went along with us, some of them with pistols tucked into their trousers and hidden by their shirts), and drove into Canton.

My memory of the trip remains hazy. I remember being part of a huge group—was it prisoners' day, or were the other people visiting the exhibition merely peasants?—all similarly attired, somewhat on the thin and haggard side. Perhaps these were commune representatives, for they looked like farmers. In any case, we all dutifully stared at the displays of photo enlargements which showed how rice and grain production had positively spiraled. The pictures showed happy, growing boys and girls shoulder-deep in golden corn, laughing and basking in contented health. (Later on, I acquired some direct experience of how such pictures were made.) Room after room after room contained such exhibits, covering almost every conceivable form of farm produce, and there seemed to be no realization, on the part of the cadres who accompanied us, of the grotesqueness of it all—for nearly all the exhibition-goers, mostly under some form of escort, were visibly hungry. Our party included some of the camp's most diligent workers, and others, like myself, whose records were the reverse of good. I was there, someone said later, because of my "high level of culture." This meant that I was able to take notes—which I did—and give my fellow workers a detailed account of what we had seen. This also I obediently did, and such was the lethargy and fear prevalent among us that no one, at any time, asked the obvious question: if food production in China had reached such a dizzyingly high level, how come we were living on bran and sawdust? To me, the most memorable thing about the exhibition was that, to prove that some at least of the food increases had been real, there were counters of food for sale. With what little money we had, we bought canned fruit, sausage, bottles of ketchup—whatever was available. The following day, I delivered my lecture about the agricultural exhibition with all the proper clichés and a straight face. My stock with the authorities went up temporarily. Then I was overheard "spreading seditious nonsense" and answering back one of the trusties, and I lost whatever merit points I accumulated from my outstandingly ortho-dox lecture.

At reveille one morning in March 1960, the trustie in charge came into our barracks and announced that everyone was to leave immediately. We were being sent away that very day. "What's going to happen to us? Where are we going?" we asked. There was no reply. Trucks were drawn up outside. Into these we climbed, and once more I headed off in an unknown direction.

We went roundabout, in order to avoid the center of town, to Canton West Station. We must have been a sight, for there were fifteen hundred of us, men and women, the men chained and shackled, all of us haggard and, I'm sure, smelling horribly strong. But by now people in Canton must have been used to such sights. Nobody paid much attention. Only a few people stopped to stare. We were then packed into boxcars, but could just peep outside through a crack in the door. I knew the direction we appeared to be heading in: this was the main Canton-Peking line. I remembered it from the stations I had been through on my way to Peking years earlier.

The journey by train lasted a little over four hours, which meant that we were, on arrival, some eighty miles north of Canton—for the train moved very slowly. The station we got off at was called Ho Tou. Few trains seemed to stop there. It was little more than a tiny village. Our guards and trusties were still with us, and, it seemed, most of our camp cadres. We formed up three abreast on the empty station platform. The surrounding countryside looked marvelous. It was cooler than in Canton, there were hills and streams. I felt good. Whatever is in store for us, I thought, it can't possibly be worse than the stone quarry. Others were not quite so cheerful. Many of the women inmates were in tears. They realized that at this distance from Canton it would be impossible for them to have their families visit them. There followed a march. At first, we had expected that we would find our new camp just round the corner from the station, but we had been walking for two hours without a break, and some of the women, bone-weary, just jettisoned the belongings they could no longer carry by the roadside when we were told there was still some way to go. The cadres kept up their antics, half drill sergeants, half sheepdogs, rounding up stragglers, urging us on with, "Not far to go, keep at it!" One of them, more humane than the rest, said to one weeping old woman: "Don't cry. The place you're going to is much, much better than the quarry. It's a real town. It has everything. You'll grow your own food and have a much better time. Don't worry."

Evening came. We were still on the march, but finally reached the banks of the North River. Sampans ferried us across. We lay flat out over one another, exhausted. As we drew nearer the north bank of the river, I could see what looked like a full-sized town, with factory chimneys, rows upon rows of dormitories and lights covering a huge area. If this was a detention camp, I thought, it must be the largest in the whole of China. In a daze, we marched once more through what looked like a ghost town, for nearly everyone in this huge detention center was by this time asleep.

CHAPTER IX

THE NEW LIFE UNITED ENTERPRISES

OUR NEW HOME was vastly different from the quarry; only gradually did I find out exactly where I was. It was more like a town, for it was a completely self-sufficient economic unit, with a large network of farms, tea estates, rice paddies and plantations of all kinds. Since prisoners were constantly being added to the labor force, and since few people ever left the place, its size grew constantly.

In the stone quarry, we had been completely cut off from the outside world. Here, gradually, I found my bearings. I knew, for instance, that the place was run under the joint supervision of the reform office of the Kwangtung Province Public Security Bureau and of various ministries. The place was called: The New Life United Enterprises, and there was absolutely nothing in its rather grand title to indicate that it was, in fact, one vast prison.

The core of the New Life United Enterprises was the town center, where we were taken that first night. Here were barracks, dormitories, a few small shops and rows and rows of small huts for married couples; a big administrative office building; a large supply depot, a school, a hospital, an army barracks for the guards, food processing factories, workshops, garages and a lime kiln. The New Life United Enterprises had its own song-and-dance troupe, a projector for showing films in the open air, even facilities for putting on plays: props, costumes, crude painted scenery. And all around the camp headquarters, over a huge area, was a network of farms and plantations, all themselves self-contained labor camps; there were experimental farms, a "tea production brigade," complete with tea factory, a sugar refinery, bamboo plantations, forestry camps and even a sulphur mine. Twenty thousand people worked in the mine alone, which itself covered a large area and consisted, in fact, of five different mines, administratively run as one unit. The tea produced by the labor camp, Ying Teh Tea, is exported to Hongkong and all over the world. Each farm, factory and workshop had its separate militia or army detachment.

The inmates of this town came under three categories. There were labor reform inmates, sentenced either for political or straightforward criminal reasons, who formed the bulk of the labor force; then there was a category called "education inmates," whose cases were not considered to be as serious as ours, but who had failed, in minor respects, to show adequate enthusiasm for their work or for political indoctrination. They were different from us in the sense that they were paid regular wages, at standard rates, and were entitled to a few days' vacation a year. Lastly, there were those who had finished their spells as education or labor reform inmates, but were "asked" to stay on in their present jobs. Since there was no choice in the matter, there was a growing population of "reformed" personnel, leading normal lives, often married and with families, but unable to leave the New Life United Enterprises.

The next morning, we paraded for a roll call and waited. As I discovered later, the new arrivals were to be farmed out to various farms, factories and workshops in the area. But first, an official who appeared quite important arrived and looked us over. "Some of you people took part in cultural work in your last camp," he said. "I want you to step forward. Anyone here who can sing, or dance, or act? Anyone here who can draw? Play a musical instrument?"

Nobody moved. We must have looked a pretty unprepossessing bunch, and the cadre looked at us dubiously. "There must be someone," he said. Like old army hands, we stood our ground. This sounded like a call for volunteers, but we would probably end up breaking stones. One lesson I had learnt from my time in prison was never to volunteer for anything.

One of the cadres who had accompanied us from the stone quarry was there, and he spoke up. "There are a few," he said. He looked at our list of names. "Let me see, X used to lead the singing. Step forward." He called out a few other names. Then I heard my name. "This girl can play the Chinese flute, and sings quite well. She's also a painter." The new cadre looked me up and down, then pointed to a propaganda poster on a barracks wall nearby, showing peasants and workers happily toiling away under the benevolent gaze of an ever youthful Chairman Mao. "Can you paint like that?" I looked at the crude poster. "If I have the right paints and brushes," I said, "I think I could do better."

"Good. Let's go." We gathered up our bundles and, as in the Army, formed up into a separate squad. We all climbed into a battered sedan, and the new cadre, whose name was Chen, drove. Nobody said anything, but I, for one, was excited and elated.

We were taken to our quarters, a spacious thatch-covered mud hut. It was clean, airy, a far cry from the barracks at the stone quarry. Our spirits rose still further. We settled in, chattering about our new assignment. One girl said: "It can't be true. I just don't believe it."

Chen appeared again. "I've got a rush job for you," he said to me. "There's a big meeting tomorrow, and we need to put up a really big banner over the entrance to the meeting hall. We've got the red cloth for background, but nobody here can do a good job of writing big-character slogans. How about you?" I said I'd try. It was a long time since I had done work of this kind, but I'd had considerable experience as a Young Vanguard at school. "You need any help?" Chen said. "You pick what you need." I selected two of the young women to come with me. We walked to the meeting hall. I rigged up a table, using a table tennis board. There were paints, brushes, scissors. I set to work with almost desperate eagerness. I made one vertical banner, copying out the slogan (about the need to work harder to make the Leap Forward even more successful) in old-style characters, supervising my two assistants as they stuck the various pieces of each character, carefully cut out in white paper strips, onto the red cloth background. As a flourish, I also completed two horizontal banners, one for each side of the entrance. Our new leader looked on with undisguised approval. He beamed. "You really do this well, don't you?" he said. "I have the feeling I've made a real find."

In the days that followed, I drew, painted and did cutouts in a never ending stream. From all over the camp came requests for my services, and leader Chen funneled the major assignments to me. He gave me a completely free hand. Not once did he criticize me, as the Canton Prison warder had done, for not giving workers a sufficiently martial and triumphant bearing. I was happier than I had been since my arrest. Chen was more like a college teacher than the supervisor of a group of prisoners. Himself a fairly cultured man, he had, I gathered from talk around me, a distinguished record in Communist guerrilla forces. Nobody—among the prisoners—had anything but praise for him. He stuck up for his "culture squad," as he called it, and used his considerable influence to get us good food, reasonable accommodations and even clothes made by the camp tailor. I once heard him arguing with another camp official, who was complaining that we were "the little lords and ladies" of the labor camp. "These are the most important people here," Chen said. "Why do you think our production records are high? It's because morale is good. And why is morale good? Because we have the best theatrical group in the whole county."

For the first few days, we were kept separate from the theatrical troupe, and I quickly realized that new arrivals were on probation. I was determined to make the grade, and painted till I dropped. Even Chen was surprised at my ability to turn out posters one after the other, until late at night. Often he would fall asleep, curled up in a corner, while I continued work in a corner of the meeting hall on my ping-pong table, surrounded by pots of paint, glue and stacks of brushes, and rolls and rolls of paper. Chen had given strict instructions that none of this was ever to be moved without my consent. This was my studio, he said. Then he'd wake up, rub his eyes, look at my work and make little admiring clucking noises.

I liked my new job, but the chief reason I worked so hard to remain a member of the theatrical troupe, after the probation period, was that we got the best food that the camp kitchens could provide. The carping official was right. We *were* the little aristocrats of the New Life United Enterprises and our food was the same as that of the cadres. Captain Chen (for we soon began calling him by his old rank) ate with us. The resources of the camp were so large that here at least there was no shortage, at least for the privileged few. Those first few days, we ate enormously, and Captain Chen looked on as we got through bowl after bowl of soup, rice, dumplings and real green vegetables we hadn't tasted for almost a year. "You're as skinny as monkeys," he said. "I want you rosy-cheeked and blooming, if ever you're going to put on stage performances. I've got you a special deal here. Nobody else in the camp gets food like that. The camp manager has agreed to this as a special favor to me. In return, I ask you to remember that, whatever your past experience, the party means to help you and wants to see that you're fit and well."

But Captain Chen knew exactly what he was doing, and while he was a thoroughly nice man, he was also a discerning one. Of the six inmates selected, I was the only one to make the grade. The others were told, kindly but firmly, that their various talents, through no fault of their own, "left something to be desired," and they were sent back to ordinary production units, mostly to outlying tea and sugar plantations. I felt fairly secure. In addition to my drawing and painting, which would have ensured me a job as the camp's official illustrator and "pictorial propagandist," as Chen put it, I could sing tolerably well, and play the flute. "We might even see what you can do in the acting line," Chen said. "You're just the kind of person we need."

One day, Chen said I was to come with him and meet the rest of the troupe, and I knew that I had made the grade. Chen helped me carry my things, and I moved into a new barracks, in the center of the labor town, adjoining the supply depot. "This," he said, "is our new member. I want you to be nice to her, and look after her. She's the best stage designer and painter we've ever had in the camp, and can do all sorts of other things as well." All the girls in the troupe were good-looking, young and obviously in good spirits. Some wore prison uniform, but even their uniforms were tailored.

The atmosphere was one of a hard-working theater and ballet school. The day started at six, with gymnastics, ballet practice and singing. After breakfast men and women of the theatrical troupe began their more serious work, rehearsing plays and ballets, dances and small sketches. After lunch and a rest, we continued rehearsals, and those with any talent whatsoever were encouraged to learn to play at least one musical instrument, to help out a rather thin orchestra. Political indoctrination came after supper, and lasted two hours. The political indoctrination classes were run by Captain Chen himself, and even here he managed to make them interesting. There was a good deal of parrotlike memorizing and editorial reading on our part, but sometimes one of the members of our crowd would get him to talk about his own experiences, and he would digress about the anti-Japanese and anti-Kuomintang war, about which he knew a good deal.

Early on, I was taken to the camp tailor and fitted out not only with fatigues and two sets of prison uniform, but also with two suits of clothes—a blouse, skirt, trousers, and a coat—which made me indistinguishable from an ordinary civilian. I asked Captain Chen what these were for. "You'll be visiting farms and factories in the area with the troupe," he said. "We don't like our performers to look like prisoners."

As I gradually discovered, our troupe was designed as a roving repertory company, to put on shows not only in farms and settlements operated by the New Life United Enterprises, but all over the area, in villages, large and small, in communes and small towns which had nothing to do with the camp and whose inhabitants didn't even know that we were, in fact, prisoners. We were provided with buses, and a truck for our scenery, stage costumes and other essential props. Apart from Captain Chen, we had no prison escort. And Captain Chen himself dropped hints that we fulfilled, indirectly, a highly important function in keeping camp relations with nearby farms, factories and workshops on a cordial basis.

A huge establishment like the New Life United Enterprises needed all sorts of things to keep going: skilled carpenters, bricklayers, bulldozers, tractors of all kinds. It also required occasional extra labor, to improve existing roads, put up new buildings, or extend the electric power grid. It consumed large quantities of coal in winter, and cement, asphalt, bricks and iron bars were constantly required. All such supplies were theoretically available from local sources, but an all-pervading bureaucracy usually caused considerable delays. The camp commander's dispatch of our troupe—as a counterpart for prompt service—worked wonders. As Captain Chen told us one day, with considerable pride: "Many local factory managers and commune directors have a stock answer when we ask them for supplies on an urgent basis. They say: "We'll give you whatever you want, provided you send us your theatrical company for a few performances."

My first performance with the troupe made no undue intellectual demands. At the time, the Kwangtung Province Party Bureau was attempting to persuade farmers to grow more Kwangtung potatoes, which bear little relation to the real thing, being tasteless and very starchy. Kwangtung potatoes are ridiculously easy to grow, and provided bulk food at a time of general shortage. The troupe went on a tour of a number of villages in the area, with a program of traditional folk songs and dances. The highlight of the show was supposed to be a brief song-and-dance sketch about Kwangtung potatoes, and Captain Chen told me to pick my team and write both the words and the music. The tune was easy enough to select; I just adapted one of the traditional jingly Cantonese folk songs. The words I unashamedly parodied from my memories of commercials on Hongkong radio. The song was performed by eight girls, all dressed up as Kwangtung peasant women.

Let's plant the Kwangtung potato
It's easy to grow, easy to harvest,
Gives strength to the young,
Sticks to the teeth of the old.
Everybody is saying how good Kwangtung potatoes are.
Let's grow some!

Our new act met with only a moderate response. The applause was perfunctory, and I doubt that a single extra potato was grown as a result.

Gradually, our lives settled down into an active, fairly enjoyable routine. Though I occasionally sang or performed, my main job was painting scenery, and, on occasion, building it, with a carpenter's help. I would also write explanatory slides, which would be flashed onto a screen during a performance to help explain what was going on on the stage. I also learnt a great deal about stage management; we built our own mobile stage in sections, and assembled it wherever we gave performances. I was also kept fairly busy copying out traditional and "political" plays and operas, for though there was a library with mimeographed scripts, there were never enough texts to go round.

When not engaged in rehearsals, we were used as an occasional mobile labor force. In winter, this meant that we unloaded stores, looked after the cleanliness of the camp, checked inventories and carried water to vegetable plots. We also swept the floors and polished the windows of the camp's impressive new office building, waxed the floors and kept the VIP guest suites, which were luxuriously furnished, in good condition. These suites had heavy mahogany furniture, armchairs upholstered in deep purple, fans, large radios, and the beds were equipped with the finest cotton sheets and nylon mosquito nets. We were the only inmates allowed inside this main building. Mostly, though, we rehearsed. To the tunes of traditional Cantonese opera, we learnt our parts in such ideologically correct plays as *The Third Sister of Liu, The Red Women's Battalion, Spring Comes to the Tea Mountain* and other works, all written recently with one end in view: to prove the strength and abnegation of the Chinese Communists and extol their past prowess in overcoming Japanese invaders, Kuomintang bandits and present-day reactionaries. Their literary merit, of course, was nil, but the tunes and dances were lively and, occasionally, beautiful. Our troupe also wrote its own play— about the "moral regeneration" of a labor reform camp inmate.

We also practiced folk dancing from Mongolia, Sinkiang, Hainan, Yunnan and Tibet.

Whenever we were ready with a new play, we put on a performance for the camp cadres, who would sit, talking loudly and picking their teeth throughout the performance. They never applauded. Only when visiting dignitaries came did they behave like model Communists, even cleaning up the auditorium and the main office buildings themselves, instead of entrusting us with the job. Once we performed in front of a four-star general. He ogled the girls throughout the performance.

Playing for the cadres was a necessary chore. But we enjoyed staging performances for the inmates, and even more, going out to neighboring farms and factories. Sometimes we would give one performance a night for a week at a time, but on an average we gave two performances a week. This entailed packing all our props and collapsible stage, and traveling in several trucks and buses—for our company, with fifteen musicians and ten performers, plus other, behind-the-scenes workers, numbered over thirty. Captain Chen invariably went with us, and such was our pride in our company that no one ever thought of escaping while on such a tour. Invariably, when we went outside the camp, we were treated like important people. At the Shaokwan Steel Works, I remember, we sat down in the workers' canteen to an elaborate meal after our performance. The workers had only watery rice and a few small pieces of dried fish.

Only once did our status as labor reform inmates cause a crisis; it happened after a performance at the Chu Jen coal mine, a vast complex of pits and workers' quarters dominated by slag heaps. We had given one performance to a large crowd of miners, some of them still black with coal dust, grinning like minstrels, and were due to give another performance the following day. The coal mine had no proper visitors' hostel and we were put up in a barracks with double-tiered beds, where the women cadres of the mine also lived. That night, two members of our troupe started quarreling. It started over who should have the lower bunk. Then one of the girls screamed at the other that she was a no-good, undisciplined, unregenerate prisoner, and should go back to Canton Prison, where she belonged.

"You bitch, I saw you flirting with Ching!"

"That's better than seducing a prison guard, you old sow!"

"And why are you here, you miserable little criminal? You'd sell your own mother on the black market!"

The cadres listened, horrified. Someone eventually called Captain Chen, who was sleeping in the men's barracks. He had only to appear, and everyone was silent. But the news spread all over the coal mine. The famous song-and-dance troupe was nothing but a bunch of labor reform inmates, common criminals, black marketeers and the like. The following morning, Captain Chen came into the barracks and said: "Pack up. We're leaving." He, too, had lost face and was quietly angry. Nobody saw us off. The two girls who had caused the commotion in the first place were punished: the first, one of our better dancers, was banished to a tea plantation. We never saw her again. The other one, who by our reckoning had been provoked, was forbidden to take part in any of our performances for three months. After that, we were specially careful to be on our best behavior and to conceal our status.

Because we were constantly on the move, we had an unrivaled overall picture of the huge labor camp. We were thus fully aware of our own privileged position, for the day-to-day lives of the ordinary inmates, especially those on remote farms and plantations, were almost as unbearable as my own life had been at the stone quarry. All farms and plantations were heavily guarded, and discipline was extremely strict. The food situation varied from farm to farm, but, contrary to what one might have expected, it was by no means easy for workers to supplement their rations by stealing small quantities of the food they themselves produced. Penalties were high, and there was a checking system, with informers, guards and trusties keeping close watch, in constant operation. Since I remained at the New Life United Enterprises for over two years, I think I saw every single one of its dependent farms and institutions. To some extent, local conditions depended on the cadres in charge, who had a considerable degree of autonomy in running their show. Some were quite as brutal as my former jailers at the stone quarry. I saw prisoners forced to work in the fields whose feet were shackled, and who could barely move without considerable pain; in some New Life farms, there were no medical facilities whatever, and the removal of a prisoner to the main hospital usually occurred when he was dying; most prisoners shivered in winter, and had to use whatever bedding they had to wrap around themselves while working in the fields. For these ordinary workers, who were nothing more than slaves, no special winter clothing was provided. I also saw considerable evidence of brutality. Cadres would slap and hit plantation workers at the slightest provocation, and I came across incontrovertible evidence of more elaborate, sadistically meted-out punishment and even torture, which occurred in the privacy of improvised "punishment" cells. There were notorious tales about some of the farm commanders' sadism, and their total indifference to their prisoners' welfare. Escape, on these farms, was practically impossible, for there were frequent roll calls and, even with money, one could not get very far: local inhabitants had been ordered to report any suspects wandering about and most of the farms were in remote areas. Members of the song-and-dance troupe were not guarded—but though opportunities for escape came, the penalties for attempting to do so were such that no one, during the two years and four months I was there, at least, even contemplated doing so.

Even among our own troupe members, there were suicide attempts, but I could never forget the days in the stone quarry and my luck at finding such a contrast in the New Life United Enterprises.

My first taste of what conditions were like in some of the outlying camps came when our company made a trip to the bamboo cutting unit on a remote mountain to the north of our "town." We spent five hours getting there, up a narrow, steep, winding path, our truck precariously rounding the corners, and found ourselves in a village inhabited by primitive country people, speaking an incomprehensible hill dialect, who had never seen a stage performance before.

The bamboo cutters were chosen from among the toughest, strongest men inmates. Theirs was considered a vital job, for the camp consumed an incredible quantity of bamboo—mainly for building purposes—and bartered its surplus for other goods in short supply. The bamboo cutters lived near the hill village, and had built themselves houses, mess halls and even a primitive irrigation system, all entirely of bamboo. They were nearly all stocky, barrel-chested men who thought nothing of carrying several-hundred-pound weights on their backs, supported by a bamboo shoulder frame. Their life was hard: up at midnight, they trekked into the forest to cut and trim poles before the sun got really hot. Then they loaded the bamboo onto their backs and carried them back to the camp. The trip back took four hours. They would do two such trips a day as normal routine, and sometimes even went back for a third trip when supplies were badly needed.

To show that we were not averse to hard work, we decided to

go out and cut bamboo. We started too late, around 5 A.M., and the sun was high in the sky when we began the struggle back to camp, lugging our lengths of bamboo. The forest was wild and beautiful, but we were exhausted as we staggered into camp. It took four of us to carry the equivalent of one bamboo cutter's load, but they were nice about it, and didn't make fun of us. The practical, organized aspect of the camp operation came to light at mealtimes. At the stone quarry, we had literally been worked to death and given totally inadequate food supplies. Here the importance of the bamboo cutters' work was recognized. They worked fantastically hard, but were valuable state property. Hence the specially picked cutters were given the best food available. Food trucks came every day with fresh supplies. There was no rationing here. Each man ate all the rice and soup he could manage to put away. We were amazed at their appetites.

That night we gave a much applauded performance to the assembled workers, and to some of the villagers, who crowded round, chattering excitedly. None of them wore shoes, and the children went naked. I felt that I was in some exotic, foreign country. This was an aspect of China I had never seen before. On our return, we loaded our trucks with a consignment of badly needed poles. "We can't tell you how glad we are that you came," said one of the bamboo cutters. "Here all we do is work, study and sleep."

The camp theatrical company was obviously a morale builder, but there were times when even we little lords and ladies of this privileged outfit were compelled to suspend our cultural activities for hard, manual labor. This occurred for a two-month period in summer, at the height of the various harvests, and during the sowing season in winter. In the official jargon of the camp, this was known as "marching to the front line of the production force to perform labor," and was regarded as beneficial and self-improving, for by doing so we were "experiencing life and discovering new material useful in our creative work." The idea behind such phrases was that by ourselves living the life of a peasant worker, those actors among us would be able to portray peasants on the stage with greater realism, and understand them better. Since then, of course, this theory has been carried to extremes and China's best dancers, singers and musicians have "voluntarily" gone to the countryside during the period of the Cultural Revolution to "learn by doing."

My own experience compels me to say that this theory is a

lot of nonsense. It could help pampered or sheltered actors. But it is usually forgotten that acting is physically exhausting at the best of times. For skilled dancers and musicians, it must be heartbreaking. Even in our own company, musicians complained that after two months of peanut harvesting, or picking tea leaves, their fingers were so stiff and so unresponsive that they could hardly play a note. Our dancers found that they had developed a new set of muscles, but failed to exercise the ones they needed to dance properly. In short, the period of "learning by doing" was regarded by all as an awful bore, to be endured and got over as best we could.

Our troupe was regarded as a mobile reserve to be sent to whichever farm was most desperately short of labor. Captain Chen, that first summer, explained that our privileged position in the camp compelled us to be an example to others. We must not only show that we were as good as the rest of the workers, but set the pace. And in fact we were able to do so, mainly because we were younger and stronger than most of the run-of-the-mill camp inmates, and—thanks to special rations—were in better physical shape to start with.

For three consecutive summers I labored at tea harvesting. It's hard work, because one has to bend over the low bushes and be sure to pick the right leaves. The pace was back-breaking; on an average, we picked some forty pounds of leaves each every day, working long hours with only a short midday break. Some "shock workers" were so skilled that they managed to pick up to a hundred pounds a day, and the members of our troupe decided to do even better. After a week, we were averaging around eighty-five pounds a day each, and were singled out for praise.

Looking back, I realize that the camp authorities cynically encouraged such competitions among the tea plantation workers in order to extract the last ounce of work from us. But at the time, I was not aware of anything except an anxiety to prove that song-and-dance workers were just as good as the regular tea pickers. I think we even despised the plantation workers for their "unconstructive" attitude towards work in general. But as one woman pointed out, muttering bitterly as she bent over the tea bushes: "It's all right for you. You'll go back to headquarters, and to your rehearsals and playacting. We have to stay here all the year round."

The times on the plantation enabled us to see how most of the agricultural workers really lived: food on all farms was in short supply, and what there was tasted awful, and at times I felt I was back in the stone quarry; we slept in overcrowded huts, with no toilet or washing facilities, and had to clean up as best we could in a nearby stagnant pool or in a river near the tea estate. We were bitten by bugs, mosquitoes and wasps and went in constant fear of leeches. From picking tea leaves, our fingers were blistered and cracked.

In between our tea picking assignments, we began harvesting peanuts, planted between the rows of tea bushes. Elsewhere, harvesting is probably done by machine, but we had no tractors, and worked with our bare hands. This was during the peak of the summer, and several members of the song-and-dance company collapsed with heat exhaustion. While the peanut harvest was going on, Captain Chen was temporarily assigned to other duties, and our new supervisor was a woman—fat, illiterate and stupid— whose sole claim to the job was that she was the wife of a fairly important cadre. She was active in public meetings, but would never herself take part in any physical work. Instead, she lay supine under a tree, fanning herself, at intervals roasting peanuts and eating them. (We, too, began eating peanuts, and eventually did so openly, despite the penalties involved.) She was almost bitten by a snake one day, and never came to the fields again. But at the end of the harvest season, she asked me whether I would mind painting a picture of her harvesting peanuts, to hang on her living room wall. She had a photograph of herself in her hand, and rather than risk offending a powerful cadre's wife, I did as she asked; a highly flattering painting was completed a few days later, and I took it to her small, comfortable house on the tea estate. Later on, presumably, she would be able to brag about her strenuous time in the fields.

One day, after Captain Chen's return, he came into our barracks and said: "Dress well tomorrow, and look your best. A film unit is coming to make a movie here and it's going to be all about you." We crowded round him. He explained. A color film was being made about the Great Leap Forward in agriculture in Kwangtung Province. It was destined for foreign buyers at the Canton Fair. The tea estate where we were was considered one of the best in the whole of China. The surrounding scenery was beautiful, and the whole setting ideal for a film. So the documentary film unit was coming—and since the best possible impression had to be made—the troupe was going to be filmed. We were the brightest, most attractive bunch of tea pickers on the whole estate, weren't we?

That night, the girls crowded round those who had mirrors, put on lipstick and tried on their clean clothes. When the film unit came, they saw, not the ragged, undernourished, dirty, evil-smelling inmates, who were the usual workers, but a song-and-dance troupe, all decked out in finery usually reserved for stage use. The movie unit spent the whole of the next day in the fields with us. Needless to say, there was little tea picking done. We smiled as we moved gracefully in front of the cameras; we sang; we even performed our improvised dance. The movie crew never saw the rest of the plantation workers, nor how they lived. I realized then how the pictures in the Canton Exhibition Hall showing the agricultural achievements of the Great Leap Forward had been possible; it was a lesson to all of us never to believe anything one might possibly be shown on film concerning China.

CHAPTER X

LOVE, SEX AND CRIME

THERE WAS AN ASPECT of our lives in the New Life United Enterprises which caused the authorities constant concern: the natural tendency of both men and women inmates to try to enjoy normal sex lives, despite the very considerable penalties involved.

In the stone quarry, the sexes had been thoroughly segregated; though men and women sometimes worked alongside each other, they were closely watched, and in any case everyone had been too exhausted and too ill to think of sex. In our new life, we were, except for harvest time, relatively well fed, and able to meet at all times of the day. There was a constant stream of visitors to the main supply depot, which was in the same compound as our own headquarters. In our song-and-dance troupe, men and women rehearsed together. Occasionally plays called for the enactment of love scenes between the men and women actors. The atmosphere was redolent of sex.

It was perfectly natural that this should be so, for many of the camp's song-and-dance troupers had been sent to labor camps for sex offenses in the first place, or for past activities which, while they would scarcely be condemned in Western society, were regarded as crimes in China. Liu Hai-lin, our leading flute player and a tolerably good dancer and actor, had been a member of an army song-and-dance team, and had been sent with a company to perform in North Vietnam. He said he had been sentenced to labor reform for seducing a Vietnamese girl while in Hanoi. Several of the girls had been sent to labor reform camps for loitering on the streets with boys and for general promiscuity. It was inevitable that there should be a constant undercurrent of sex in our song-and-dance company, and even the cadres who looked after us, and who were supposed to report the slightest flirtatious behavior among the prisoners, were themselves vulnerable. This was the case of the camp's guard commander, Major Tien, who a week after his wife's death (she died in childbirth), began spending all his spare time with our song-and-dance troupe, neglecting his real duties to watch us rehearse.

Shamelessly, some of the girls in the troupe took advantage of this to flirt with him openly. He was, after all, a powerful figure in the camp hierarchy and might prove to be a good ally if needed. So during rehearsals, the girls would ask him to help them fix their clothes. "Major, is my waistband all right?" "Major, do I have too much lipstick on?" The corpulent major was delighted to be the center of such attentions. He would insist on making up girls' faces himself, would stand obediently around, carrying stage accessories until they were needed, and he would contrive to have his arm around girls, or to touch them, while giving the impression that he was being helpful. He was never found out, and it was never known whether he had or not actually slept with any of the girls. But one evening, while I was operating a projector, showing slides during a Cantonese opera performance, he sidled up to me and, in the dark, squeezed my thighs. I kicked him, nearly knocking over the projector. Alarmed, he moved away.

The biggest rake in the song-and-dance company was undoubtedly Liu Hai-lin, and he was hated by most of the company for his arrogance. Since his crime had been of a sexual nature, and not "political," he looked down on all political prisoners, and constantly reported on them to the cadres, thus earning their approval. His army background served him in good stead: he knew exactly how to handle his superiors, how to display the proper disciplined, respectful attitude. He spouted Mao Tse-tung by the yard, was servile to his superiors and a born sneak and bully. He was also quite unrepentant about his "crime" and conscious of his somewhat flashy good looks. He was convinced that all the girls in the troupe were secretly in love with him and chased them all, displaying consummate ability to conceal this side of his personality from the authorities. His chief target was the troupe's prettiest dancer, a nineteen-year-old girl called Yen Shiu-lan, who had been sent to the camp for stealing.

When not in rehearsal it was our duty to look after the warehouse and unload incoming stores. One afternoon we were unloading bales of sugar from trucks which had just arrived from the refinery. Inside the warehouse, there were two small dormitories, partitioned off from the storeroom proper with sacking. Dizzy from carrying the heavy loads, I nearly fainted, and Captain Chen authorized me to go and lie down on a bed in one of the empty dormitories. I lay there, almost asleep. I could hear the sounds of the sugar being stacked next-door. I could hear other sounds, too; in the other dormitory, it was obvious that a couple was making love. It was none of my business, and—being a "reactionary" individualist, I failed to report the incident—as I should in fact have done. Indeed, I soon forgot about it altogether. But then, several weeks later, while we were out tea harvesting, Liu did a foolish thing: he slipped a love letter into Yen's tea basket while she wasn't looking. But she didn't notice this, and emptied the love letter, along with the tea leaves, into the machine where the tea leaves were sorted and dried. The worker operating the machine spotted the letter, and good, obedient worker that he was, handed it over to one of the cadres. The cadre began an investigation. He traced the day's harvest to our song-and-dance team, and handed the letter over to Captain Chen, who identified Liu's handwriting.

Captain Chen had had his doubts about Liu and Yen, and sent her away to be questioned by a woman officer. Then, in her absence, he summoned a general meeting of the troupe. "Something very serious has happened," he said. "Listen to this." And he began reading Liu's love letter. It was a sentimental, mushy kind of letter, and—knowing what kind of man Liu was—we made no attempt to conceal our feelings. The girls tittered, and some of the men made crude jokes—but not loud enough for Captain Chen to hear. Chen read the letter through slowly, and then repeated the key passage in it. "My love, I have a feeling that we have been found out," he read. "Whatever happens, you must never admit anything concerning that afternoon in the warehouse." Everyone present knew that Liu would come under relentless cross-examination until he spoke up and explained what had happened in the warehouse. This was the usual Communist practice. I was entrusted with the minutes of the ensuing "criticism" meeting. I began taking notes.

Prisoners were not allowed to fall in love, and to have a sexual encounter was a serious crime, punishable by several years extension of one's original sentence. But Liu didn't look at all concerned. He probably thought he could brazen his way out of it, owing to his past record as an orthodox, politically reliable prisoner. "It was nothing," he said. "Nothing at all. Just a joke."

But Captain Chen was firm. "I'm not moving from this room until all the facts are known," he said. And with considerable acumen he added: "We will all stay up all night if necessary to get to the bottom of this." He knew our feelings towards Liu, and he knew we would not let him off so easily.

"It was that evening we were unloading sugar," Liu said. "I went up to Yen and kissed her, that's all. There's not much harm in that, is there? All right, I did wrong. I sincerely repent. Now may I please go?"

Other prisoners began to get in the act. Normally no one would have behaved this way, but we all hated Liu. "This is simply not true," said one of the men prisoners. "If Liu had merely kissed her, he wouldn't have been so anxious to conceal the fact by writing her a note. There was something more. Confess! Confess!"

But Liu wouldn't confess. He just sat there, a slight, arrogant smile on his lips. "These are all immoral, reactionary people," he said, turning to Captain Chen. "Surely, as one soldier to another, you don't take their word against mine, do you?"

Chen, who didn't especially like Liu, became angry. "It is you who are being criticized right now, not your fellow workers," he said. "I don't believe your story. You'll stay here until you choose to talk."

At that point Yen, pale and obviously on the verge of collapse, entered the room and sat down quietly. Captain Chen pretended not to have seen her.

"Since Liu doesn't want to do any talking this evening, let me do some for him," he said, taking out a bulky file from a brief case. "Some of you think that Liu's sole crime was that affair in Hanoi, when he seduced a girl while on an official cultural mission to a friendly country. Perhaps I should put the record straight." Captain Chen then read out a court verdict on Liu, who had been sentenced to eight years in a labor camp not only for the business in Hanoi, but for consistently chasing after girls while in the People's Liberation Army cultural troupe. "The accused is a menace to all women around him," the verdict said. "He is constantly causing trouble and is not a fit person to be allowed at large. His attempts to seduce and even rape girls make him a potentially dangerous criminal."

Yen had been listening to all this. She screamed at Liu: "You bastard! You just did to me what you did to all those other girls. You don't love me at all. You were just afraid others would find you out, that's all." She burst into tears. The meeting degenerated into an uproar. All those whom Liu had in the past reported to cadres—and most of us had figured in his reports at one time or another—started shouting at him. Captain Chen made no effort to calm anyone. Some had to be restrained from hitting Liu. He cringed, and bowed his head.

At last, Captain Chen called the meeting to order. "Well," he said, "I expect your full written confession before morning. Don't think you can get away with anything any more around here. Your confession will be forwarded to the disciplinary committee. You may go." Liu slunk away. He was stripped of his title of "group leader," and another year was added to his sentence. He no longer dared to lord it over the rest of us. Nobody spoke to him, except on official business. But Yen was also punished, as was invariably the case in such matters. She, too, got an additional year's sentence.

But during the second summer I spent in the camp, Captain Chen himself got into trouble, and the cause of his own downfall was a girl. We were harvesting peanuts, and Captain Chen was working with us. One of our dancers, Liang Chun-hsiao, complained of a headache and asked whether she might go back to the dormitory and lie down. Curtly, Captain Chen said she could. Liang was twenty, but looked about fifteen. Her parents had had her sent to the camp, complaining that she was constantly running around with boys and had become completely unmanageable. She danced beautifully, and was a talented actress. Captain Chen seemed to treat her like a small girl. He would help her put on make-up before her stage performances, and chuck her under the chin. He sometimes called her, in fun, the troupe's "problem child."

We were working late that evening and no one noticed Captain Chen's disappearance. A car drove up, and one of the senior camp managers emerged. "Where's Captain Chen? I need him in my office right away."

Captain Chen was gone. The manager said: "I'll go and look for him back at the barracks. You"—he pointed to one of our girls—"show me the way." Afterwards she told us what had happened. They looked first in his office, which was empty. Then they went through the dormitories. The manager had a flashlight. It was already dark. As they were walking through the women's dormitory, the manager shone his flashlight on the row of beds. There, hidden by a mosquito net, but with his bare feet protruding, was Captain Chen, in his underwear, kissing a near naked Liang. The manager told the girl who had shown him the way back to the office to leave. She didn't know what had happened after that.

We returned to our dormitory around midnight. Liang was on her bed, crying her eyes out. We sat about, talking in hushed whispers, wondering what would happen. We knew that Captain Chen and the manager were close friends. Perhaps the whole thing would be hushed up.

But we never saw Captain Chen again, and nobody was ever able to find out exactly what happened to him. For weeks we had no one to look after us. We worked in the fields along with the other prisoners, and sat about despondently after our work was done, wondering whether he would ever come back. We all agreed he was the only Communist cadre we had ever felt any respect and affection for. We blamed Liang for what had happened, for she was always flirting with all the men. When the harvest time was over, a new captain took charge. He was a thick-headed lump of a man, who knew nothing about music or the theater, and admitted as much. "But I do know about discipline," he said. "From now on, things are going to be different." We had political indoctrination meetings for hours every night, and bitterly regretted the good old days. The new captain only dropped one hint about his predecessor. We were all collectively responsible, he said, for leading a highly respected cadre along the path of "degenerate corruption." We suspected that Captain Chen might himself have landed in a labor camp, probably in a remote area so that he would never meet any of those formerly in his charge.

If the camp authorities were rigidly opposed to sex relations between prisoners, they encouraged marriages between those people who were compelled to remain in the camp after their sentences had expired. This guaranteed the permanence of a stable working force. Couples who did get married in this fashion were there for good, and didn't stand the slightest chance of leaving, ever.

This didn't deter people from marrying. The supply depot, near our headquarters, was a favorite spot for men and women to meet. There was a café, a store, a photo studio, a cycle repair shop and a slaughterhouse. Outlying farms and workshops got all their supplies from the main warehouse. Here people would come from all over the New Life United Enterprises on their day off, to shop, to have their hair cut or simply to hang around and to meet.

Often prisoners who met this way, and liked each other, would make arrangements to marry as soon as their sentences had expired. Countless times, I helped prepare for such weddings by working in the sewing room, stitching together two mosquito nets or two single cotton quilts so that people could sleep together. Such couples, about to be married, followed a fixed routine: they would consult their cadres to find out whether their prospective mates were politically reliable, and would then formally ask the camp manager's permission. They would then take the manager's written certificate, allowing them to get married, for registration at the Ying Teh People's Commune Branch, which acted as a registrar of all births, marriages and deaths. This was all that was required. As soon as the commune had been informed, the couple was regarded as being legally married. They then posed for their picture together at the camp's photo shop. This was, in fact, the only function which came close to being a ceremony.

When a couple from the same production team got married, they were usually given a tiny room furnished with a board bed and two benches. They occasionally got a small stove as well, or managed to buy one. To go to a communal farm and buy food to cook in your own room on holidays was a luxury. With couples from different production teams, there was no real attempt made to unite them, and husband and wife usually worked without seeing each other, sleeping as before in communal dormitories. They would then meet once every two weeks and try and find a room to be together in for a day. It wasn't always easy. When a marriage broke up, which happened often enough, the girl would return to her dormitory.

In our troupe, men and women were constantly together during the day and got to know each other well before marriage. For members of the troupe, a wedding was a more formal occasion; I would decorate the theater where we performed with large signs signifying "Happiness" on either side of the large portrait of Chairman Mao which dominated the theater hall. The table where I worked to paint scenery would be covered with a red cotton tablecloth, and we would somehow obtain tea, candy and biscuits from the supply depot. The bride and groom would each wear a big red paper flower and, entering the hall, would bow low before Mao's portrait. One of the senior members of the company would then make a short speech, and everyone would adjourn to the buffet table, nibble sweets and peanuts and drink tea. Then, almost always, one of the girls in the troupe would say: "Now tell us the full story. How did you fall in love? When did you know you were made for each other?" And there would be other frank and sometimes crude questions. The bride and groom would blush, and try and wriggle out of the ordeal, but the assembled company would be as relentless in pursuing their questions as they were during a "struggle" meeting.

Actually, we knew the full stories of such love matches almost as well as the parties concerned, for living cheek by jowl with one another, we could scarcely fail to notice when a couple fell in love. I had filled notebooks with minutes of struggle meetings, in which couples were criticized, and sometimes punished, for falling in love while still serving their sentences. In most cases, "engaged" couples tacitly assumed they would get married as soon as their sentences expired, and whenever possible, indulged in sexual relations and even occasionally lived together, with the complicity of the rest of the troupe. Only when the local authorities found out about such goings-on did we stage struggle meetings, and then put on a show of indignation to give the cadres a good impression. Except when they concerned unpopular members of the troupe, such struggle meetings were part of the empty ritual of Communist discipline. The "guilty" couple would promise to make amends and to refrain from sex relations until their sentences were completed. In actual fact, they were constantly thinking, even during their "confessions," of ways and means of coming together again. And when weddings were actually celebrated, at our modest tea parties, members of the theatrical company took delight in recalling, sometimes in fairly plain terms, the circumstances of the couple's first meetings and the ways in which they had circumvented the camp rules.

Frequently, such marriages went wrong. Probably this was due to our confined environment. Ex-prisoners who got married knew nothing about each other's pre-prison past. They soon began quarreling, and even newly married women often moved back to their communal dormitory after just a taste of married life. There were pathetic case histories in our theater troupe. One girl married an ex-prisoner when she was five months pregnant, only to find that her new husband was brutal and openly reproached her for tricking him this way into marrying her. Another girl, a dancer, married one of the troupe's accordion players, had a baby and, after medical complications, was compelled to stop working in the troupe. She stayed in her hut and gradually lapsed into inarticulate misery, occasionally making some money by selling some of the camp's surplus vegetables on the local market, while her husband, a notorious woman-chaser, had a good time. She repeatedly asked the authorities for a divorce but none was ever granted.

There were girls, too, who took cruel advantage of men. One of our troupe members was an attractive girl called Wu Liu-ching. One of the camp's accountants, an official, not an ex-prisoner, fell in love with her. She played him along like a fish. She said they would need money to buy a home, so as a token of his love the accountant transferred his savings to Wu. Then, quite unexpectedly, Wu learnt that she was being released and could return home. Without saying anything to anybody, she left, taking the accountant's money with her. She later wrote to him, breaking off their engagement, but she never returned the money.

There were also touching scenes of enduring love and devotion among couples who rarely saw each other more than once a year. It was sometimes possible for relatives to make the long journey from Canton to see us, though mine never did. Chang Ping-ju, a former layout editor for a Communist Party daily paper in Kwangtung Province, was in our troupe and one of our best singers. She was small, lively and beautiful in a delicate, boyish sort of way. She had been sentenced to four years labor reform for corruption. She once told me that she had offended some powerful party figure on the staff of the paper, who had sent in an anonymous report on her and got rid of her this way.

We were miles away from the camp, picking tea, when her husband came with their two small children. He was an engineer, trained in the United States, and we crowded round our three visitors. Chang fetched a basin of water and washed her children's faces and feet, for they were dirty and exhausted by their long trip by train, bus and then on foot, hitchhiking rides on tractors for the last few miles. They sat and talked for half an hour, and ate rice cakes her husband had brought. It had been their hope that the family would remain together at least that night (it had taken them nearly sixteen hours to get to the camp), but a cadre came back, a little shamefaced. "Comrade," he said, "you'll have to go when the last tractor returns to the factory. You can spend the night in the New Life United Enterprises but not here. Tomorrow you'll take the train back to Canton."

Moments later, Ping-ju's husband and her two children climbed onto a tractor. "Take care. Don't worry. I'll look after everything."

Ping-ju nodded, and tears streamed down her face. She kissed the children. "Listen to what your father says. Don't be naughty."

One of the small boys said: "Why can't you come too?"

"I'll be back soon."

The tractor started up and they were gone.

Ping-ju knew better than to complain. Other visitors got the same treatment. Sometimes it was worse. I saw a group call on one of the women laborers on the tea plantation. As in the stone quarry, the visiting relatives had to spread out all the gifts they were bringing on the ground for inspection. The woman prisoner

had to squat motionless in one spot, and the visitors remained
under constant supervision all the time. A cadre sent them all
away after fifteen minutes' conversation. The visitors had spent all
day getting to the camp and had walked for the last four hours,
but it made no difference. The camp authorities did not formally
ban all visits, but they discouraged them by allowing visitors to
stay such a short time that the journey must have seemed almost
in vain.

Finally, although conditions were more bearable than in the
stone quarry, confinement in the camp resulted in a crop of suicides, and an escape attempt led to the public execution by firing
squad of a woman inmate.

I remember two such suicides well; in any normal, humane
society, they could have been prevented, for they both resulted
from an obvious manifestation of mental disturbance. In the camp,
what counted was the individual's productive capacity. When he
broke down, he was merely given another, more menial task to do.
Nervous breakdowns—which were frequent—were in themselves
a crime. Hu Chiao was a highly educated former university instructor. His father had been Nanking's best-known doctor before
being sent away to a labor camp, where he died. In 1957, as a
result of the "Anti-Rightist Campaign," Hu Chiao was demoted
in the university hierarchy and his salary was reduced to a mere
nine U.S. dollars a month, which he could barely live on. Then
his fiancée left him, at the request of the local party headquarters,
which had ruled that he was a bad "class" figure. Hu Chiao,
heartbroken, just ran away. A security police squad found him
wandering in the countryside and brought him back. He was assigned to looking after the pigs on the university farm. Shortly afterwards, he was caught stealing the four volumes which made up
Romain Rolland's classic *Jean Christophe*. "I just wandered into
the Foreign Languages Bookstore, saw the books and took them,"
he once told me. "Nobody was likely to buy them. I certainly
couldn't afford them. They cost nearly two months of my salary.
It seemed a pity to leave the books where no one would read or
appreciate them." He was caught, and sent to the labor camp.

Here he became increasingly eccentric in his ways. He hit a
prison guard who was ill-treating an old man, and got sentenced
to a spell in solitary confinement. He stole bread from the camp
kitchens and handed it out to prisoners. He was put to work on a
vegetable plot but threw down his spade and told a warder: "De-
bussy once said that gardening was the most stupid occupation on

earth." He refused to uproot weeds or disturb "nature's natural growth," as he called it.

Then he was put in charge of a flock of sheep and deliberately turned them loose, explaining that he wanted to save their lives from the slaughterhouse. Each of his eccentricities cost him a longer spell in solitary confinement, and after emerging from them, he would mutter to himself all day long. He would stop and talk to other inmates, embarking on a long, rambling story of his life, and of the "betrayal" of the girl he loved. "I return her to the party," then he would shout. "She is theirs. They can keep her."

Hu Chiao was still made to work on the simplest projects inside the camp, such as digging ditches. One day, he broke away from a working party and began running. Two guards tried to catch him, but he escaped. He ran and ran. At one end of the camp there was a ledge, giving onto rocks some fifty feet below. Hu Chiao stood on the edge of this ledge, shouting and screaming. Then, deliberately, he threw himself over, and died.

A girl in our own theatrical troupe became increasingly worried about her family and withdrew into an inner world of her own. At first, we noticed that she remained silent during group singing. Then she seemed to be in a constant trance. She had been through a rough time during political sessions in the camp, and had been forced to write confession after confession, acknowledging her "backward" political stand. Her husband was also in a camp, somewhere in China, and she had received news from one of her relatives that her children had run wild in Canton and had been taken to a delinquents' home. The whole family had thus been broken up and incarcerated in various government institutions. One night, she left the dormitory where we were all asleep, and threw herself down a well. Her body was found a few days later. She had taken off all her clothes before jumping into the well, and on the bundle, neatly tied, she had left a note. It said: *"I no longer even have the freedom to breathe."*

There was little serious crime inside the camp, for discipline was such that even hardened criminals (there were a few) thought twice about breaking the camp laws. But I remember one hideous case, which showed what could happen when one despaired of ever leaving the place. A camp cadre, Ho, had a grudge against Li Yung, one of the camp carpenters. Ho had put Li Yung in solitary confinement over and over again, mostly on trumped-up charges. As a result, Li Yung hated Ho, and his hatred became a form of madness. One day, working on a new building, he saw Ho walking below and threw a wooden window frame down on him, shouting curses. But a tree broke the fall and Ho was unhurt. Li Yung went to the camp stockade again. When he emerged, he swore vengeance.

He bided his time. Then, one morning, he waited near the cadres' living quarters. He waited until the time was right, then made off with Ho's five-year-old daughter, who was playing in a lane, took her into the fields and raped her.

He was arrested, and confessed. There was a public investigation and trial, at which he was sentenced to death. Ho himself conducted the case for the prosecution. "Why did you do this?" he said.

Li Yung replied, "Why did you keep putting me in solitary confinement?"

Ho said, "All right. You wanted to hurt me. Why hurt my daughter?"

"You're her father, aren't you? Anything that happened to her would make you feel bad, wouldn't it? I wanted you to hurt. I wanted you to feel like me."

"But do you think it's worth the death penalty to get even with me?" Ho asked. Li Yung looked at Ho, then laughed and laughed.

"What is life worth to us prisoners?" he said. "There are thousands of us, buried in the fields near the Hsiuts'ai Mountain. You think life is precious? So it may be, to you people, cadres, officials, members of the party. Not for us. No. It was worth it. To me."

The carpenter was not shot immediately. He was sentenced to a two-year spell of extra-hard labor first—and he was not reprieved.

But the event which caused the most excitement in the camp was what we referred to as the Photo Studio Conspiracy. The photo shop was a focal point in the life of the huge camp. It was in the center of camp, near the supply depot, and it was always busy. People like having their pictures taken, no matter what their appearance, and the cost was reasonable. Cadres and their families patronized the studio even more than the prisoners and ex-prisoners. It was simply a room, equipped with a chair and some strong lights, with a small darkroom leading off it. In a corner of the studio a woman prisoner called Li Wei-lun altered and mended clothes for the cadres and ex-prisoners. It was Li Wei-lun, a tough, strong-minded woman, and the wife of a

Kuomintang army officer who had fled to Taiwan, who was the instigator of the conspiracy and the brains behind it.

Li Wei-lun believed in fortunetellers, and a famous Canton fortuneteller had once told her, a long time ago, that she would achieve fame, fortune and happiness in middle age. She was then in her late thirties, and her prospects were not good. But she was a scheming, tenacious woman. Her sentence was a long one. She and her husband had been "hard-core" Kuomintang cadres, and her goal was to escape first to Hongkong, and then, possibly, to Taiwan. But before she could attempt this, she had to make contact with her daughter, aged seventeen, who lived in Canton on money regularly remitted to her from relatives in Hongkong.

The head of the photo studio was another former Kuomintang man, Kao An. He also wanted to escape but had resigned himself to a life-long stay at the camp. When no one was around the photo shop, Kao An and Li Wei-lun would sit and talk about the good old days. Little by little, Li Wei-lun spoke to Kao An of her hopes, and of what the fortuneteller had said. Kao An introduced Li Wei-lun to a friend of his, a paroled prisoner called Chin who occasionally got permission to visit relatives in Canton. Chin had served his sentence for operating a clandestine night club in a Canton basement, and he had a way with girls. He left for a five-day leave in Canton bearing a letter of introduction to Li Wei-lun's young daughter. She fell in love with him. Eventually, owing to Chin's good connections with some party cadres in the camp, this daughter, Hsiao Yun, was allowed to come and visit him, on the grounds that they were engaged to be married.

Li Wei-lun had planned the match, but the reason why she wanted her daughter to visit the camp was to act as courier. On her instructions, Hsiao Yun wrote to relatives in Hongkong, asking for money and making plans. Li Wei-lun claimed that her husband still had anti-Communist contacts in China, who would be ready to help them. If they failed, they decided they would try and make their way to Kwangsi Province and link up with some anti-Communist guerrillas in the area.

Li Wei-lun's scheme became more ambitious as time went on. She had already decided to escape with her future son-in-law, and with Kao An, the photo shop manager. The latter suggested they also include a friend of his, nicknamed Old Lao, who was a storekeeper in the camp's chemical engineering plant. Among the stores Old Lao handled were explosives, and when Li heard of this, she decided they might as well be hanged for a sheep as a lamb. Her new plan was to blow up the main administrative building in the camp and take advantage of the ensuing confusion to escape. This act of sabotage, she told the others, would ensure their fame. Taiwan authorities would welcome them as heroes. Such was her eloquence that the others eventually agreed.

They got as far as accumulating stolen ration cards, to buy food on the way and proper clothes, so that they would not be taken for ordinary camp inmates, and planning their escape route, but had not got round to stealing the explosives when someone talked. One night, soldiers carried out raids all over the camp and arrested scores of people. The key plotters were arrested, and a lot of innocent people as well, whose sole crime was that they had known the members of the Photo Shop Conspiracy. The avowed policy of the cadres, in cases such as these, was to arrest anyone remotely suspicious, in fear that the guilty ones might otherwise escape. Li Wei-lun's daughter was also arrested, in Canton, and sent up to the camp to be questioned. The prisoners were handcuffed and shackled in special disciplinary cells. The inquiries went on and on.

Nine months later, when memories of the initial arrest had faded, a huge public trial took place. I had to prepare the posters displayed on this occasion, and I remember most of them: "Firmly punish counterrevolutionary elements who remain stubborn to the end." "For those who resist reform, there can be only death." "Those who dream of restoring the old, of escaping, of creating trouble and of indulging in sabotage will come to no good end."

As with all trials in China, this one merely promulgated a sentence, and there were no pleas in favor of the accused. Thousands of people crowded into the main hall to watch the trial. The prisoners, when they were brought in, were unrecognizable. Li Wei-lun now looked like a haggard old woman, and had to be half carried to her place. To me it seemed that she was dying of beriberi, and she seemed only partially aware of what was going on. The other prisoners were in almost as bad shape. Li Wei-lun was carried out of the court and shot by a firing squad in the middle of a thunderstorm. Her daughter was compelled to sit with the court and watch the whole proceedings. When the sentence was announced, she fell into a dead faint. Chin, the dashing young man, was sentenced to death with the chance of a reprieve if he repented. Kao An, the photo studio manager, got a life sentence. Old Lao was sentenced to twenty years' hard labor. The "hero" of the day was a man called Yang Chi-ko, a close friend of Chin's, who had betrayed the group to the authorities. He was called upon to make a speech at the end of the trial, praising the camp authorities for their "leniency." He stammered and shook with fright, and stopped halfway, while the assembled prisoners stared at him with undisguised loathing. The senior judge told him he was excused.

The execution of Li Wei-lun was the first time, to anyone's knowledge, that a woman had been executed in the labor camp. From then onwards, security precautions were tightened: letters were censored more carefully, former prisoners were searched before they were allowed to leave the camp and such leave was heavily curtailed. The camp guard was reinforced, searchlights and barbed wired were brought in to strengthen the camp's perimeter and stricter control was maintained over working parties leaving the main enclosure for work outside. More soldiers and guards arrived, and armed detachments now accompanied the prisoners who went out on working parties in the fields, though the song-and-dance company was still allowed to travel around the countryside on its own. The betrayal of the gang by a close friend of one of the chief plotters also showed us all that no one could really be trusted. The long-term result was to drive us all into greater moral isolation, confiding in no one.

CHAPTER XI

THE PRICE OF RELEASE

THE MONTHS and then the years slipped by, and by the summer of 1963, I had completed my sentence, staying out of trouble, keeping the minutes of all the troupe's struggle meetings, altogether the model prisoner. I immediately asked to be sent home, only to be given the classic reply. I was here to serve the state. The state, in the form of the New Life United Enterprises, needed me. Who else was there to paint and assemble stage scenery, cut out big characters to make into posters, or keep records of our meetings? The only difference in my new status as an ex-prisoner was that I got paid: about ten U.S. dollars a month. I was still regarded by the camp authorities with suspicion. As a former political prisoner, I was denied the few advantages enjoyed by the others. My mail, of course, remained heavily censored. Applications for leave to go to Canton were turned down.

I had almost given up hope and wondered whether I would ever see Canton again when, one morning, one of the cadres came up to me and, speaking softly in my ear, said that I was to stay behind after our working party had completed its task. We were busy helping to lay out a new basketball court. Instead of returning to the dormitory with the others to wash up before our midday meal, I went to one of the cadre offices, as I had been told. The cadre who dealt with security matters, Wu, was there.

"You are being transferred to a new post," he said. "I can't say any more than that. While the others are eating, you are to pack your things, come with me and leave."

"Please tell me where I'm going."

"I can't do that. You'll find out soon enough. Hurry up. You haven't got much time."

"Shall I take my cotton uniforms I was issued here?" I asked. These were prisoner's clothes, and would not be needed if my destination was Canton.

"I said, take everything." He added, seeing my face fall: "Clothes are in short supply everywhere. You may need them, wherever you may be." He looked at his watch. "Report back in half an hour."

There were three cadres in Wu's office when I came back with my belongings—a battered old suitcase and a bundle containing my bedding, a mosquito net and some books. A woman cadre went through all my things with care. Throughout my peregrinations, I had managed to keep a silk cheongsam from Hongkong, and she held this up and looked at it with surprise. "You must be a young miss from Hongkong," she said. "Nobody would say so to look at you today." This was meant as a compliment, and I smiled and made a small bow.

I decided to try my luck again. "Shall I keep the cotton uniforms or hand them in?"

"These belong to the government. I don't think you'll need them. You can leave them here." My hopes rose.

One of the cadres loaded my suitcase and bedding roll onto the back of his bicycle and we set off for the ferry, the cadre wheeling his bicycle, I on foot. "We've got to hurry," he said. "The train leaves at one-thirty." Wu, the security officer, saw me off as far as the ferry. I passed inmates I knew on the way. They looked at me in wonder, but didn't say anything. In Wu's presence, they dared not ask me where I was going. On the other side of the ferry there were two people waiting, a man and a woman. The man's face seemed vaguely familiar. The cadre who had helped me with my luggage whispered to him, then left without saying anything to me.

The man waiting for me said: "You don't remember me, do you? Well, you have changed too. Labor reform seems to have done you a great deal of good." The woman chimed in: "As our leader says, in our new society human beings can be changed for the better. This is especially true of young people, and you are young, aren't you?"

I didn't know what to say, and just stood there. The man said: "My name is Judge Li. This is Comrade Liang. You may call us comrades. We have asked you to come with us because of certain things that happened to you in the past, and also because you may be able to be of use to us in the future."

The woman said, "We want to put you to the test, to see whether you have really recognized your errors and now hate the crimes you were guilty of."

I then realized that the vast bureaucracy of the state had never really let me out of its grip. I had felt, during my last few years, in the camp, that I had been forgotten. All the time, reports about me must have been forwarded, regularly, to the security branch which had been responsible for my original arrest and conviction. I didn't know whether to be pleased or frightened by the circumstances of the move. The two cadres were obviously trying to be nice to me, which was not in itself a bad sign. Li said: "We are taking the train. Don't talk to any of the passengers. Don't say who you are. If they ask you where you're going, say: on official business to Canton. Don't move from your seat. If you want to go to the toilet, let me know first. When the train arrives at its destination, let the other passengers off first. Stay behind with us. Don't worry. Trust the party and the government, and you'll be all right."

The train was Canton-bound. My hopes rose again. I did just as Li had said. The fact that I was allowed to call them comrade was a good sign. It meant that I was no longer regarded as a pariah. They ordered supper for me on the train. We ate silently.

Several hours later, we arrived at Canton Station, and I waited obediently. There was a Jeep outside, and we got into it. The driver seemed to know where to go. I knew better, by now, than to pester my escorts with questions.

To my surprise, we didn't go far. The Jeep stopped in front of the East Asia Hotel, in the center of town. Li helped me unload my luggage. Without registering, we all took the elevator to the fifth floor. Li led the way. There was a large hotel suite. Two men were waiting inside. Li introduced us: "This is Section Chief Yang. This is Comrade Liu." Tea was poured. I waited for someone to begin.

Section Chief Yang spoke slowly, with a strong country accent. His eyes never left me, and I could see he was watching carefully to study my reactions. By now I, too, was experienced in hiding my true feelings.

"Comrades Li and Liang were sent to bring you here because we have a specific task in mind for you. I hope you will seriously consider the proposal that the government, with its customary benevolence, is about to make. You have been treated with great leniency, and have enjoyed considerable privileges during the latter part of your labor reform. Few young people guilty of crimes can have been treated more generously. Now your future is at stake. You are still young, and capable, we think, of complete reform. We would be interested in hearing your views on the subject."

"I am indeed grateful that the government, in its customary generous fashion, should have enabled me to reform and put me once more on the right path. The instructions from the party and from the government are infallible and must be obeyed implicitly. In my own small way, I would like to have the opportunity of serving the people as an ordinary citizen. In order to be able to do this, it is my fond hope that the party, showing its customary generosity and understanding, will allow me to return home."

It was Comrade Liu's turn. "Whether you return home to Canton or not will eventually be in your hands. We feel, in your case, that it may be a little premature. We want you to review your past and your present thinking to see whether you are now able to fulfill a useful function in our new society. Our comrades here are ready to help you at all times. If there is anything that, in earlier days, you withheld from the government, you must say so. If there is anything you would like to add to your confession of five years ago, you must let us know. Your political viewpoint must have changed in the last five years. You have reached a higher level of political consciousness. You must think about these things."

They got up and left. All but Liang, who said: "I stay here with you. Have a bath. Go to bed. Rest, you must be tired." She saw the men out. After they had left, she locked the door on the inside.

For two days I remained alone with Liang in the hotel suite. She went out twice a day for food, and each time she left, she locked me in. We hardly talked. I knew I was back in the net of the security police again, but in easier circumstances. I was being handled with kid gloves. Why? My vague apprehensions were somewhat stilled by my present luxurious confinement.

The bed was soft, the sheets clean and I bathed in a real bath—several times a day. Li, I recalled, must have been one of the officials who had questioned me those five long years ago. Was the whole process going to start all over again? If so, whatever could I say that I hadn't said already? There was no sense in discussing all this with Liang. She was quite obviously a minor cog in the machine. Moreover, she was tired and ill. When she undressed that first night to sleep in the bed next to mine, I noticed that she was several months pregnant. She, too, was delighted with her present assignment. Most of the day she sat in the comfortable armchair of the sitting room, resting. The only orders she gave me were not to talk to the hotel staff. They must have wondered who we were, and why I never left my room. I thought hard about what I should say when the three men returned.

They came back on the evening of the third day. Yang said, once we were seated and sipping tea, "Well, how about it?"

I made a short, well-prepared little speech. I said that my labor reform had taught me that I had been wrong to pretend, as I had done five years ago, that there was no connection between politics and religion. Of course religion and politics were inseparable. "I deeply regret that I allowed myself to be used by the imperialists to do bad things against the people and against the state. As I now realize, my capitalist upbringing was the cause of all my errors. I am grateful to the party and to the government for allowing me to shake off the bad bourgeois influence during my last few years through productive work and labor reform."

As I spoke, Yang and Liu nodded. Yang said, "It's obvious to us all that your ideological standards have been considerably improved. Only through deep repentance and thorough self-criticism can real reform occur." I had passed my first test with flying colors. "You are leaving here soon," Yang said. "You needn't take all your things. Just a change of clothes will do. The rest of your luggage you will leave with us. Your wishes may come true, but you must first undergo a fresh course of study. If you study well, then things may go as you wish. If not, things will not be good for you at all. In the meantime, we need a fresh, full confession of your initial crimes in the light of your new, heightened political awareness. This you will complete later on. Then you will write a comment on your crimes, and suggest a possible course of study to improve your cultural level still further."

The next evening Li and the same Jeep driver came. Liang came too. The tarpaulin of the Jeep was lowered and I had no idea where we were headed for. I knew that we were leaving Canton by the North Gate, and were heading north. The road was bad, and we bumped around a lot. Nobody said anything.

We stopped outside a fairly large house, which appeared deserted. It was dark. Inside the house there was a small room, with two beds, each with a mosquito net. Li said a few words, which I couldn't catch, to Liang and left. We went to bed early, without saying anything.

The next morning Liang briefed me about the place. The building we were living in, she said, belonged to the New Life Brick and Machinery Factory, a plant where former labor reform prisoners continued their "re-education." "We don't eat here," she said, "but in the headquarters of the Kwangtung Province Labor Reform Office, which comes under the Public Security Bureau. All the people you will see there are fairly senior cadres. The fact that you are allowed to have your meals there with them shows the extent of our trust in you. But you mustn't speak to them. If you come across someone you may have met in the past, you must tell me straight away. If you recognize any prisoners, just ignore them. If anyone asks you why you have come here, just say: for work and study. Stay in your room and don't go out unless it's absolutely necessary."

I began writing my confession. By now I knew the form well. Essentially, it would be no different from my original one, except that I threw in every possible bit of Communist jargon I knew. It was obvious, I wrote in a long preamble, that the Church was the secret arm of the imperialists, aimed at gullible elements of the bourgeoisie like myself. I no longer felt any qualms of conscience about this. To achieve freedom, it was necessary to write this way. I felt sure God would understand.

I wrote morning, noon and night. Liang escorted me to the toilet and to the communal bathhouse. While I was writing she slept. After I had finished writing my confession, I was asked to thumb through a catalogue of known and suspected Catholic "agents" in Canton. I recognized none of them. Then, Liang said, I must once more write my detailed life story. Liang read what I had written page by page before passing it on to Li and Liu, who had also arrived, but were living somewhere else. In the evening I was allowed to go for a walk in the paddy fields with Liang, and to watch television. I was not allowed to write to my family and had no idea how long this "thought-remolding" process would continue.

From the grounds of the house I lived in, I could see both the brick and the machinery factories in a valley below. The place was a hive of activity all day. The bricks were mostly exported, and the machine shops produced a famous brand of Chinese electric fans, popular in Hongkong because of their low price. On Sundays, dependents came to visit the ex-prisoners, and Liang told me not to go out of doors then. She was afraid that someone might recognize me.

I wrote and rewrote my confession and my life story during the course of those weeks, and was supplied with all sorts of Communist literature concerning the Catholic Church, which I used to flesh out my story, quoting long chunks of the books I had been lent. Liang, Yang and Liu used to come and see me from time to time, and occasionally we had a meal or drank tea together. The Moon Festival came and went. My three Public Security escorts brought me moon cakes and sweets. It got colder. They saw to it that I got warm clothes. I desperately wanted to go home, but didn't dare broach the subject openly. I had the feeling that time was beginning to lay heavy on Liang's hands, too, and that she, too, wanted to go back to her family. Her husband, she told me in a rare confiding mood, was an important man—a judge on one of the Canton People's Courts. From her identity card, which I saw once while she was looking for something in her bag, I had already noticed that she was a full-fledged official of the Public Security Bureau.

I had finished my writing, and had nothing to do. Liang's pregnancy was getting more and more advanced. I hadn't dared write to anyone, or transgress any of the rules my three new jailers had laid down. But I was getting increasingly anxious. One day Liang was not feeling well. She was afraid, she told me, that her baby might have rickets owing to a calcium deficiency. Would I go to the nearest village and buy some pork bones? She would ask the cook to make some special broth for her. She gave me a Chinese* dollar. I bought the bones from a butcher's shop, and received ten cents change. On impulse, I bought a sheet of paper, an envelope and an eight-cent stamp with what was left—I had no money of my own. I addressed it to a friend of mine in Canton, but deliberately left the note unsigned. She would recognize my handwriting. I simply said: "I have been transferred to another place for further study. I may be home soon, if things work out." I had been quick about all this, and Liang never found out what I had done. It was the only letter I wrote during the whole time I was in the cadres' house.

All this time, as I was to find out, Li and Liu were carrying out detailed inquiries about me. They talked to survivors of the stone quarry, and to all my closest colleagues in the song-and-dance troupe I had just left. Li returned one day from the New Life United Enterprises and started writing his own report. I was good at my work, and obeyed the camp discipline well, he said, but from his observations and questioning he had discovered that I still left a lot to be desired. According to him, from what other members of the troupe had said, I still had a petit-bourgeois

* One Chinese (Jenminpao) dollar is equal to 0.42 U.S. dollars.—Editors.

mentality, still kept my faith in "religious superstitions" and was "full of pride."

I accepted these comments with outward humility. In my own mind, I wondered whether Liu had any understanding of the motivations of the people he talked to in the camp. Did he not realize that they in turn were out to give the cadres a good impression of themselves, even if this meant slandering a fellow prisoner?

A new "religious expert" appeared on the scene, a section chief called Ko. He smiled all the time, and was too friendly to be sincere. The report from the troupe must have worried them. They wanted to be certain that I would not revert back to my old ways.

Section Chief Ko sat down in my room one day. "We've got to get this straight," he said. "Do you believe in a so-called God or not?"

I said, "I can't lie to you. I do believe in the existence of a supreme being. This has nothing to do with the crimes of the Church. It is just a belief which is firmly rooted in my mind."

Everyone looked disappointed. Liu said, "Do you mean to say that all these last few months have been for nothing?"

I said, "I have made a full and sincere confession about espionage in the guise of religion. I hate people who do that. But I can't give up my belief in God. The two things are quite separate."

Li said, "Will you go to church if you are free once more?"

"If you say: don't go to church, I won't go, obviously. If you see no harm in it, then, yes, I would like to go to church occasionally."

One of the security men started to say something, but Ko cut him short. "That's fine," he said. "We won't prevent her from going to church. But"—he turned to me—"we must know all about what goes on during and after the services, do you understand? You must keep your eyes and ears open. Anything suspicious you must report to us immediately." No one had ever spelled out my future task quite so bluntly. In order to be free, I was prepared to promise anything. Now it looked as though my release was near. What was I to do?

I hung my head, and said: "I understand."

Everyone in the room cheered up. Ko said: "That's good. I know we can rely on you. Now I'll tell you a piece of extraordinarily good news. We are in a position now to make the atom bomb. Do you realize what this means? It's a crushing blow for Soviet revisionism and American imperialism. Peking is the revolutionary center of the world. We are the giants in the world revolution. How happy and glorious it is to be Chinese, and to live in the present era!" I smiled somewhat wanly. They were all excited and Ko was almost in a trance. This was ten months before China's first atomic explosion occurred. Ko was proud of being in the possession of such important news. It set him apart as a cadre of undisputed importance. He deliberately made this announcement in front of me to show that he was no subordinate hack.

The days went by, and I despaired of getting home in time for the new year. Then, on New Year's Eve, Li and Liu arrived at our little house burdened with parcels. "We're going to have a banquet," Li said, "and celebrate the new year and your own departure, and at the same time wish you every form of happiness in your new life." I could hardly believe it. I laughed and cried, hugged them all and thanked each one of them. Liang and I prepared the meal, and such a meal! Chicken, roast pork, spiced meat, Tsientsin cabbage, green vegetables, sausage—there was enough food for a dozen people at least. But the meal was not just a formality. Afterwards, for the last time, we sat down for a long, practical briefing session.

First of all, Li handed over my census card. This was an identity card, with which one could get food ration cards. Without it, one could not hope to survive in China. It was issued by the Ying Teh Public Security Office, dated December 31, 1963. I was not to mention to anyone how I had spent the last three months. If anyone should ask questions, I was to say that I had been a member of a workers' song-and-dance troupe in Ying Teh. There had been considerable change in my family, Li said. My grandmother had died a year ago. All the remaining members of my family had obtained legal permission to go to Hongkong, and they were living there. I would, in fact, be alone in Canton. I was considerably upset by this—but it was typical of them to have withheld this news all along. I was to become more upset by what followed.

"You are still remembered by the Catholics in Canton," Li said. "They have a very high regard for you. So your job will be to renew your acquaintance with them, go to church, mix with them, and find out all you can about them. You will report on what you see and hear. Anything that strikes you as being reactionary in word, thought or deed must be noted. We shall be getting in touch with you regularly through your local street committee, and the local police station, but nobody will know what our relations really are. In an emergency, or if you have something particularly urgent to communicate, here is a telephone number. It is Comrade Liang's office. Memorize it, don't write it down."

Li handed me an envelope. "Here are some rice ration cards, for twelve kilos, and thirty dollars. You had better write to your relatives in Hongkong and ask for money. Don't be in too much of a hurry to look for a job. You'll have to apply in Canton, and your records will show you've been in a labor camp, so it may be difficult at first. But don't worry. If you get into trouble, phone Comrade Liang. Have you understood all this?"

I nodded. Li and Liang then embarked on a formal little speech. They said the motherland needed me, and that I should not let the government or the party down. They reminded me that I was the object of enormous favors. How many labor reform inmates had been allowed home so soon after their sentences had come to an end? The three months I had been privileged to enjoy were usually set aside only for cadres about to embark on confidential work. I should remember all this, and be grateful. Then they said good night and I was once more alone with Liang. The next morning, we both left by ferry, and took the train from Hsitsun to Canton. There, at the station, I found my belongings. Liang had checked them into the station cloakroom three months ago, and produced the necessary receipts. I carried my luggage outside, and Liang called a pedicab. I waved good-by. At last I was on my way home.

CHAPTER XII

THE RETURN

I CLIMBED INTO A pedicab and gave my address. It was a long way and I felt sorry for the old man. "Take your time, drive as slowly as you wish. I haven't seen Canton for years and years and don't mind how long it takes," I said.

"I'll take you through the city center," he said. "That way you'll see the bright lights for the new year. But first, I must give you your receipt." He consulted a dog-eared sheet. "That'll be eighty cents," he said, and began writing out a receipt on a thin slip of paper.

"But I don't need a receipt."

"That shows how long you've been away," he said. "Everyone has to have a receipt." He explained that this was a new way of ensuring that pedicab operators didn't make money on the side. "Any policeman or party member can stop me on the way and ask to see your receipt," he said. "If you don't have one, I'm in trouble."

"Is the pedicab yours?" I asked.

"It is, in a sense. But we've been unionized. You may say it belongs to the union now." He went on to explain that under new regulations, pedicab owners were compelled to pool their resources, and were not allowed to operate their pedicabs for more than eight hours a day. The rest of the time, they were loaned out to other members of the union, who didn't have pedicabs of their own. "They say it's to prevent us from working too hard," he said. Actually, it's to share what work there is. Can't really make both ends meet working only half a day, specially with no tips allowed, and fixed rates for every trip. Luckily, my wife and my sons work too. I'll rest when I'm dead."

I noticed that despite the bright lights in certain central city streets, the rest of the city seemed dimmer than when I had left it. "Yes," the pedicab driver said. "The lights are for the new year and the tourists. But the ordinary street lighting has been dimmed. To save electric power. We save everything now."

And it was true: my first impressions of Canton were of a city of incredible thrift. Everything was saved, repaired, and even when apparently broken and useless, it still had value. A broken plastic toy car was worth one cent; an empty toothpaste tube, two cents; five kilos of broken glass were enough for a bus fare across town. Copper from dismantled electric fittings sold at one dollar (U.S.) the pound. Chicken and duck feathers turned in at government agencies entitled one to extra cloth rations. People saved dried banana peel for fuel; saucepans were patched up and made to serve when apparently broken; and of course most people went around in patched and heavily darned clothes. Some of these habits had been instilled into the Cantonese during the shortages of the Great Leap Forward. Some were simply due to the prevalent low wages and high prices—over a week's wages for a pair of shoes or a pair of men's trousers; a bicycle was the equivalent of five months' wages.

All this I discovered in my first few days of real freedom. The homecoming had been a letdown. A few neighbors had been there to welcome me, and we had kissed. I didn't specifically say where I had been, but they guessed. The question was never put to me. Too many people had disappeared in Canton over the last few years, only to emerge again as I had done, subdued, incommunicative and thin.

Our house was no longer strictly ours. After my grandmother's death and that of an aunt who lived in a small apartment above us, the Canton municipal authorities had decided that it was far too big a place for the rest of my family. New tenants had moved in. One of them, a staunch party man, was the local street committee leader. All that was left that was ours was a small apartment, with some of our salvaged furniture. The new tenants paid almost nominal rent, and in my new chastened mood, having listened for years to the crimes of capitalists and landlords, I felt almost guilty that we had in fact once owned the house, and would not have dreamt of complaining that complete strangers were now living practically rent-free in what was by rights my house, using my furniture and treating the place as their own.

Difficulties began when I started trying to buy little things for my new small apartment—a saucepan, some dishcloths, a washer for a leaking tap. The shop attendants would either shrug and move away, or else ask: "You have your tickets?" I eventually asked a neighbor, and soon I was as ticket-conscious as most Cantonese.

Tickets were a bonus given as a form of supplementary wages to workers of all kinds and without them it was impossible to buy any consumer items. To buy a tube of toothpaste, for instance, required one ticket—and an empty tube, to prove that one wasn't hoarding or in the black market toothpaste business. A watch cost two hundred tickets.

Though I was unemployed in those first few weeks after my release, I was among the privileged few—my parents kept sending me money from Hongkong and with each hundred-dollar (HK) remittance—which I exchanged for a hard currency voucher, valid in any "overseas Chinese special commodity store" —I received a batch of tickets as well as supplementary ration and cloth cards.

This was one of the paradoxes of Canton in 1964: it was full of remittance men, and women, idling away their lives, eking out a relatively privileged existence on the proceeds of what the capitalists in Hongkong sent them. One could hardly fail to notice the number of idle people in Canton, all seemingly well fed and even comfortably off. They sat in parks during the day, reading newspapers. They filled cafés and whiled away the time at food stalls. Nowhere in China, I was told, were there so many people on the streets during working days. The living standards of the Cantonese must have been higher than anywhere else in China, for almost everyone, it turned out, had a relative in Hongkong—and even the smallest remittance went a long way.

For a monthly remittance of a hundred Hongkong dollars (U.S. $17) was, in Canton at least, enough to ensure one a decent standard of living. It meant that with the exchange certificates turned in at local banks, you could shop at special overseas Chinese shops for unrationed goods, at admittedly higher prices, but of a quality rarely seen in ordinary shops; it meant that as a bonus, one received quantities of "industrial tickets," with which one could in turn acquire common household goods which it took ordinary citizens sometimes years to acquire. And some people living on remittances from abroad had no qualms about wheeling and dealing in surplus tickets, making a profitable living out of it. The authorities must have known of such practices, for they knew almost everything that was going on. My private feeling was that in 1964, after the failure of the Great Leap Forward, hard currency was so badly needed in China that the government and local municipal bodies were prepared to wink at all kinds of abuses as long as the Hongkong dollars kept rolling in.

But for those who had no such additional income, life was still very hard indeed—though there was widespread agreement that things were far, far better than during the Great Leap Forward, when there had been almost nothing in the shops, and practically no food.

I soon caught the hang of all this, and learnt to shop as the Cantonese did; I learnt to line up outside a food shop whenever I saw other people doing so—this invariably meant there was a limited but unusual supply of food to be had there. People stood in line for hours for fish, beef and certain vegetables—but everyone I met commented on the increasing supplies in the shops and the contrast to the years of the Great Leap Forward. I wanted to get used to my new freedom again, and simply the fact of being able to walk the streets of the city I knew and loved, of being able to shop, to rest, to read when I felt like it were luxuries enough.

These were relatively carefree months, though I had a vague premonition that I had better make the most of them, for things might change for the worse. Also, I was in love. Long ago, before my nightmare began, I had met Kang, a young student—and relative of some distant relatives of ours. We had, at the time, corresponded and even flirted a little. He was a medical student at Wuhan, a brilliant student, they said, with a brilliant future. I had been in Wuhan in 1956 visiting friends, and he had acted as guide. When the time had come for me to leave, he had said, "Perhaps one day I'll get a job in Canton." We had corresponded after that, until my arrest. For five years I had heard nothing from him. I, of course, could not write. He did not at first know what had happened to me. Eventually he heard, but was cautioned against writing; it would, his friends said, ruin his career. He was a qualified doctor by now, working in a research laboratory.

Then, out of the blue, only a few weeks after my return to Canton, I got a letter from him—warm, tender, chatty. He had not forgotten me, he said. He joked about our match-making cousins—for my relatives in Wuhan had obviously introduced us with marriage in view—and discreetly hinted that he hoped my "foolishness" was over. He was in Sian now, had a good job and would soon be a party member.

He obtained a few days leave, and permission to travel to

Canton. We met, fell in love and decided to marry—provided he obtained permission from his superiors. He went back to Sian, and from then on we corresponded several times a week. I no longer felt alone, and with Kang, I felt, I might even settle down in China and become, after all, a loyal, hard-working citizen. We were determined to get married as soon as possible.

But the laboratory authorities in Sian were not at all pleased at what had happened. Kang was one of their most promising cadres. What the devil did he need to go and fall in love with a former counterrevolutionary element for? A subtle campaign was mounted against me: his colleagues, his friends, his party mentors all tried to convince him that he was making a huge mistake. By marrying me, they pointed out, he would be jeopardizing his whole career. His chances of joining the party would be nil. He might even find himself unable to get a qualified job anywhere in China, and it was by no means certain that he would ever be able to live in Canton or that I would be allowed to go to Sian. Why get involved in a "gray element," when there were so many "orthodox" girls in Sian with excellent political records and unimpeachable workers' backgrounds?

There was a stubborn streak in Kang, however, and having set his mind on marrying me, he was determined to do so. He described the sessions to me. He had tried to claim that I had only "worked for the imperialists" because I had been young and ignorant, and deserved a chance to make good. The fact that I had been released proved, he said, that I had undergone satisfactory "thought reform." Was it not government policy to help redeem those who had erred?

Reluctantly, the party authorities in Sian gave their consent, and the wedding was planned for September. Kang had tried to extract from his superiors the promise that I would be allowed to come to Sian and live with him. He wrote that no pledge to that effect had actually been made, but the authorization to marry had been, in itself, as he put it, "an immense concession" on the part of the local Communist cadres, and he was confident they would be won round to his point of view. Poor Kang! He did not know that the fight he was putting up on my behalf was hopelessly discrediting him in the eyes of his superiors. Granted, he was one of the brightest and most valued young scientists on the staff, with a brilliant future in research ahead of him. This was as nothing when put in the balance and measured

against his infatuation for a suspect, convicted labor reform inmate. Needless to say, I had no inkling of the situation as it
really was. Had I known what I discovered later, I would
have had the strength, I think, to prevent Kang from making
such a costly mistake—for it was, in the long run, heartbreaking
for both of us. At the time, my release, my falling in love,
the fact that someone like Kang even considered marrying
someone with a labor camp record all made me feel that, after
all, everything was right with the world and that China—despite
my past experiences—was where I belonged.

That summer, then, was a happy one, and I looked forward
to my new life in Sian. At the back of my mind there was
another, perhaps cold-blooded, but perfectly valid reason for
getting married and leaving Canton: I would no longer have
to go through the pretense of reporting on fellow Catholics to
the Public Security Department.

For in various ways, the presence in Canton of my "liberators"
was making itself felt. In the first few weeks after my return
to freedom, I heard nothing from any of the comrades, and
the fear that they might demand immediate results receded.
But a few weeks after I had returned home, I received a message
from the street committee. I was to phone Comrade Liang.
She had had her baby, she said, and was back to work. We
chatted inconsequentially about things, and I congratulated her
on the birth of a son. Her real purpose in getting me to call
her was to make an appointment for lunch, in a remarkably good
Canton restaurant, where we sat, unobserved, behind screens.

Perhaps I had half expected what followed, but my blood
still ran cold. In Canton, Liang said, there was a Chinese Catholic
priest who still heard confession. He was suspect. She wanted
me to go to him and confess, and in the course of my confession say bad things about the regime and the way Catholics
were treated, in order to test his reactions.

"I can always try," I said, "but there's absolutely no certainty
that he'll speak up against the government. If he doesn't say
anything, I can't force him, can I?"

Liang was patient. "You can try," she said, "and you must.
It is your duty."

It was, of course, out of the question for me to behave as
she had suggested. To my mind, apart from the horror of being
an *agent provocateur,* the secret of the confessional worked
both ways; even if the priest had ranted and raved at Chairman

Mao and at communism in general, it would have been unheard of for a Catholic to report him to anyone. In fact, Liang's approach to me was proof that, despite the huge and efficient bureaucratic machinery of the Public Security Bureau, its members were hopelessly misdirected and naïve if they expected a priest to mention, to a stranger, his troubles and his doubts about the regime. Catholics knew better than to speak up in public, even before Catholics they knew and trusted; they were well aware that attempts, far subtler than Liang's, were being made to infiltrate their midst. In any case, the attitude of such priests was one of resignation and quiet determination to pursue their work—not anger and resentment. But how could I explain all this to Liang, who really believed all she had read about the evils of the Church as an agent of imperialism?

So I went to Father X's church, and confessed. Later, I met Liang, in the same restaurant. "He didn't say anything," I said. "He didn't seem to trust me. He just gave me his benediction and closed the window, sharp." Liang said nothing, but sat there. She ate almost nothing, and never said a word. We parted coolly.

But I was not to be let off that easily. A neighbor in my street had a visitor from Hongkong, and Liang again left a message for me. This time she was curt, and didn't bother about any social niceties. I was to keep a close watch on the visitor from Hongkong. He was suspect. I was to report on comings and goings, and if possible talk to the man myself, and test him by hinting that I, too, had had my troubles with the government. Again, my report was negative, and the man returned safely to Hongkong. Liang didn't conceal her disappointment.

Liang tried to induce me to perform more satisfactorily by dangling an additional carrot in front of my eyes. My next rendezvous with Liang was in a luxurious tea house in a Canton suburb. We sat in a private room, sipped green tea and ate sticky sweet cakes. Despite my obvious ill luck on my two earlier assignments, Liang said, the Public Security Bureau still had hopes for me. In order to prove its trust and love, Liang and her colleagues had decided to help me find a job, and even—a very great mark of favor—to obtain an art degree for me. She produced some forms. "Fill these out," she said. "In the biographical section," she added pointedly, "our leaders have decided, after giving considerable thought to the matter, that you need not mention your years in a labor camp. Just say that you engaged in study at home and obtained occasional designing and illustrating jobs. Return these to us, and we'll see what we can do to get you a full-time job as a painter or illustrator."

The proposal pleased, but also disturbed me. I had, on my own, attempted to obtain a job as an artist. I had called on state publishing houses, cultural bureaus and other organizations begging to be taken on as a probationary artist. In all cases I was told that holders of degrees in art were given priority whenever vacancies occurred. Moreover, as one official put it, "There are too many artists in Canton. They're not holding examinations or giving degrees any more." Some questioned me about my background, and invariably, when I mentioned the fact that I had been in a labor camp—for to conceal the fact would have been a serious crime—I was curtly shown the door. Now the Public Security Bureau was going to all this trouble to obtain an art degree for me, cutting across all the local red tape, and concealing the fact that I had been a labor reform inmate into the bargain. It sounded too good to be true. "What do I say if my employers, or anyone else, ever finds out the truth?"

"Don't worry," Liang said, "we'll see to that side of things."

There was no doubt in my mind that there would be a price to pay for the papers she had promised me. And as a kind of afterthought, Liang said: "By the way, you may have heard of a round-up of Catholics in Canton." (Indeed I had. Several hundreds were taken away in the middle of the night for indoctrination in a special camp outside the city. The course lasted for several weeks and was a barely disguised warning to all Canton Catholics to drop their religious affiliations and their church going or face the consequences of being branded as "class enemies" and "counterrevolutionaries.")

"Well," she went on, "these people will be returning to the city soon and we are awfully interested in what they have to say about their valuable experiences. You haven't been terribly active lately, have you? Well, go to church, chat with fellow Catholics, mingle with people after the services. Ask them about their stay in camp. Get them to talk freely about their indoctrination sessions. Don't hold back anything. All we want to do is to get these people to see the errors of their ways. Report on everything you hear—the favorable as well as the unfavorable side of things." I looked glum. "My dear"—she laid her hand on mine—"you really must show your loyalty to the government, mustn't you? If you don't, how are we to know whose side you're really on?" She paid and left. I sat alone, wondering how on earth I was going to wriggle out of this one.

Since it was almost certain that I was being watched, I did as I was told, went to church and stayed after services making polite desultory conversation with people I knew. But when I reported back to Liang, I could report only that Catholics refused to talk to me, because they knew I had been to a labor camp and regarded me as a "bad element." The truth was something else: I refused to enter into any real contact with any of my fellow Catholics. When anti-government talk occurred, I abruptly broke off all conversation and retired into my shell. Indeed, Catholic friends of mine were convinced that, as a result of my years undergoing forced labor, I had become eccentric and a bit of a recluse.

This was in fact the end of any hopes Liang and the security bureau may have had in me. "The comrades are sad," Liang said, "very sad. We had placed great faith in you." This time there was no dinner, just a brief meeting in a tea shop. My apprehension was tempered by my forthcoming marriage. I thought: soon I'll be out of your clutches. You won't go on bothering me all my life, not after I'm married to a promising party aspirant. Needless to say, my papers granting me an official artist's certificate—and the job—never materialized. By this time I would have welcomed a steady job, for I realized I couldn't go on being a burden on my parents forever, but thought it wiser not to ask Comrade Liang what had happened to her promises. I dimly hoped that she might have forgotten about me.

But I had other things to think about. Kang came to Canton with all the necessary papers, and my mother and two of my brothers arrived from Hongkong. I had not seen her for five years, and at first we were almost like strangers. She wept, then laughed, then wept again. She refrained from the obvious comment: I told you not to go to Canton. But I knew she was of two minds about my marriage. She liked Kang, but was sad at the idea of my living for good in China. We registered and filed our wedding papers at the local municipal office. Afterwards, with a few of our closest relatives and friends, we had a rather grand dinner party in one of Canton's better restaurants. That night, Kang and I moved into one of Canton's tourist hotels, while my mother and my brothers occupied our small apartment.

Canton residents are not supposed even to enter the better-class, tourist hotels. To this day I don't know how my husband obtained a room there. He had gotten two weeks leave, and then had to go back to Sian. For the time being, he still didn't have permission to take me back with him.

Those two weeks passed in a moment. We visited the few friends we knew well, and trusted, and went on picnics and excursions. I shall always treasure the memory of those weeks, for they were among the happiest in my life. We made plans for the future, we laughed and joked like children. I cried when Kang left, and eagerly awaited his letters. The first said: "I am very happy to have you as my wife. I shall always love you as I do now." I lived in daily, then in weekly, expectation of being allowed to move to Sian to be with him.

But summer turned into autumn, and still there was no news of when I might leave. Worse, my husband's letters were becoming colder and colder, and more and more infrequent. I had to face the terrible fact: back in Sian, he was being taken in hand by his fellow scientists, the party cadres he respected and his superiors at the research laboratory. They worked on him as the police had worked on me when I was first arrested. The first consequence of his daring to come to Canton and marry me was that he was removed from his responsible post and given a minor, low-grade appointment which any semi-skilled laboratory technician could have held down. Kang loved his work, and the party had found the one means of pressure which could usefully be put on him. I was never explicitly told anything, but his letters, after a month or two, hinted that a deal could yet be concluded; my husband was of course bitterly disappointed at his undeserved demotion, and would have accepted almost any humiliation, any sacrifice, to get back in the party's good books and to resume his former job. After a month or two, I realized who was in danger of being sacrificed. "Give up your wife," the authorities in Sian were in effect saying to Kang, "and we will overlook this youthful indiscretion of yours." Reading between the lines of his letters, I began to realize that despite his earlier warmth and genuine love for me, he was prepared to enter into such a bargain—and this despite the fact that by this time I was pregnant.

So life dragged on for me, and it was almost as bad as being in a labor camp again. I had to face the prospect of not seeing Kang again—and consequently I made plans, baby or no baby, to try to escape. This was the time that all young Chinese, on orders from Chairman Mao himself, were encouraged to try their hand at such tough, militarily useful sports as swimming, hiking and mountaineering, and I began putting in hours at the local swimming pool. Soon I could swim for hours at a time without too much effort. At least, I thought, I'll train and train so as to be in good shape if ever I do have to put myself to the test. But soon my condition no longer allowed me to do even this. Mostly, I stayed at home, sketching and painting for myself, seeing nobody, just waiting for the blow which, obscurely, I knew was about to fall. In October one minor piece of good luck came my way: I got a temporary job as an assistant at a local museum, and was able to spend time actually copying examples of classical Chinese art on display there.

In December, my nightmare began all over again: one day, out of the blue, I got a summons from the local police station. Shaking with apprehension, I went there, and an official, a clerk, told me that they had had instructions from above: from now on I was a member of the "Four Black Categories"* and would from now on be under special restraints and constant surveillance.

Who could have been responsible for this? I begged the clerk to tell me. "I'm not supposed to tell you," the clerk said. "But I don't mind. If you must know, its the Public Security Bureau. You may go, but remember: from now onwards you'll be required for various tasks—self-criticism and political indoctrination at least once a week, corrective manual labor in the city and so on. We'll be getting in touch with you. Oh, by the way, one last thing: don't on any account try to leave the city. That would be fatal."

I was crying as I left the police station, and went to a public phone. Comrade Liang's number had changed. But a few days later she sent me a message. We met in a suite in the Aikun Hotel.

This time I was no longer in the mood for fencing and maneuvering; tearfully, I explained what had happened, and how it would affect my whole life. It was tantamount to going back to labor reform camp again, I said. What had I done to deserve this? Granted, my work for them hadn't been successful, but was this my fault, or only bad luck? I couldn't very well invent details simply in order to get people convicted, could I? Now I

---

* Former landlords, counterrevolutionary elements, "bad," i.e., criminal elements and rightists.

risked losing my job—this in fact happened a few days later and I was once more branded as an enemy of the state, just at a time when I felt that my period of probation was nearing its end.

Liang was not alone. She had brought Section Chief Yang with her. He was no longer smiling. Quite unmoved, he listened with ostentatious boredom, looking up at the ceiling, a contemptuous smile on his face. Finally, he stubbed out a cigarette. He motioned me to stop. "You should know enough by now to realize that this is a kind of a test," he said. It didn't mean that I stood condemned in their eyes, but rather, my new status would bring me into even further contact with Catholics and suspects, and make my "cover" that much more credible. "But we won't lie to you," Yang said. "We have been most disappointed, and our only inference is that your thinking is unstable, very unstable. We are still not absolutely convinced that you are in fact a reformed character. You should know, without having to be told, the full reasons for making you a Four Black Categories person. This will be a thorough test of your revolutionary will. We will soon see whether you are genuine or not. In the meantime"—he looked at his watch—"we must leave. If we need you, we will contact you." He paused. "Don't telephone us any more. We're busy, so don't bother us unless it's a really urgent matter or you have something of vital importance to say." They filed out.

I did see them once again. This was several months later. I had had my baby by this time, and had got a new, part-time job, painting toy designs for a local toy factory—work which enabled me to stay at home most of the time. The message came from the police station, asking me to call a new number. Liang answered, and made an appointment to meet me later that day at Canton's famous Peking Restaurant.

She led me up to a private room on the fourth floor, where an elaborate meal was waiting, along with Section Chief Yang. This time I knew better than to cry and rant. I told them, calmly and dispassionately, about my new life: how, every week, I went to the police station with other Black Category members for thought reform and self-criticism, how, at least once a week, I helped sweep the streets or collect garbage or dig drains. Remembering my past experience in the labor camps, I thanked them all for enabling me to show my zeal and my loyalty in new circumstances. I didn't complain about the back-breaking physical work, or the apparent injustice of it all. I tried to give the impression, once more, of a totally obedient and dedicated person. They ate while I talked. Yang said: "We're very gratified to hear all this. But tell me . . . we've heard reports that you're secretly making preparations to escape to Hongkong? Is this true?"

I vehemently denied this. "But be frank with us," Liang said. "Isn't it a fact that around the time you learnt of your new status, the thought did cross your mind: I would be better off in Hongkong?"

They were closing in now, and I had no way of fighting back, except to try to show that I was not worried by what they had to say. So, though I didn't feel like eating, I deliberately selected a piece of chicken, munched on it unconcernedly, thinking all the while that a really guilty person wouldn't show any appetite at a time like this. "The chicken soup is really delicious," I said to Liang. "I've only been able to afford dumplings here before." Then, after a pause, I said: "Quite honestly, the thought never crossed my mind. Escaping to Hongkong? What an absurd idea! What would I do there, I'd like to know? Do you really have such a low opinion of me as a person? Haven't I told you that my loyalty to the state is as firm as a rock? Besides, if I were to ask you, you would probably give me a temporary exit permit," I added, thinking—in the back of my mind—now I am calling their bluff: they might just do that. "In fact I was going to bring this up; not that I particularly want to see Hongkong again, but I would like to see my family. I thought your faith in me was sufficient to warrant a favor of this kind. Now," I said primly, "I'm glad I didn't ask for one. God knows what you might have suspected!"

This argument appeared to have shaken them a little. Perhaps they had expected vehemence, more tears or overt signs of guilt.

"We certainly won't give you a temporary exit visa to Hongkong," Yang said. "Despite your considerable reform, there's always the danger you might get involved with the espionage people again—not necessarily through any fault of your own," he added hastily. "I'm glad you're not thinking of leaving by any other way. Remember, Hongkong is part of China too. One day we will recover it. Then where would you go? In Hongkong we have several million loyal Chinese citizens. It's normal that you should want to see your family, but it's much simpler for them to come here. In any case, remember: if ever the thought *did* cross your mind, you'd certainly be caught, for we have agents all over the place. And then there'd be no one to bail you out—not after five, fifteen, or fifty years." They finished the meal in silence. I never saw either of them again.

After the meal, I went back to my room, to my baby and to my thoughts. I was not overimpressed by their threats. I knew too much to believe that everyone was caught who tried to escape. They had no real grounds for believing that I was planning escape. But from that day onwards, I thought, I certainly will give it a thought. Either I go to Sian with my husband, and try and make a go of things here in China: or else, if he gives in to his party superiors, if he fails me, I'll leave. I'd love to see the faces of Comrades Liang and Yang. They might get into trouble if I did slip through their fingers. Why, they might even end up in a labor camp themselves. And, remembering their hypocrisy, their false friendliness and their utter disregard for human beings, I thought to myself: it would make the trip worthwhile.

As soon as the weather became warm enough, I resumed my long-distance swimming practice.

EDITOR'S NOTE

by Edward Behr

AS IS CLEAR by now from Lai Ying's story, it really does seem as though she had, after her marriage at least, decided to settle in China after all, despite everything she had been through. Talking with her about this was difficult; after all, to admit to thoughts of escape would be to admit that, from the first, her marriage was a temporary expedient.

I'm convinced this was not the case. Lai Ying was much too straightforward a person for that. True, in her talk with us she was not very forthcoming about that period of her life when she and her husband were together in Canton. The whole experience, in retrospect, was possibly more painful, and more personal, than that of the stone quarry or the prisons.

Beyond this, there is the question of her child: Lai Ying eventually, as she later explains, made the cruel decision to leave her baby daughter behind when she embarked on her escape bid. To some, her attitude may seem callous in the extreme. But to anyone who comes to know Lai Ying, as I did, it was apparent that her thoughts constantly revolved around her baby daughter and that the loss of her child was the real tragedy of her life—a far greater tragedy than her sufferings in the camps. Often, when talking about her child, she blinked away tears—and we felt reluctant to cause her additional pain by continued questioning. I still feel that Lai Ying is not resigned to the loss of her daughter, even though she says she is. At the back of her mind, I'm convinced, she has the notion that one day things will change and they will be reunited. Her deepest fear is that her daughter may grow up to hate her "counterrevolutionary" mother.

The fact that Lai Ying had a child is, to my mind, proof enough that she did intend to stay in Canton if she possibly could. Over the years, the shock of arrest and the horrors of the camps and jails had gradually faded. Lai Ying had survived some of the worst that China could offer and I'm convinced she was, after her marriage, determined to stay if she was able to enjoy the minimum security of a normal family existence. Had she married an individualist, a rebel like herself, it's likely that escape would have been a joint—if almost unspoken—compact between them. Lai Ying's husband, on the contrary, was an ambitious young party worker. Poor fellow: his association with Lai Ying proved fatal to his career. The latest reports are that he was dismissed from his laboratory job, was then consigned to remote Sinkiang Province in a subordinate position not at all commensurate with his ability, and finally removed to some unknown destination.

At the time Lai Ying married, however, China was not as remote, or as frightening a place as it later became. I spent two months in China in August and September 1964, traveling the length and breadth of the country with a French television team, and I was struck by how normal—outwardly at least—things were: in parks and squares, young couples strolled hand in hand; there was a peaceful, tranquil, leisurely air about Peking and though political indoctrination used up a great deal of time, nobody appeared to be working too hard. There was plenty of food in the shops, people looked well fed, and they were not as drab as I had been led to expect them to be. There was, of course, constant radio propaganda, but non-political movies and traditional opera shows could be seen; in a few areas of Peking, jugglers, magicians and storytellers still delighted audiences and a fabulously expert circus performed nightly near Tien An Men Square—I remember that all their acts save one final "tableau" were non-political.

Indeed, until the Cultural Revolution began in 1966, travel to China had become relatively easy, for non-Americans at least, and it had always been easy for Hongkong-resident Chinese. At the time of Lai Ying's marriage, her mother came to Canton and stayed a month.

Since the Cultural Revolution, or aspects of it, caused Lai Ying to try to escape from China, it's essential to explain it. Our knowledge of the byways of Chinese power politics is still spotty, but here is a rough-and-ready, somewhat oversimplified account of what it was all about.

It seems that at some stage in the early sixties, Mao Tse-tung was placed in a minority within the party's Central Committee and was in danger of being not only ignored and bypassed, but even conceivably retired—i.e., deposed. The movements against Mao were disparate. There were those, high up in the party hierarchy, who had never regarded the break with the Soviet Union with anything but apprehension; to many high-ranking officers of the Chinese People's Liberation Army, it meant that the flow of

sophisticated modern weapons ceased; there were those, too, who
—timidly following the post-Stalin example—were beginning to
argue the case for more consumer goods and less harsh economic
discipline. There were those who remembered the failures of the
Great Leap Forward—and few really agreed with the official explanation that its failures had been due to counterrevolutionary
sabotage. Many privately blamed Mao for embarking without sufficient preparation on a grandiose plan lacking all reality.

On Mao's side, there was an equally strong feeling that all
was not right with China, but for diametrically opposite reasons.
Under the normal, rational, consumer-oriented system of government we are used to, it is assumed that growing prosperity is good
in itself. Mao Tse-tung, however, certainly does not. Maoism is
romantic and puritanical, and deeply distrustful of anything which
might impair revolutionary fervor anywhere. It is an axiom of
Mao's communism that any material benefits for the individual
must wait until revolutionary movements have succeeded all over
the world. There is, of course, a case to be made for Mao as the
true heir of Marx, Engels and Lenin, whose theories have been
"perverted" by modern Communist leaders. Be this as it may, it's
quite certain that Mao was horrified at the spectacle of changes in
the Communist world outside China, as he observed them after
Stalin's death in 1953.

It must have become an obsessional preoccupation for him to
try to answer the question: how was it possible for the Soviet
Union, which had experienced its revolution in 1917, and had been
in the grip of a leader of Stalin's strength and single-mindedness,
to have sunk so low in Mao's eyes? In Chinese Communist par-
lance, the natural enemies are of course the capitalists and imperialists, in open or disguised forms. But since 1965 the real
venom of Chinese insults has been reserved for those who, like the
Russians, appeared in Chinese eyes to have betrayed the cause of
true communism. These former friends are, if anything, considered to be worse than the hated capitalists themselves. For here
were nations on the threshold of a new revolutionary experience
which had suddenly drawn back and—in Chinese eyes at least
—were becoming just as contaminated as the capitalist countries
themselves. Worse, their example was contagious: of all the Communist countries in Europe, only tiny Albania maintained the
China-approved orthodox traditions.

Since the disease of "goulash communism" was so catching,
what could Mao do to prevent the virus from spreading to China

—and was it not already too late? During my visit to China in 1964, I happened to be included, by the greatest of good luck, among the small group of people who—as delegates to the French Industrial Fair in Peking—were received by Mao in his country house at Hangchow. The conversation lasted three hours. Part of it—relevant to this story—concerned Mao's attitude towards China's youth. At dinner I asked him whether he was satisfied with present-day Chinese youth as a whole. He paused briefly, then said: "Not necessarily. They are not all in favor of communism by any means. There are still big bourgeois elements among the students. They have not been exposed to any real tests, such as war, as their elders have." He spoke scathingly of the atmosphere prevalent in Peking's Peitah University. It was, he said, a "very bad university." The French ambassador in Peking, Lucien Paye, who was present, said something about his recent visit there. He had been most impressed by the university, he said, and had met several students who knew Mao's works by heart. "They recite parrot-fashion," said Mao. "They were telling you what they thought you would like to hear. A bad university," he repeated, and again, "a bad, bad university."

Remarks such as these should have warned of the storm to come. Still more direct were his comments to another French visitor, André Malraux, who saw Mao the following year. China had been officially communist for nearly twenty years, Mao said. Yet there were parts of China where Communist Party officials still lorded it over the people like the corrupt mandarin officials of old. Chinese peasants, he added, had an innate tendency towards conservatism.

I can testify as to the arrogance of two minor Communist cadres who accompanied me on part of my 1964 visit to China. We were filming nomads in Chinese Mongolia. Both the cadres were from the South, and were obviously ill at ease. Together with a Mongol-speaking interpreter, they sat in their goatskin tents and were waited on hand and foot. Hospitality was lavish, for the nomad "commune" had obviously put itself out to honor the guests from afar, but the two Communist cadres treated the likable, beaming Mongol commune officials with clear condescension. After a particularly succulent farewell banquet, I turned to one of the cadres and asked him if I could go and thank the cook. "Don't worry," was the reply, "we will have him brought over here." It was with difficulty that I managed to go round to the kitchen and thank him myself. I had the wry satisfaction of telling the cadres that to have produced the cook, cap in hand, as they intended, was tantamount to lording it over him as in the "old society" which they constantly decried.

There were, of course, many other reasons to explain why the Cultural Revolution occurred, and why it took the form it did. In China, the Communist Party was an extraordinarily well-organized tentacular bureaucracy, and within the party, as within any huge administration, a mafia had come into being: officials of the same origin, who had had common experiences, who came from the same districts, who had been through the same purges, the same wars and the same promotions, inevitably tended to protect each other. It may seem absurd to think of lobbies existing in Communist China—but the fact is that they were particularly powerful. Time and again, as the story of the purge of this or that high-ranking official unfolded, it became apparent that for each top-ranking official there was a host of henchmen, who served no clear purpose other than that of constituting a kind of court. It was all very Chinese—for the court derived considerable advantages from its leader—and communism had very little to do with it.

The party members, as such, were only a small proportion of China's total population and this alone tended to set them apart from the rest of the country. China's managerial class—so essential to any modern industrial society—was expanding as China modernized herself, and it was from this managerial class, usually composed of party members anyway, that the greatest threat to Maoism was seen to come. In the interests of efficiency, the managers naturally wished to introduce techniques such as bonuses and overtime which no orthodox Maoist could agree to; soon, it might have led to their cutting down on the time given over to political indoctrination and study of Mao's thought as interfering with productivity!

This managerial class had, even in China, by 1965 acquired considerable material benefits. One has only to remember Lai Ying's description of those managers she encountered to recall just how far apart they were from ordinary workers and peasants. Salaries might not seem tremendously disproportionate, but salaries were the least of the discrepancies: many managers, whether party members or not, had comfortable living quarters, expense accounts in restaurants, chauffeur-driven cars and rights to shop in certain well-stocked stores. Some even had servants on a scale few Western capitalists could afford.

All this was driving a large wedge into the Maoist concept of a truly egalitarian society, and it was months, if not years, before Mao acted. He had, since 1965, been very preoccupied with these questions—and increasingly out of the public eye. Rumor had it that he was severely ill, perhaps even dead. Then he made his much-publicized swim in the Yangtse River, in August 1966, and this marked the end of his meditative period. Action soon followed which plunged China into chaos but effectively blocked, for a time at least, the possibility of China following the Soviet Union's example in becoming a consumer-oriented nation.

The outside world first became aware of the inner stresses and strains affecting the Chinese leadership with the disgrace of Peng Chen, the powerful, outspoken, publicity-conscious Mayor of Peking. It was quickly apparent that Peng Chen and his henchmen were but secondary targets; the real figure aimed at was Liu Shao-chi, the President and nominal head of state, and—through him —the whole of the efficient and ubiquitous party machinery.

In retrospect, the way devised by Mao to oust his opponents— who were, in the party at least, in a majority—has an element of brilliant simplicity about it: rather like General de Gaulle appealing directly to the "people" without any intermediaries, Mao made a scarcely disguised appeal to the one category of the population which could be relied upon to display intense fervor— Chinese youth. Taking advantage of a certain amount of turmoil in Peking's Peitah University and of a small-scale revolt against some of the older, more established teachers there, Mao himself penned a poster—later displayed on the university's walls and soon copied all over China—with the words: *Bombard the Authorities.* The Chinese are used to oblique commands, and Mao's own spokesmen probably spelled out his real intentions to a select few, in any case. Soon, the "revolutionary" students were taking over the universities all over China, dismissing, intimidating and often severely manhandling their erstwhile teachers (the universities have remained closed for formal instruction—though they do now teach Mao's thought, to the exclusion of everything else). At the same time, first in Peking, and then all over China, the Red Guard movement began, with an apparent spontaneity which can have surprised no one in China itself—for how could anything spontaneous occur in the China portrayed by Lai Ying?

At first, the Red Guards or "little generals," as they were called, had as their target only certain selected figures of the party establishment. But soon their offensive broadened to include factory managers, all party officials, government servants and nearly all those in authority—save, of course, Mao himself. The very word "specialist" became a term of abuse. *"The only specialist,"* said a Red Guard poster, *"worth his name is a specialist in the thought of Mao Tse-tung."* The Red Guard movement attempted to prove that all of China's ills had been caused by the managers, the party officials and those who had neglected the ordinary people. But the most extraordinary thing about the movement was the peak of mass hysteria reached in the cult of Mao Tse-tung. Perhaps never in history had one living mortal received such adulation and been the subject of such religious devotion. To live in China at the start of the Cultural Revolution was to take part in a gigantic happening whose sole theme was the worship of Mao, the living God. Those papers which continued to appear in China after the start of the revolution printed stories attempting to prove that close attention to the thought of Mao Tse-tung could literally enable one to perform miracles: doctors wrote how, after reading Mao's little red book, they had managed to perform surgical feats previously deemed impossible; unskilled workers wrote in to report that after applying Mao's thought, they increased their factory's production beyond anyone's wildest dreams; one medical orderly wrote to say that constant meditation on Mao's thought had cured him of inoperable, fatal cancer.

The Red Guards happening was not confined to the big cities. Young people poured into Peking, of course, to take part in the revolution, to "exchange revolutionary experiences." For weeks, the whole life of the capital was tied up, with hundreds of thousands of youths sleeping in improvised dormitories or in the open. The two main railroad stations in Peking were closed to normal traffic and passengers and totally given over to the transport of Red Guards. Feeding and housing the millions who came to Peking presented formidable problems—but these were nothing compared to those which were to arise when the whole Red Guard movement started getting out of hand. For the Red Guards did not everywhere meet with the response they had hoped for; in most cases, the workers on communal farms saw the brash teen-agers as interlopers, coming in to eat their food and meddle with their lives. Since the Red Guards preached revolt against established authority, with Mao's explicit blessing, the commune leaders often found themselves threatened. In most cases the peasant workers rallied around their own commune workers—just as the factory workers defended their own managements: cases of Red Guards thrown out of farm communes and factories—in some cases after pitched battles and considerable loss of life—became so common that such news was even reported on Red Guard posters.

In a sense the Red Guard phenomenon was an explosion of young idealists who had been prevented from expressing themselves all their young lives; but an uglier note soon crept into the proceedings. The clashes on the communal farms were just the beginning of a series of disasters. As was to be expected, the hardworking peasants assumed that they, too, should have the freedom to go out on free junkets to join in exchanging revolutionary experiences.

In many cases, commune farm leaders deliberately added confusion to chaos by issuing tickets, travel allowances and food. But the farm workers soon learnt to their bewilderment that what was considered opportune for schoolboys and youths was not considered right for them. The peasants were needed down on the farms to ensure that agricultural production, at least, was not too disrupted. The injustice of this was soon brought home. Some of the peasant marches were put down by force. Similar clashes in factories brought China to the brink of civil war and led to sizeable economic upheavals inside China. The Red Guards, too, started behaving more like the teen-agers they were than like paragons of Maoism: rival Red Guard groups sprang up all over China, each challenging the others and claiming to be "truly Red." In Canton alone, at one point, there were over two hundred groups of mutually antagonistic Red Guards, and the struggles they engaged in were by no means verbal. There was severe street fighting, and terrified inhabitants in several districts of Canton put up barricades and organized themselves into vigilante committees to keep troublemakers—and all Red Guards—out. Increasingly, Mao found it necessary to call on the Army to restore order. Eventually, the Red Guards lost their importance and were, in 1968, on the point of vanishing into limbo altogether; their usefulness was over, and by 1969–70 millions of former Red Guards, older and doubtless wiser, were themselves working in agricultural "communes" under the close supervision of army units.

The outside world can have little idea of what it must have been like to experience the Cultural Revolution at first hand; the inmates of the concentration camps described by Lai Ying were at one point turned loose as a result of the prevailing anarchy. They descended on Canton like angry locusts, only to be cut down and hanged, sometimes after being tortured to death on Canton's streets. The breakdown in law and order was almost total in many areas. It is Lai Ying's impression that most, if not all, of the officials and people in authority she dealt with during her prison years have been either disgraced or arrested.

Lai Ying herself witnessed the beginning of the Cultural Revolution—and in her case it took the form, which it did everywhere at first, of a tightening of regulations and a more rigid attitude towards all those already considered guilty of political shortcomings. Her experience left her in no doubt as to what her ultimate fate would be. There is every reason to believe that, had she not escaped when she did, she would once more be in a labor camp. And her timing could scarcely have been bettered: only a few months later, the Portuguese authorities, under constant Communist pressure, began returning escapees to the Chinese guards across the border. Some reports suggest that the penalty for attempting to escape is now summary execution if caught. This may explain why shackled corpses have, of late, been discovered floating in the China Sea close to the Hongkong and Macao shores.

E.B.

CHAPTER XIII

I LEAVE CANTON

AS A MEMBER OF the Four Black Categories, I was the lowest possible form of life in China. Elsewhere a prison sentence might not count against one for the rest of one's life. Innocent or guilty, punishment served, bygones could become bygones. But not in China. My crime was twofold: I was known to be a Catholic, and I had been to jail on a trumped-up charge of espionage. No matter how absurd this charge had been, I was, in consequence, regarded as a counterrevolutionary and was, therefore, irrecuperable. For the rest of my life I would be under constant surveillance. For the rest of my life I would have no basic rights whatsoever.

When I had left the labor camp, the residents committee responsible for the street where I lived in Canton had received a report on me. The committee is theoretically under the supervision of the party, but in fact it works hand in glove with the local police station. It issues ration cards and is supposed to look after the welfare of those living in the area of its jurisdiction—usually just a few streets—but it is above all an invaluable police adjunct: it reports to the police on strangers in the area, on unfamiliar comings and goings, on suspicious gatherings in people's homes. Its members also call on people, unannounced, seemingly just to pass the time of day but really in order to test out political enthusiasm and reliability.

As a member of the Four Black Categories with a counterrevolutionary record, I had to report to the local police station if I absented myself from my room for more than four hours for any purpose other than that of going to work. All my incoming mail was censored by the residents committee and I was supposed to report on all those who came to visit me, with a summary of what we had said. The committee relayed instructions as they came down from the police station. Additionally, I learnt that I was required to report every Monday and Wednesday to the police station for political indoctrination—an evening session which mainly involved reading the *People's Daily* editorials out loud. In my group, I realized, I was the youngest by far. Most of the people summoned with me were elderly people who appeared quite in-offensive, if somewhat weary, wretched and downtrodden. Most of them were former bourgeois residents who had attracted offi-cial displeasure in some way, probably by once speaking out against the new order and talking nostalgically about the past.

Even before the Great Proletarian Cultural Revolution began, our fate was unenviable. Not only were we spied upon and kept under a form of semipermanent house arrest, but we were an ideal—and dirt-cheap—labor force. We could be called out at any time by the municipal authorities to do any unpleasant job that needed doing, such as digging drains, mending roads or white-washing buildings, all, of course, without pay and in our own time—in addition to our normal work. Whatever technical or aca-demic qualifications any of our lot possessed were of no use; we were barred, for all time, from any skilled jobs or from anything which required a measure of responsbility. Even on holidays, when others stopped work, we were treated differently; in some cases, we had to report to our local police stations and spend the day in political study sessions there, and in some cases we were warned, by local police officials, to remain indoors—as a pre-cautionary measure, I was once told, against possible beatings-up by "patriotic elements." But mostly, on public holidays, we were worked to the bone; apart from our three-day stint a month of manual labor (which usually meant cleaning the streets), holidays meant that I was up at dawn, having been warned the night before by a member of the street committee (itself an offshoot of the residents committee), and often I didn't come home till mid-night. Whenever holidays occurred, then was the time, the police decided, to clean up Canton—and our pathetic task force was at it all day, on May 1, October 1, and during Chinese New Year, scrubbing, whitewashing and cleaning from dawn to dusk. It gave the party authorities considerable satisfaction to watch their van-quished enemies humbly at work while the good people of Canton took their ease.

The twice-yearly Canton Trade Fair was also a pretext to get us out on the streets to clean up the town, and when the summons had come, it was no use trying to avoid it. I was told, early on, that it had absolute priority over any other kind of work—even if one ran the risk of losing one's regular job as a result. I some-times wonder whether the foreign visitors to the Canton Fair realize that this is how the town is made so spick and span. While working without pay in this manner, we of course lost part of our livelihood, and had to pay for our own food.

The Cultural Revolution made things much worse: study sessions became more frequent. We were, not unnaturally, a prime target for the young Red Guards. It was in early August 1966 that I heard stories of people being paraded in the streets with shaming inscriptions painted on boards tied to their chests, of girls having their hair cut off, of families standing helplessly by while Red Guards ransacked their homes. Canton, in August, was also full of stories of people who had committed suicide as a result of such persecution and humiliation. A friend of mine saw three bodies in the street, and was told that the man had jumped into the street from the top of a building.

Then, on September 3, I was summoned in the evening by a member of the street committee to a special meeting at the local police station. I was there early, for to be late was a serious crime, and I recognized, also waiting with me, a number of people who had taken part in earlier study sessions. We were all local Black Categories people, but some of them looked different. A few women I noticed, had scarves over their heads. They had been shorn. An old man, a Taoist scholar, had also had his hair and beard cut off, and sat listlessly, mumbling to himself. A few people whispered to each other. I listened, and asked a neighbor what was going on. "X has disappeared," he said. "Red Guards came last night and took him away. I think he's gone to a labor camp." Someone else was describing how, a few nights previously, Guards had burst into her family's room: "They tore up our twenty-year-old wedding photos," she said. "They took our ration cards, and our cloth coupons. They had no right to do that." "They took our money too," said one woman. A middle-aged man said that, without any kind of warning, he had just been dismissed from his factory job. "There was nothing personal about it," he said. "I hadn't done anything wrong. It's just that they said they could no longer keep anyone who was a member of the Black Categories."

The meeting was late, because only a senior police official had the authority to hold the meeting and he was busy elsewhere. When he came, we all stood up and trooped into the police station. He spoke harshly, in a staccato voice, curiously expressionless and stereotyped. "You people have seen what's going on," he said. "Now, you must recognize the importance and the value of the Cultural Revolution." We stood facing him, motionless and gaping. "Now, I want you all to confess your sins. I know you haven't been supporting the Cultural Revolution. You must confess your failings, and speak up in praise of the Cultural Revolution."

We were used to taking part in confessions of this kind, and usually we made things easy for officials—and for ourselves—by admitting our sins. A normal confession would involve my getting up and saying: "Instructor [we were not allowed to call him comrade, for we were outcasts], I will do my best to support government policy. I'll try and reform, and enthusiastically mend my ways." In Chinese the expression for all this is "doffing one's cap."

But this time, it seemed, none of us was able to do this. We were angry at what we had just heard, angry at the injustice of it all, and when the official said, "Well?"—waiting for one of us to speak—there was prolonged silence. He was not used to this, and we probably took him by surprise. It would have been difficult for him to arrest all seventy of us then and there.

Luckily, the meeting was adjourned unexpectedly. "Comrade, you are needed across the street," said one policeman. The official glared at us, left the room and we waited in silence. Meanwhile, as we could hear from outside, some kind of a meeting was going on and someone was being shouted down.

Eventually he came back. "All right," he said. "You can go. But first, I have some news for you. From now on, whenever you leave your homes, you will wear a special board. You can make it yourselves out of cardboard. It has got to be thirteen by eighteen centimeters. Those are the regulations. On the board you will write, in big characters, your name, address, age and which category of the Black Group you belong to." A roll call followed. My name was called. "Category: counterrevolutionary," he said. "You have two days to comply with my instructions. There will be no disobeying these orders." When I returned home, a large black and white board was already stuck on the door of the house where I lived. It gave my name, age and sex and the same infamous category: counterrevolutionary. Rather than comply with the police official's instructions, I thought, I won't go out, that's all.

I was glad I didn't, for from September 5 onwards, in Canton, those wearing boards were dragged about by Red Guards, spat on, made to stand for hours in the sun and sometimes seriously beaten. People wearing such boards were forbidden to use public transport, or public telephones, or enter restaurants or other public places, or walk in parks. In some cases they lost their jobs. I was lucky: a neighbor, Fang, helped look after me, did the shopping and all errands. My job—painting toy designs—could be done at home, and a friend volunteered to take my paintings back to the factory and take away a fresh lot of designs.

Everyone, I heard from those who visited me, was taking hasty precautions to avoid incurring the wrath of the Red Guards, getting rid of all objects of value, including books, which might appear old-fashioned, bourgeois or counterrevolutionary. I did the same. First I smashed the old dragon-and-phoenix-patterned vases which had been part of my mother's dowry. Then I burnt a collection of Christmas cards from friends, which I had received over the years, as well as my most treasured possession: a large collection of colored picture postcards of famous painters from Piero della Francesca to Van Gogh. I also removed the picture of Jesus Christ which hung above my bed. In the empty frame I dutifully inserted one of Chairman Mao. I also festooned my room with big-character quotations of his works. I did so with rage in my heart, but this was simply a precautionary measure, a means of survival.

I stared at the walls of the room, now decorated in an acceptable manner with Mao-think. I knew that I could not stand another spell in a labor camp, and I knew that my arrest was only a matter of weeks, perhaps days. Even if my health stood up to the back-breaking work and inadequate food, I had no will to live out such a soul-destroying existence once more. I asked myself what I had to live for in China. My husband? The party had sent him to Sinkiang, and there compelled him to divorce me. Did my ex-husband want me back? From his letters, which were becoming increasingly distant in the last few months, I realized this was unlikely. He knew now he had made a mistake, he said, and that the party had been right to insist on a divorce. The divorce at least had enabled him to prove his loyalty to Chairman Mao and to the party. Although he didn't say so in so many words, I knew that he now realized that by marrying a counterrevolutionary he had made an almost irreparable mistake, and that he bitterly regretted ever having done so. He had certainly been in love with me, and in a rash moment had thought that he could overcome all the difficulties in our path. The system had proved him wrong. He had never even seen our daughter, Hsiao Ray. Though he inquired about her perfunctorily in his letters, I knew that I had lost him, and his love, for good. As for Hsiao Ray, I knew, too, that if I were arrested once more, I would never see her again. As it was, I had had to let my neighbor look after her because I worked in my small room all day, and—no longer being able to go out—I could no longer take care of her. Though she came to see me often enough, I felt that she was, in a sense, no longer mine.

The more I thought about all this, during those long summer days and nights, the more I came to the conclusion that my one hope was escape. I knew that on an average only one person in ten made it. Despite this, and the hideous penalties for being caught, I had to try.

Having made this decision, I first made a number of costly mistakes. There were people in Canton with experience in smuggling people out of China, but they were mostly shady characters, interested only in the money they earned this way. My first attempts to contact them ended in disaster.

Not being able to leave my room, I had to do all the negotiations through intermediaries. There was almost no one I could trust. The first smugglers, once contacted, demanded "tea money"—to buy strong walking shoes and bicycle inner tubes for improvised life belts. I sent the money and they disappeared. This happened several times, and there was, of course, no means of redress.

Then, one day, Hsu came to see me. He and I had been in the same labor camp. Hsu was one year younger than I and had, while still a boy, been a promising musician. After his release he had played the cello in the Canton Symphony Orchestra and been a member of a musical ensemble which recorded music for the movies, but he was now desperately poor and out of a job, for the Canton Symphony Orchestra had been disbanded and he had been warned, along with his colleagues, against playing rotten capitalist music. He still earned a little money giving private music lessons, but was finding such work increasingly difficult to obtain.

Hsu liked painting, too, and came to my room to help me work on my factory designs. As we painted, we talked. In our years in the labor camp, we had hardly ever exchanged more than a few words. Now we had plenty of time. Now I saw that Hsu also wanted to escape. As the days went by, we made new plans.

It was obvious, we agreed, that we would never make it on our own; it was essential to find experienced, reliable guides.

Hsu said he would try to find some. Since he had no money at all, I gave him some, and told him he could have more. I would pay all the costs of the trip, I said, for several persons, if necessary.

Hsu was himself at a disadvantage: having been sentenced to a spell in a labor camp, he was suspect and liable to arrest. But things were easier for him, in those confused days, simply because he owned an old army uniform, which had once belonged to his brother. This he wore constantly, and everyone assumed he was some kind of Red Guard. Without the uniform he would not have been able to move around at all.

At first I had thought of Hsu as a good-natured dreamer, for he had an unpractical streak in him, but he began making arrangements for our escape with considerable thoroughness. He rode his bicycle outside Canton, into Chungshan County, the district nearest Macao, looking for possible routes and contacts. He met a man we all got to know well later; his name was simply Fatty (nobody knew him by anything except this somewhat obvious nickname) and he was one of Canton's most prosperous and successful black marketeers.

At first, Fatty seemed uninterested in helping us. "There's someone I know," he told Hsu, "a peddlar called Longfellow. Why don't you see him? He might want to go himself." Fatty introduced Hsu to Longfellow, and our chances of escaping immediately brightened.

Longfellow was just the man we needed to come along with us on this trip. He knew the area well, and—even more important—he could provide us with an excellent cover, for he had both a sampan and a means of livelihood which regularly took him all over Chungshan County.

Longfellow was a quack and he could have stepped straight out of an old Chinese adventure story. He had a long, thin body, an inexhaustible fund of stories and boundless self-assurance. He was a magician, fortuneteller and raconteur, and when he had attracted an audience with his tricks and stories he sold them a strange-smelling patent medicine which he made himself "out of mysterious, health-giving herbs." He called his mixture Tall Bamboo. Tall Bamboo, he said, would cure everything from rheumatism to impotence. How people like Longfellow survived in China was always a mystery to me, for he was everything the regime abhorred—an arrant individualist, a rebel, a cynic and, in a small way, a capitalist.

Longfellow even had an apprentice, a young farm boy from Chungshan County whom he had promised to teach the secrets of herbal medicine, and the apprentice, Mok, was also a good person to have around. He was strong, and could row a sampan for hours without getting tired.

Longfellow, it turned out, had been in trouble with the authorities before, and had been warned several times about his "undesirable way of life." China's huge, cumbersome bureaucracy had so far failed to catch him in its net. But it could only be a matter of time. Longfellow and Mok were aware of this.

At first, Longfellow was a little suspicious of Hsu, thinking that he might be a police informer. But he was reassured, and the three of them began planning our joint escape and drawing up a list of things we would need: four new pairs of oars for the sampan, gongs, cymbals for Longfellow's act and a fresh batch of herbs for Tall Bamboo, to camouflage the trip as an ordinary business tour; clothing, food reserves, bicycle tire inner tubes. It was an expensive list. Longfellow and Mok said that their food must also be paid for during the actual escape. I let Hsu do the negotiating. Their terms were reasonable, and Hsu trusted them.

For the first few meetings, Hsu didn't mention my name, though he had told them that a fourth person would be coming along. Eventually Longfellow said, "All right. Who's the mysterious stranger? Who's your boss?"

Hsu had already made up his mind what he should reply. He said unhesitatingly, "I'm bringing a woman. She's my wife and her parents live in Hongkong. She has the money and she'll pay for everything."

Longfellow said, "If she's your wife, that's okay. But can she stand the trip? It's going to be very tiring. Can she climb mountains on an empty stomach? Can she swim? If she's a soft and fine lady from some la-de-da family, leave her behind."

Hsu thought about our years in the labor camp. He said, "She can take it. She's very strong. She's a very good swimmer. I took her swimming at Shihman recently, to test her. She swam almost twelve miles. Why, she's better than Chairman Mao himself." Longfellow laughed, and said he hoped it would be all right.

To leave Canton we still had to have papers and travel documents. This was where Fatty came in. He was interested only in money, and obviously made a good living in Canton, but he, too, wanted to leave at some point. How he had got away with his black marketeering so far amazed me. He had contacts, he said, and proved he was not boasting. For the equivalent of four U.S. dollars a head, he got police travel permits for us all from a local police station, and for a few dollars more he bought some communal farm letterhead paper, on which we composed a letter explaining that we were traveling on commune business. "All the crows in the world are black," he told Hsu. "For money, you can get service from the devil himself." He had utter contempt for the officials he dealt with; they all had their price, like all men. Fatty himself decided to come with us at the last minute.

All too quickly, it seemed, everything was ready. The first Sunday in September was my father's birthday, and that night we would go. About 3 P.M. my neighbor brought my baby daughter over to see me. Hsiao Ray was an exceptionally pretty girl. She wore a skirt with a red heart embroidered on it, which I had made for her, and apple-green shoes. She was excited and jumped up and down. She tried on my slippers and shoes, and played with them on the floor. We played together and I kept looking at her, to remember her for all time. Then I held her tight and kissed her. My neighbor came and took her away, and I cried until I had no tears left.

I loved my baby daughter and knew I would never see her again. I cried, thinking that she might grow up to be a Red Guard, and perhaps hate and despise her mother; I cried because I was all alone, because my husband had been sent away; I cried because I was scared of what lay ahead, and tired of being scared. I cried, too, because I knew that however much I tried, my memories of Hsiao Ray would fade, and she in turn would change. I would be remembering a baby girl long after she had grown. The crying left me weak and drained of any feeling whatsoever.

My neighbor returned, having put Hsiao Ray to bed. "Sister Fang, look after Hsiao Ray," I said. "All my life I'll be grateful to you. I shall never forget, whatever happens." I kissed her, and started crying again.

Hsu arrived and found us together. She turned to Hsu and looked at us both. "Let me see your faces in the light," she said. "I'll tell your fortune." She looked at us for a long time and said, "Both of you will have good luck. I know you will make it. I'll miss you." She then grabbed Hsu's hand and said, "Look after her. She's a good girl. I regard her as I would my own daughter."

Hsu blushed. "I'll look after her," he said. When my neighbor had gone, Hsu said, "I meant what I said. I swear, if there's any danger, I won't leave you, even if the others do."

That evening I wrote two letters—one to my husband in Sinkiang, one to my parents in Hongkong. I didn't say where I was going. All I said was: if anything happens to me, I hope you can take care of Hsiao Ray. Hsu posted these letters for me.

That day I had another visitor—a neighbor who knew my plans. She urged me not to go. "You have a lovely daughter," she said. "I have nothing. My husband is dead and I'm consumptive. We are victims, you and I, and there's nothing we can do about it." I said I'd made up my mind. "I'll bring you something to eat then," she said. "You must eat. Hunger will make you thin and ill. They are delighted to see people like us die. Don't give them that satisfaction." So I ate the rice and vegetables she brought me from the communal mess hall, had a bath and changed into a clean blouse, blue cotton slacks and tennis shoes. I looked at myself in a mirror. Hideous. The day before, an official of the street committee had said that all women must cut their braids. I asked my neighbor to cut mine and she had done a bad job. My head looked like a fuzzy chicken's nest.

I put my money in a silk stocking and tied the stocking around my waist. Then I put on the gold ring my mother had given me. I also put on my wristwatch. I was the only person in the group with a watch, Hsu had said. Then I waited. There was nothing else to do, until it was time for me to meet Hsu in the town.

Another visitor appeared—the husband of a former classmate of mine. Wei came from the North, was a veteran Communist guerrilla fighter and had won a chestful of medals for bravery during the civil war and later in Korea. He had had a responsible job as security chief in a district in Kiangsi Province and seemed all set for a thoroughly comfortable life gradually moving up in the party hierarchy. Then he met my classmate, fell in love with her and lost everything—his job, his party affiliation, his friends. The girl was a Christian, with parents in Taiwan, and his party superiors refused him permission to marry. He argued and pleaded, and they still said no. He was so furious that one day he threw a cup of tea at the police chief. "I've fought all my life for the party," he shouted. "I have twenty years of fighting behind me, and scars all over my body. And still you don't trust me, you bastards. I quit." He was sacked, on the spot. He married my classmate but became, as time went on, increasingly ill tempered. He could talk about only one thing: his regret at having given twenty years of his life to the party. He earned a living doing odd jobs, repairing sewing machines and mending taps. By this time he hated the party, and Chairman Mao, with almost visceral hatred.

Wei also urged me not to try to leave China. "I can't stand the idea of your running such risks," he told me. "For the sake of your daughter, stay in Canton. Think what will happen if you're caught. I know the Communists. They'll never forgive you."

"It's too late to turn back now. All arrangements have been made. I'm leaving in thirty minutes."

Wei stared at the floor. "You don't know what you're letting yourself in for."

"Look, I've had enough. Anything is better than this. It's a gamble. What have I got to lose? Instead of arguing, you might wish me luck."

Wei grabbed both my hands. "Wish . . . you . . . luck," he said, almost in tears himself. Then he added, "Look: just in case, I'll try and put some money aside every month. Then I'll be able to send you things if you get caught and go to a labor camp." He left.

I sat still until the appointed time. Then I got up, walked down the staircase and through the front door. The representative of the street committee for the apartment house where I lived was chatting with neighbors on the pavement outside. "Chief," I said, "I'm just going to get my daughter and bring her home with me. Won't be long." He nodded and I walked briskly away, without looking back.

CHAPTER XIV

ESCAPE (1)

IT FELT STRANGE walking in the streets after having been confined to a small room for so many days. I tried to behave as though I were used to it all, but I was staring at what I saw as though this were my first visit to Canton.

The town seemed to be in the grips of some collective hysteria. Despite the fact that it was late, trucks thundered through the streets, packed with Red Guards who showered leaflets and pamphlets onto bewildered pedestrians. In front of Exhibition Hall, where the Canton Trade Fair is held twice a year, another large group of Guards were smashing old, and presumably bourgeois, crockery. Nearby, more Red Guards, stern and self-satisfied, were parading a group of Black Categories, who wore not only the regulation-size board on their chests but pointed dunce's caps as well.

I was supposed to meet Hsu in Haichu Square, only a few blocks away. Luckily, he was there. He saw me and we walked side by side. "We can't stay here," he said. "It's extremely unsafe. You'll have to come to my place. I have tickets for Fushan County. We leave the bus station at five forty-five A.M. Now listen: my name is Liu Chih. Your name is Teng Li-hsing. We are husband and wife. I'm thirty and you are twenty-nine. Our home town is Yiyang and our police substation is East River at Tungshan District. My occupation is hostel manager. You are a clerk. We are visiting relatives at Shihlien Brigade, Soukwan Commune in Chungshan County. On our way there we have permission to visit our uncle, my mother's brother, who lives at Chiangmen. Can you remember all that?"

Hsu lived a long way from Haichu Square, but we decided to walk. It was safer, and besides, in the bus we would have had to join in the reading of Mao quotations and in compulsory singing of revolutionary songs. At the corner of Tanan Road, a group of Red Guards surrounded us. Their leader said: "You will recite a quotation from Chairman Mao." That was easy enough. Quite by accident, Hsu and I recited the same phrase in unison: "Be resolute, fear no sacrifice and surmount every difficulty to win victory." We did not quite mean this in the way that it was intended, but they let us go. They were stopping everyone in the street.

Further on, in Wenteh Road, more Red Guards tried to detain us. "You must help us," one of them said. "This miserable creature"—he pointed to a middle-aged man surrounded by jeering teen-agers—"can neither recite a quotation from Chairman Mao, nor is he able to learn one by heart. You must help us teach him."

Hsu, luckily, was wearing his uniform and I suppose I, too, could have looked like a party cadre. Hsu said: "Little comrades, we can't help you because we have an important meeting. Please be patient and reason with this unfortunate man until he learns to quote from the works of Chairman Mao." They let us go, but we were stopped once more by another group of teen-agers.

This time I recited, to their apparent satisfaction: "In times of difficulty we must not lose sight of our achievements, must see the bright future and pluck up our courage."

Finally we reached Hsu's place. His cousin was waiting for us. We sat on the stairs. He had brought some apples and we ate these in complete silence. Then he got up, shook hands with us and said, "I'll be sleeping at a friend's house. You stay here. Wish you good luck and bon voyage. Try and let me know if you get you-know-where." After Hsu's cousin left, we dared not go up to Hsu's room until much later, because we knew that the police could burst in at any time to check people's papers. So we wandered up and down the streets outside.

The Red Guards had finally gone to bed, and we were able to talk quietly. Our walk took us past the Canton Prison at Huanghua Road and I told Hsu that I had spent some time inside—months I would never forget. He told me that he had recently been in love with a girl but her parents had turned her against him—claiming that he was a "bad element." "It's all over now," Hsu said. "Soon we'll be free." Just before we turned back to go to Hsu's room, we walked past the Garrison Command Headquarters. In front of the gate we could see a typical Cantonese scene: two wretched-looking men were standing on a table in the open air, surrounded by screaming, yelling youths. It was a so-called struggle meeting, and the two men on the table would, I suppose, eventually be dragged out, wearing dunce's caps, and paraded through the streets.

When we got back to Hsu's place, everyone was asleep. Hsu

lived with relatives in a tiny apartment, and there were men and women, in their underwear, sleeping all over the main room. It was exceedingly hot and humid. Hsu had a tiny room to himself. He told me to sleep on the bed. He slept on some matting on the floor.

But I couldn't sleep. I kept thinking about what lay ahead, and I couldn't get used to sharing a room with a boy I knew only moderately well. Instead, I listened to the tick-tock of a large alarm clock and thought: only a few more hours to go, and we'll be leaving for good.

At 4:30 A.M. just after I had finally dozed off, Hsu woke me. I washed my face and hands and ate a roll I had brought with me the night before. Hsu said we should try and assume some kind of primitive disguise, and he gave me his spectacles to wear. We slipped out of the building unnoticed. There were beggars sleeping on the sidewalk, but they didn't pay any attention to us.

Dawn came. Food stalls opened their doors. It was a long way to the bus station, and we walked fast. I couldn't see properly, for Hsu was quite near-sighted. Passers-by looked like blurred ghosts and the street itself seemed to curve away from me. I was glad when we reached the North Station at Haichu Square. We got on the bus and I took his spectacles off.

Without looking round, Hsu nodded to me, indicating that we were not alone in the bus. I turned round. In the rear row of seats, there was an immensely fat man, with a ruddy complexion and broad, squashed features. He looked like a healthy, self-satisfied pig. This must be Fatty. As I watched, a tall, thin man entered the bus and, without looking at anyone, sat down next to Fatty. As he sat down, he nudged him with his elbow. Long-fellow. I gestured to Hsu, and he nodded.

The bus moved off and for the one-hour journey through the lush green fields I was happy. Though we had not escaped, this was my first day of real freedom and we seemed to be making progress. Nobody had expressed any interest in us and at intervals of looking at the countryside I tried to memorize the details of my new identity. We didn't speak. It was pleasantly cool in the bus, and Hsu, too, was smiling to himself. It was like a trip to the countryside with old friends—something I had often done in the past, before my arrest. Except that now a party cadre, also on the bus, stood up and said: "Everyone sing: 'Sailing the seas depends upon the Great Helmsman.'" We sang lustily, though I could scarcely prevent myself from bursting into hysterical laughter as I heard, from the back of the bus, Fatty and Longfellow singing in loud, toneless, hideous bass voices. After singing, we had to recite Mao's quotations again, all together, like children learning to read.

At six-thirty we arrived at Fushan Station and changed buses. I felt slightly queasy and Hsu went to a small shop and bought me some preserved plums and salted ginger. At six forty-five we were on our way again, this time to Chiangmen. It was a three-hour journey, and the bus was exceedingly crowded. I sat beside the window and Hsu was next to me. We watched the countryside go by but didn't talk. I was scared: a middle-aged man in cadre's uniform sitting in front of us kept turning round to stare at me. Had he spotted something suspicious about us? Was he following us? Or was he just staring at me because he always stared at girls? Eventually he got off the bus and I heaved a sigh of relief.

It was just past 11 A.M. when we reached Chiangmen. At the station Hsu unobtrusively got together with Fatty and Longfellow and agreed to meet them an hour later at a food stall. Hsu and I then walked to the Huatu Hotel. The streets were full of big-character posters and here, too, there were Red Guards shouting slogans. Many people seemed scared.

Booking in at the hotel was something I dreaded. The party cadre on duty examined our papers closely, and asked Hsu detailed questions about our trip. I was afraid I would say the wrong thing if he questioned me, so I told him I was very tired, and that my husband would reply to all his questions. Hsu filled in both our registration cards and I was allowed to go upstairs. I was in fact extremely tired, for I had had no sleep the previous night and we already seemed to have done a considerable amount of walking.

Soon afterwards, Hsu joined me. "Fatty and Longfellow are waiting for us," he said. "We'll meet them, have lunch and then see whether Mok has arrived with the sampan."

The restaurant was packed, but from where we sat we could see Fatty, Longfellow and a third person—a young man. That must be Mok. They were eating silently. We waited till they had finished, then paid. They got up to leave, and so did we. We followed them at some distance. They wore Chinese-type shirts and trousers, like those worn by peasants of Kwangtung Province, and we didn't want to catch up with them where we could be seen, because we were dressed differently, Hsu in his uniform and

I like a party cadre. Mok turned round to see whether we were following, and shook his head from side to side. He looked glum.

"There must be some trouble," Hsu whispered to me. "Mok's usually a cheerful fellow. You'll like him. But something's wrong right now."

I told Hsu I was worried. "You know I have no place to go if this fails," I said. "I can't go back to Canton now."

"I thought about all this. I was talking to Fatty, some while back. If things don't work out as they should, we could always walk to Kiangsi Province, and earn our living as laborers there. I won't let you down." But I knew that Hsu was saying this to keep my spirits up, and that he felt as worried as I looked. I didn't answer.

Chiangmen has three main streets, but the back streets are narrow, dirty and strangely quiet. They were empty. We followed the three men for about half an hour, through back streets, until we came to a park. It was a beautiful place, with lots of weeping willows, lakes and flowers. At this hour, it was quite deserted and we had the whole place to ourselves. At last, we all sat down next to a small garden pavilion on a grassy hill. I heard Hsu say, "Well, fellows, this is Lai Ying my wife." Nobody said anything. Hsu said, "Well, what's the matter?"

Longfellow puffed on a cigarette. Fatty's face was quite drained of color. He still looked rather like a pig, but like a very worried pig. Only Mok grinned as though everything were all right.

Mok was the one to speak. "Let's pack up and go home," he said. "Everything has gone wrong. Last night I paid twenty-five dollars and was ready to pick up the sampan. Then the maintenance man said he must have written permission from the party committee of the commune we were from. He said the boat was too small for five people, and wanted to know what we wanted four pairs of oars for. Said he didn't want to take responsibility in case we were smuggling things. Said we'd have to wait until we got written clearance, if we really were what we said we were." My throat was dry. Mok went on, quite cheerfully: "So I said, 'Look comrade, how do you expect us to get word from the commune? I don't have any money for my return journey there. So why don't I go back there and get the necessary papers, and you give me back the money I've just given you so that I can pay for my trip back?' But the bastard wouldn't do that either. He only gave me back five dollars and kept the rest on account for when I return. Look, here's his receipt. I think I'd better drop the whole idea and go back to my village and become a militia leader again."

"By the way," he added inconsequentially, "they're having a display here tomorrow, the militia, I mean. D'you want to see the shooting competition and the drilling?"

By this time, I thought that Mok was more than a little mad. But Longfellow brought us all back to the matter on hand. "There's no hope of getting a fake document for the sampan," he said. "It would take ages. Let's try and make it on foot, through the mountains."

Fatty looked even more distressed. "We can't do that," he said. "We'd be caught. They have dogs and things. The nearer one gets to the frontier, the more guards there are around. Besides, one has to swim that last stretch. Hundreds of people have been drowned that way." He babbled on, raising objection after objection. The local people would spot us right away; we would be carrying heavy loads, for food; we weren't fit enough to try.

I thought I should speak up. "Sampan or walking's all the same to me," I said.

"You're not afraid of walking?"

"No, I'm not. Besides, it's all right for you. But I can't go back to Canton. So what choice is there?"

Hsu looked more cheerful. "That settles that," he said. "This means we have to start right now. In a week's time, there'll be a moon. And we can't wait another month. Where would we all stay?" Nobody said anything. "Can we stay in your village to make the necessary preparations for this new move?" Hsu asked, turning to Fatty. Fatty grunted, but didn't reply. Hsu felt that not everyone was convinced. "Look," he said, "we've got to get started as soon as possible. If we leave it any longer, we'll freeze to death when the time comes for us to make that swim. I agree with Longfellow. We've got to walk." And he added in a firm voice: "Besides, if you people are scared to come, we'll make it on our own, Lai and I."

"That's right," I said. "I have about two hundred dollars left, and that's enough to buy food, clothes and all the extra stuff we'll need. Let's make a list of what we want, shall we?"

Longfellow and Mok looked relieved, but Fatty was as white as ever. It was clear that he must be overruled.

"Let's get on with it, then," Hsu said. "Lai, get the money out." I went behind a tree and undid the silk stocking round my waist. I took out $150, but kept $50 for a final emergency. I also took out some rice ration cards I had bought on the black market in Canton some time back. We decided that we should all buy separate items that we needed, but spread our purchases over several shops, in order not to arouse suspicion, when we returned to town. Fatty, Longfellow and Mok walked ahead, and we soon lost sight of them. Hsu and I followed, more slowly. Neither of us dared say anything. We knew that, since we no longer could travel by sampan, we would have to make at least two trips by ferry near the border area, where police checks were bound to be thorough.

We had worked out that the trip would take us five days of hard walking, with a long swim at the end of it. We bought five pounds of sweet cakes each, preserved plums and salted ginger. I had pointed out that we must keep our loads down to an absolute minimum. We would be climbing mountains most of the time. One pound of food a day per person should be enough. While in one store, I bought a length of plastic clothesline. The man in the store who served me was a "former capitalist." At least, that's what was written on the black board tied to his chest. He looked miserable but there was nothing I could say to make him feel better.

Hsu asked, "What's the string for?"

I said, "It's to tie us together in the water. I'm scared of being washed away by the currents."

We had our evening meal, and I went up to my room to rest. Hsu was out, making further arrangements, for though we had decided to walk, we must first take a ferry from Chiangmen to Taipiewei, and here, much more than on our bus ride, we ran the risk of an identity check by police or militia. I tried not to think about it. I tried not to worry about Hsu, but in my mind's eye I saw him being arrested in Chiangmen along with Longfellow and Fatty as they tried to buy ferry tickets. There was a sharp knock on the door, and I started in terror.

"Who's there?"

"Comrade, tonight there is hot water. The bathroom is at the end of the corridor, if you want a bath." The footsteps went away.

Eventually, Hsu turned up, in high spirits, with his sweet cakes, and an ice on a stick for me. He waved some flimsy pieces of paper. "Our tickets. We take the ferry at nine-thirty tomorrow morning. Now let's rest. After all, what did Chairman Mao say? To work well you must know first how to rest well."

It was dark, and we had to get some sleep. There was only

one bed, of course, and one mosquito net. Hsu said, "You sleep on the bed. I can sleep on the floor."

I said, "That wouldn't be right. The mosquitoes bite like hell here. Besides, we're supposed to be married. What would the police think if they were to come to look at our papers, and see you sleeping on the floor? This bed's big enough for both of us."

We kept our clothes on. It was in any case too hot to be close to one another. The mosquitoes were very active, and I didn't dare roll up the net.

I knew Hsu much better now, but it was strange to share his bed, and neither of us, it seemed, could sleep any better than the night before. "I'll tell you a story," said Hsu, and embarked on a long, rambling account of a short story he had once read in a magazine called *Translations from Foreign Literature*. It was all about a young woman who left her husband and child to run off with another man, and an old woman who spent her time watching others gamble, in some kind of a watering resort, either in Germany or Russia. Could it have been a story by Tchekhov? In the end, the old woman saved a young man from suicide, after he had lost all his money, but insisted that she sleep with him afterwards. I was dead tired.

All I could think of to say was: "There are plenty of casinos in Macao. You must take me there, when . . . if . . ." It was bad luck to talk this way, and I didn't finish the sentence. "Let's sleep," I said. "We'll never have the strength to see this through if we spend all the night talking."

The next morning, we were at the ferry with half an hour to spare, and bought some breakfast at a food stall. Even here, there were political struggles going on, and I saw a group of Black Categories being pushed along the streets, wearing their boards and dunce's caps. Sickened, I turned away to stare at the Pearl River. We boarded the ferry without any trouble. There was no identity check.

The two-hour journey was uneventful, though I was constantly on the lookout for police. Mok kept up a stream of banter, and at lunchtime, ate enormously. It was hot, and we were packed like sardines. The seats were littered with handbills and I read them to pass the time. They all consisted of "urgent orders" from the local party committee, mostly urging people to work harder for the Cultural Revolution. Some were police notices, listing the names and descriptions of "known counterrevolutionaries." All ended: "Long live Chairman Mao." Longfellow and Fatty were on another part of the boat, and we only caught a glimpse of them. At one stage in the trip, Mok went to the toilet. When he returned, he passed me a strip of cigarette paper, which I read and then destroyed. It said: "This evening, we meet at Matoutanto, at the bridge just before the entrance to the village. If no one is there, ask for a Kung Shih-lun in Matou village." I repeated this to myself over and over again, to memorize it as I had memorized the details of my new identity. There was nothing else to do.

At eleven-thirty we arrived at Taipiewei. The boat couldn't approach the wharf, and sampans ferried the passengers to dry land. It was the most spectacularly beautiful part of China I had ever seen, with small old stone bridges over tiny streams. A mother was washing her small son in the river mud, the traditional peasant way of curing ringworm.

Mok's mother lived in a village near Taipiewei, and our plan was to split up into two groups. Hsu, Mok and I would walk to his village, where we would divide up our recent purchases and arrange them into more portable loads. Mok would say good-by to his mother. Then we would take yet another ferry, and meet up with the rest of the party that same evening at Matoutanto. At least, that was what we decided.

Hsu was impatient to get started, and hustled me on. "It's a long walk," he said, "and our ferry leaves at three-thirty." Mok was already ahead. As he walked, he sang a popular revolutionary song which had been introduced a few weeks before. It was called: "Go Back to the Village and Take Part in Front-line Agricultural Work." He sang with a heavily rural Cantonese accent, fully aware of the irony of it all, which made me laugh. That, and his imitations of Cantonese party cadres, kept us in good humor most of the way.

At one point in our journey we crossed a stretch of water by boat. The man who rowed us over, a fine old man with a deeply tanned, wrinkled face, obviously knew Mok well. "How are you, Mok?" he said. "Coming over for market day, are you?"

Mok said, "No, I've been visiting my uncle at Chiangmen. These"—he waved towards us—"are relatives of my uncle and have orders from the party to look at the state of farm work here. So, because I know this area, they asked me to come along too." Mok obviously wanted to impress the old man. "Comrade Hsu," he said, "you've been a member of the cultural troupe of Canton Military Command: what about a song?" Hsu shook his head, but I remembered a Kiangsi folk song, strangely appropriate. I sang:

"One rapid after another lies ahead of us.
We fear no hardship and no difficulty.
As long as the water runs in the river
We will make a breakthrough some day."

We reached the shore on the other side, said good-by to the boatman, and walked on. From notices on the small co-operative shops lining the road in the village we were now entering, this was part of Panfu Commune, in Chungshan County, the border area. This was also Mok's home ground, and everyone, it seemed, knew him. He waved to friends, or stopped to chat with them. In between greeting old acquaintances, he said to me, "Here's the street. The last hut on the right is my home." He was obviously under a strain, afraid that those who knew him well might ask him embarrassing questions about us.

It was hot and dry in the village. This was a part of China no visitors ever saw; the houses were tiny bamboo and plaster huts, and the people seemed desperately poor. Naked children played in the dust, and their mothers, who must have been in their thirties or younger, were old women, wrinkled and bent from work in the fields. That, I thought, is what I'll look like if I'm sent to a labor camp again.

Several old men and women sat in front of Mok's hut. They were peasants who, because of their great age, were excused from work in the fields. Mok's cousin, the local militia leader, was away —taking part in the all-county drill competition. No one paid any attention to us as we walked inside. After a quick cup of tea, we sorted out our belongings. Everything inessential to the hard climb ahead we left behind, in a corner of the hut—a welcome windfall for Mok's mother, if she could dispose of it. We burnt the papers we had used to register at the hotel in Chiangmen, and, on a blank piece of letterhead paper stolen from the Chiangmen Pharmaceutical Company, which Fatty had somehow laid his hands on, we wrote out our new identification, as follows:

To whom it may concern:

This is to certify that Comrades Liu Chih and Teng Li-hsin are assigned to investigate the condition of medical stores

and equipment at nearby Hsenwan. Any assistance by organizations in the area to help them complete their mission
will be appreciated.

Then we put the day's date on the letter, folded it carefully
and entrusted it to Hsu, who hid it in his purse. We were ready
to leave—and the sooner the better.

But this was reckoning without Mok's mother, who kept up a
steady stream of questions. "Why such a brief stay?" she asked
Mok. "Can't you stay to supper? When are you coming home
again? I hardly ever see you these days."

Mok said, "Mama, I've got to take these two friends of mine
back to the ferry." He spoke in a loud voice so that his aged
relatives outside might hear. He dared not, of course, say where he
was going, nor that he would, in all probability, never see his
mother again. At last we managed to say good-by. We were far
behind schedule, and I tried not to look at my watch too often.

We had our bundles with us, and I knew, so near the frontier,
we must look a strange trio. Some fishermen mending their nets
eyed us suspiciously as we left Mok's village.

We were too late, of course. Our ferry had just left. Mok
blamed us for not walking fast enough, though he had delayed us
as much as anything by talking to his mother. He was nervous
and on edge, but outwardly controlled himself.

"There is another way to Matoutanto," Mok said. "It means
taking a ferry to Wuchou, then a walk along the main Shihch'i-
Macao road. We have no choice—if we want to meet up together tonight."

Again, the ferry crossing presented no difficulties, and no one
asked for our papers. But once we were on the other side, our
trouble began. Mok explained that bicycle taxis were usually
available on the Shihch'i-Macao road. To supplement the bus
services in this densely populated area, those with bicycles
transported passengers, riding pillion, into Matoutanto for a
small fee. But we were out of luck. One cyclist went by, and sometimes two, but never three together—and we couldn't afford to
split up into two groups, for neither Hsu nor I knew the way,
or where exactly we should go to meet up with Fatty and Longfellow.

By this time, I think, we were all really scared, for it seemed
obvious that with our neatly tied bundles we must look like
an escaping party. "As a last resort," Mok said, "we could

take the Shihch'i-Macao bus* and get out at Matoutanto. We would still be on time for our rendezvous. It should stop here just after five P.M."

Hsu didn't reply. I knew what he was thinking: a bus so near the frontier, actually crossing the border into Macao, must be subject to repeated searches. "I know some of the bus drivers," Mok said, "and it's just possible there'll be no identity checks. We have papers, don't we?" And, as if to compel us to make up our minds, he added, "My cousin, the militia leader, will be coming down this same road in an hour's time. If you can't make up your minds, I'll be going back with him, and have my supper at home."

We said we'd take the bus, and moved our belongings under the shade of a tree, to be less conspicuous. A sugar-water peddler passed by, and we drank some apricot tea and ate some cakes. They were delicious.

The bus was on time. Mok bought three tickets, speaking the local dialect, which neither Hsu nor I understood. There were few passengers on the bus, and most of these, it seemed from their clothes, were Macao residents returning home after visiting relatives in China. Mok chatted with the conductor, to my very great anxiety, for—not understanding what he was saying —I was afraid he would let slip some trivial remark which would make him suspicious. There were no police or militiamen on the bus, and we were not stopped once. Eventually Mok nodded, and at the next stop we got out. It was raining as we walked to the meeting place near the bridge where we were to find Longfellow and Fatty.

They were not there. Three farmers were washing themselves under the bridge after their day's work, and eyed us curiously. We waited and waited, feeling more conspicuous all the time. Then, thinking Longfellow and Fatty might have gotten tired waiting for us, and gone to the other alternative rendezvous in the village, we decided to walk to the village ourselves and try to locate our contact man there, Longfellow's friend Kung Shih-lun. None of us knew what he looked like, nor where he lived, for Mok had never come across him in his previous hawking trips with Longfellow.

It turned out to be a tiny village, with only some twenty

---

* This bus only takes passengers with valid travel documents across the frontier. Mostly they are Macao residents allowed into China to see relatives.—Editor's note.

huts in all. As in all small places, people seemed intensely suspicious towards strangers, and we were followed by a crowd of boys. Hsu asked one where Kung's place was, and he said he would show us. By now we were part of a noisy procession of kids.

Kung was squatting inside his hut, cutting his hair with a pair of rusty scissors. He looked up, and I realized that he, too, was scared. Hsu was of course in his usual ragged army uniform, and I had done my best to look like a party cadre. To him, we smelled trouble. Our disguise was too successful. Or else he had not been warned to expect us.

Hsu said, "Comrade, you know Longfellow, the Tall Bamboo salesman?"

Kung shook his head.

"What about Fatty?"

"I haven't seen them. I don't know anything about them." Kung spoke in a high, squeaky voice. "They haven't been here for ages."

The crowd outside Kung's hut was considerable now. It was dinnertime, and some women wandered over to the hut, rice bowls in hand, to watch the fun. I was thinking: we made a dreadful mistake leaving the bridge to come to Kung's hut, when, out of the corner of my eye, I saw four people striding straight towards us. One looked like a local man, and the other three were real militiamen in uniform.

CHAPTER XV

ESCAPE (2)

THIS IS IT, I thought. I looked at Hsu and Mok and was surprised at how calm they appeared. I was glad I was wearing trousers, for my legs were trembling uncontrollably.

The senior militiamen came up to us. "Who are you? Where are you from? What do you want with Kung? Show me your papers."

Hsu took out his purse and unfolded the letter. He spoke in a relaxed, conversational tone of voice. "We are cadres from Chiangmen Pharmaceutical Company on official business, comrade," he said. "We missed the ferry and asked this commune worker here"—he pointed at Mok—"to help us on our way. Kung in your village has done business with this man Longfellow. We want to find Longfellow because he owes the company some money for some herbal medicines he bought and hasn't yet paid for. So we decided to call on Kung to ask him if he knew Longfellow's whereabouts." The militiamen were expressionless. "By the way," Hsu went on, "maybe the cadres in your village can help. We would like you to notify our unit if you catch up with this Longfellow person. He owes the state money. It's a serious matter."

The cadre and the militiamen looked at the letter. Mok pointed at the old village rooftop tiles, with designs of fishes and dragons on them. "In our commune at Panfu," he said with considerable self-assurance, "these old things were taken down a long time ago. Why don't you do the same?" It was the militiamen's turn to look uneasy. Their chief returned our document, and said that Longfellow often came to the village to sell Tall Bamboo and sometimes spent a few nights there, sleeping in Kung's hut. But nobody had seen him for a long time. They noted the address of our pharmaceutical company and promised to let us know as soon as they saw him again. One of the militiamen asked us to stay and share their evening meal. Hsu thanked them all with somewhat officious dignity, but said we had already notified the Hsenwan militia that we would be spending the night there, and they had made arrangements to feed us. We couldn't waste their food, could we?

Another militiaman said it was ten miles to Hsenwan, and that they could accompany us part of the way. With profuse thanks, we declined, saying that we knew the way. We were followed out of the village by an escort of small children but they soon returned to their huts when we left the village. I realized how close we had been to disaster, had the militiamen been more persistent. It was only then that I understood how near we'd been to arrest, for had the militiamen searched our belongings, they would have found plenty of evidence of our intention to escape.

Back at the bridge again, Longfellow and Fatty still had not shown up.

Now we were in a quandary, for we could not return to the village and spend the night with Kung—even assuming that he had been warned of our arrival and understood by now that we were not real party cadres. On the other hand, we couldn't leave without Longfellow, for only he knew the way over the mountains. Mok suggested we walk to Hsenwan—to give some credibility to our story, for the militiamen might still be around—and return to the bridge after dark. "If Longfellow doesn't show up," said Mok, "I'm going home. I don't know the way over these mountains like he does." His morale was obviously low, and he had been more shaken than he cared to admit by our recent encounter.

I whispered to Hsu, "What on earth will we do if Mok lets us down?"

"We'll make it on our own," he said. "No sense in waiting any further. As a matter of fact, we might as well leave now. It's only some twenty-five miles, and we can find the right direction by the stars."

I was less convinced. "Give me a number at random, and I'll see what the stars say," I said. I'd learnt this trick from a Taoist while I was in prison. Hsu gave me a number and I made the necessary calculations, working out the various lunar and stellar ascendencies for this time of year, scribbling sums on a scrap of paper. My verdict: "Luck in a small way—enough to overcome routine difficulties." I didn't really believe in any of this. Nevertheless, we decided to wait a little longer.

Then, as we had given up hope, Longfellow and Fatty came walking down the road. They looked as if they hadn't a care in the world. We were so glad to see them that we almost forgot to be angry. They explained that they had stopped for dinner on the way with one of Longfellow's cronies, and, not having a watch, they had not realized how late they were. They listened to our story of our encounter with the militiamen and we all agreed we must make for the hills right away. For if the militia came across us with Longfellow after the story we had told them, they were bound to arrest us.

Longfellow was now in his element. He and Fatty would lead the way. Mok would follow, some distance behind. Hsu and I would be last. At all times, we must keep our eyes and ears open, and hide in the bushes at the first sign of trouble. We changed our clothes, for we had all, except Hsu, been wearing white shirts, and now we put on black cotton shirts we had brought specially for walking at night. We divided up our loads, shouldered our packs and started walking steeply uphill, with Longfellow going first.

He led us straight through thick shrub and trees, and when we reached the first hilltop, we saw ahead of us, in the diminishing light, range after range of hills and mountains. The valley below was a bottomless black pit. There was a wind, and a noise of rustling leaves.

"Pay attention," Longfellow said. "You see that part of the mountain, which looks a little lighter than the rest of the ridge? Right behind it are the lights of Macao. As long as one keeps going in that direction, one can't get lost."

We moved on, down a valley, up another hill and were halfway up the second slope when Longfellow whispered to us to halt. He had seen a distant light behind us. That would be the militia, he said. They patrolled regular hours, from 8 to 11 P.M., but they stuck to mountain paths and seldom bothered to climb to the top of the hills they were supposed to search. There were two reasons for this: they were not all that energetic, and they were afraid of being ambushed on the hilltops by smuggler gangs. There had been several cases, Longfellow said, of smugglers killing a four-man patrol, so the higher up the hill we were, the safer we would be. We moved on, faster than before, and clambered up the hill, our lungs bursting. The pack on my back felt like a ton, but the dancing intermittent lights behind us—probably flashlights—seemed nearer than before. There was a huge rock ahead and Longfellow told us to hide behind it. "If you keep absolutely quiet," he said, "the patrol won't bother to come this far."

We watched two groups come nearer and nearer. Counting

the flashlights, it seemed there must be eight persons in all. They made a lot of noise as they came up the path. Luckily they had no dogs with them. We huddled together, and Fatty chose this moment to put his hand round my legs. Careful not to make the slightest noise, I pushed him away. The lights stopped some ten yards down the path from where we were. There was some kind of consultation, and then the patrol turned and walked downhill again. As Longfellow had said, they were on a routine patrol and not interested in climbing any further than need be. But as they left, from the noise they made crashing into branches, we realized that they carried rifles, and that a struggle would have been out of the question.

We waited until they were far away, and resumed our climb, then walked down the other side through a broader, wilder valley. There were tall grasses, weeds, wild vine and other vegetation, most of it growing higher than our own height, and the ground underfoot was soggy, and soon turned into a swamp. We moved very slowly, and had to be careful not to sink in the mud. There were brambles and thorns, too, and the going was very difficult.

Longfellow alone was pleased. As we struggled to push ahead, he explained that we were safe in this valley. The height of the vegetation proved that people never came as far as this, so there would be no intruders gathering wood. Not for the first time that night, I admired Longfellow's practical cunning and his knowledge of such things. I was dog-tired, and said so. My watch showed it was 4:50 A.M. After daybreak, we should not be able to move at all, and this was a good place to stop and rest. Mok took our solitary water flask to fill. The rest of us built a hideout, cutting brambles and branches to seal off the entrance, though it was unlikely that anyone would come our way. Longfellow insisted we make ourselves invisible from the air, too, and put the finishing touches to our nest by covering it with thick branches, making it sun- and light-proof. I felt safer than at any time since I had left my room in Canton.

We were in a tiny hollow, but the ground was covered with sharp stones. I was so relieved no longer to be climbing that I didn't mind this at all, and wallowed in the luxury of just sitting there. We opened up our bundles and ate some of the cakes we had brought, and drank the rather brackish water that Mok had brought back. Then we tried to sleep, huddled together. It started to rain and we all covered our heads with plastic sheets we had with us. The rain pelted down on our legs, and the ground became soggy. It was impossible to sleep sitting up in this position, and we talked. Hsu said, "Are you all right? You don't regret having come?"

"Why should I regret anything? I would have been arrested this week or next, that's for sure. You've been very kind."

Hsu said, "Listen." Above the sound of the rain pelting down on our groundsheets, Fatty and Longfellow were snoring heavily. "The escapers' symphony."

Eventually the rain stopped. It was day again. The sun gradually dried our soaked clothes. We repacked our bags, and went to sleep. We slept all day. Then we waited until darkness was complete, and began walking again.

This second night's walk was worse than the first. Perhaps because I was still exhausted from the first night, I found I couldn't see straight, and stumbled continuously. Mok and Hsu took turns at guiding me and holding my arm. I was a burden to them but I was too tired to worry about this. We had seen, from the top of a hill, that there was a stream in the valley below, and had agreed to stop there, to drink some water and eat more of our dry cakes. But as we got near the creek, Longfellow hid in the grass, and we all followed suit. "Cattle hoof marks," said Longfellow. "They're fresh. This must be a known watering place. We can't stay here."

Suddenly there were sounds from the other side of the river, quite near, and we saw flashlights being used and coming our way. In the dark, it was impossible to say how far off they were, but soon they seemed agonizingly close. Longfellow said: "Quick! Up the hill. Try not to make any noise. Keep in the undergrowth." They were gone. I tried to follow, but I slipped and found myself floundering in a small swamp. I was sinking, thrashing about and making an enormous noise. Hsu came back and hauled me out. A beam of light flickered near where we were. Hsu grasped my hand and pulled me along with him. Eventually, we staggered into a clearing, where Longfellow was waiting. He was angry. "Damn fool," he said to me. "Your muddy footprints are all over the mountain. All they have to do is to follow them."

With Longfellow in the lead, we struggled on uphill, our faces scratched and torn by brambles. We came to a huge rock. Mok climbed up first—there were some footholds, but it was almost vertical—and somehow or other Mok and Hsu half pushed, half carried me up, over and down the other side. Whoever had been following us was left far behind, and though we stopped and looked, we could no longer see any trace of lights. After a brief rest, we began climbing again.

By now I was completely exhausted, and stopped again, unable to move. Fatty started grumbling. "I knew it," he said. "She's holding us up. It'll be her fault if we're caught." The others said nothing, but Hsu took off my pack and carried it along with his own. After that, I moved faster.

So intent were we on getting away from the voices and flashlights that we had blundered up the mountainside where the undergrowth was thickest, without really bothering about the direction we were going in. But now our progress was halted. We were skirting what appeared, in the darkness, to be a huge precipice. There was no sense in going on, for we were lost, and it was dangerous to move without seeing where we were going. We lay down on a small grassy slope near the precipice, and waited for light. We had made almost no progress whatever that night. I looked at my watch. 3:30 A.M.

When it was light, no longer obeying our own rules, which were to lay up during daylight, we skirted the precipice, and Longfellow led us up another slope, having, he said, found the way at last. We had climbed high, for now it was bitterly cold on the hilltop. Mok was sneezing and coughing a good deal, and I covered myself with my mosquito net, using it as a huge scarf. The mosquito net had been a good idea, prompted by my previous experience in Canton Prison; then, after my arrest, I had been almost bitten to death and I recalled now that my determination to carry a mosquito net on this expedition was prompted by the pessimistic feeling that if I was arrested again this time, at least I would keep the mosquitoes out. After climbing some more, we decided to rest awhile. And we all huddled together, using the mosquito net not for protection but for warmth.

After a brief rest, Longfellow got us going again. "We can't stay here," he said. "Too exposed. I've just noticed there's some kind of a path nearby and that means people may come walking by. We must find a real hiding place." We walked along the trail for a bit, and eventually Longfellow selected a shrub-covered gully where we could all hide. Feeling I had done this all my life, I helped cut branches to conceal our nest from possible prying eyes. We all crawled inside, and, despite a profusion of ants, earwigs and every conceivable variety of crawling insect, I felt comfortable, and at peace.

I had dozed off, and Hsu was shaking me awake and at the same time warning that I should not make a sound. There were people only a few feet away. A man's voice said, "Look: someone has been here already." A woman's voice replied, "That's impossible. We're the first up here. Nobody else has gathered any firewood from this place. It's too early." The man's voice mumbled something about it not being people from the village, but maybe someone on the run.

We were holding our breath, and I noticed that Mok, fearing he might sneeze, had wrapped his head in a towel to stifle any possible noise. Despite myself, I felt like laughing. Shortly afterwards, the footsteps went away and there was silence.

When we were absolutely certain that we could no longer be heard, we started talking again. Hsu wanted us to move on immediately, fearing that the firewood-gathering couple was on its way to the village to report us to the militia. Fatty was in favor of a move too. But I was against the idea. There was no proof that we had been spotted. If we stayed in our hiding place, we were relatively safe. But if we made a move now, in broad daylight, we were almost certain to be discovered, since the villagers obviously regularly came as far as this to gather firewood. Longfellow agreed, and we stayed where we were. We were still arguing when the crackle of branches indicated that more intruders were on their way. We froze. For some time, there were noises of people hacking down branches and occasional small talk between peasants, but they didn't come near us. When they, too, had gone, I took off my shoes and socks, which were full of mud, to dry them in the sun. I also tried to scrape some of the mud off my clothes. Mosquitoes were active now, and I wrapped a towel round my bare feet and slept.

I was awakened by familiar pangs of hunger. The men were all fast asleep, with Longfellow and Fatty snoring as usual. I looked in a small mirror, and hardly recognized myself. My face was dirty and scratched, my clothes filthy, my hair plastered with mud and dust. I must wash, I thought, whatever happens I should try and clean up a little. Longfellow had said we were near a spring. I decided to slip out of our hiding place alone, without waking the others, and find it. Taking soap, my towel and my spare pair of underclothes, I crawled out and soon came across a stream, about thirty yards further down the slope. I stripped, and washed all over. The water was cold and clear, and tasted wonderful. I felt this was the best thing that had ever happened to me. I would insist that the men wash too. It would improve their morale no end. Besides, they stank and it would be better for all of us, sleeping huddled together as we did, to take every available opportunity to clean up. As I dressed, I noticed that Hsu was standing a few yards away, watching. I was furious.

Hsu explained that my crawling out of the hiding place had woken everybody up. From the sounds they could hear, they thought I must be washing in the stream and sent Hsu over to bring me back. It was dangerous, they said, to leave our hiding place while there was still light. Hsu hadn't wanted to go. The others said he was hen-pecked. "If you won't go," Fatty had said, "I will. What's the matter with you?" So Hsu had followed me, but had allowed me to have my bath without being disturbed.

"They say you've got to come back now," Hsu said.

My bath had filled me with boundless self-confidence. "I won't come back," I said. "Tell the others to come down here. The water's marvelous. They need a wash too." Eventually, one by one, they emerged, but no one stripped. One by one, they washed their faces, hands and feet.

Afterwards we went back into our hiding place and unpacked our bags for a meal. One four-pound bag of cakes had been lost, and there was a good deal of quarreling about who was responsible for this. Longfellow cut recriminations short. "All right," he said, "all it means is that from now on we've got to be extra careful about food. We don't have too much left, and we can't buy any up here." Up to now everyone had helped himself, and while I nibbled at my cakes, Fatty had wolfed his down, and then eaten some of mine. This time we divided the cakes up equally. Fatty looked glum.

The third night we started off by making good progress. By now our muscles were attuned to the climbing and we got off to a brisk start. The hill we now climbed was almost bare, except for stones and grass, and while this made us more vulnerable, if spotted, it also made for faster progress. I was, however, more conscious of my unquenchable thirst than on the previous two nights. We only had one water bottle and Longfellow had decreed: no drinking during climbing. So, while we rested at intervals, I could only take a single swallow, and even this was frowned on.

On the way down into yet another valley, we came across a deserted tomb. What happened then showed me how great a gulf there was between Hsu and me, brought up to despise all traditional superstitions, and the rest of our party. For Fatty immediately knelt by the tomb, and reverently kowtowed; Mok bowed a few times, and said a brief prayer. Even Longfellow folded his palms together, in a somewhat self-conscious gesture. Hsu and I stood by, and did nothing. The others were all country-bred, and despite all the indoctrination they had been subjected to, they firmly believed that if one came across a tomb like this, it was essential to pay one's respects. For country people in China still believe that if the dead are treated with deference, their spirits can help the living. If contempt is shown, then the spirits can harm you, and do you untold damage. Then even I, knowing this to be superstition, said a brief prayer, whether to the spirits of the dead man whose tomb we had accidentally stumbled on or to God, I don't know. "Please," I thought, "see to it that we reach Macao safely."

We moved on, into the valley. It was pitch-dark and we blundered into a small swamp, thinking it was a patch of grass. Taking immense pains to be absolutely quiet, we crossed what appeared to be a main road and moved ahead, through scrubland and occasional fields, to the foot of yet another mountain.

We began climbing again, more expertly this time, and the air became cooler until it was quite cold. At last, we reached the top. What we saw made us realize that this was the highest mountain we had yet climbed, for far away in the distance, for the first time, we could actually see Macao. In a small sea of yellow lights there were neon red and green spots. It looked like a huge metropolis to us, tantalizingly near, desperately far.

"Now that I've seen those lights," said Hsu, "I know we'll make it."

"See that white mist around Macao?" Fatty said. "That's the sea. I'm not as good a swimmer as the rest of you. I'm scared."

Longfellow asked me the time. It was 4 A.M. Past experience showed us that militia patrols seldom came this high, and there was no reason for local inhabitants to come this far—unless it was to have a look at Macao's bright lights. There was still time enough to make a little further progress before dawn came.

After a brief rest, during which I fell asleep, we began slithering downhill. It was quite a wrench to tear ourselves away from the first glimpse of Macao.

We didn't go far, for an hour later, from a fairly safe distance, we saw tiny dots in the valley below making for the scrub below us. These were villagers on their way to cut wood for fuel, and we looked for a suitable hiding place once more. We found a small hollow under a clump of bushes, and remained there all day, sweltering in the heat, while the woodcutters worked around us. By this time we were used to people moving near us in broad daylight, and scarcely felt afraid, except once, on hearing a woman's voice almost at my feet. "Look," the voice said, "a red plastic cup." "That's a lucky find," said another voice. "You'll be able to give it to your daughter." It was my cup, which I had forgotten to pick up after our dawn snack. Mok's coughing got worse, but luckily his worst bouts occurred when there was no one around to become suspicious. Far worse than the woodcutters' presence was the almost unendurable heat.

In the afternoon, the villagers all went down to the bottom of the valley with their bundles of wood, and it was quiet again. We were hungry, thirsty and tired. We unpacked our bags for our evening meal. There wasn't much left. I said, "I still have some money. Let's try and buy some food tomorrow." No one answered. We slept again, until it was pitch dark once more.

All too soon, we started on our march. We found a trail which skirted round the hill we were climbing, and Macao's lights came into view again. But after a long walk along the trail, we realized there was something wrong. We appeared to be walking away from Macao, for the lights were behind us now. We couldn't afford further delay. We all knew our food situation was desperate and it was obviously going to take us much longer than the five days we had bargained for. At last we decided to leave the trail, easy though it might be, and move south, cross-country. At least this way we knew we'd keep moving in the right direction. Over to our left, far away, were two isolated red lights, and Longfellow reassured us. "Those lights," he said, "are the entrance to Macao Harbor. We're all right. And this," he said, waving to the hill ahead of us, "is Pine Tree Mountain."

From the top of Pine Tree Mountain, we could see the lights

of Macao a little more distinctly, and we could even make out the moving headlamps of cars. But at the foot of the mountain, near where we had to cross in the valley below, there was an army barracks and several sentry posts. We could just make out the dim lights in the barracks, and the outline of a basketball court. If we failed to cross the valley before sunrise, we would be in trouble, for we would have to lay up during the whole of the next day and try again at night. And we just didn't have enough food to keep going. After a brief pause, to get our strength back, we drank some water and moved on.

It was a clear night, and stars winked at us from above. The slope we were on was so steep that we slid down it like children playing on a slide. To keep ourselves from crashing down, we held on to branches and hugged tree trunks. My palms were soon scratched and bleeding. Fatty swore as he ripped his trousers on a branch, and Mok gave a sharp cry when he slipped and crashed headlong into a tree. "Wait for me. I can't see any more," he hissed, and we had to guide him down because he had really had a nasty jolt. The side of his face was swollen, and his left eye was smarting and red.

Longfellow had warned us that the valley was patrolled by a unit at least one battalion strong. Fear gave us unsuspected added energy and we picked our way through the bushes and scrub with unaccustomed silence. But it was impossible to keep absolutely quiet and soon we heard dogs barking. We were in the sugarcane area now, and this, Longfellow whispered, was a good thing, for sugarcane fields made ideal hiding places— as long as one didn't get lost in them. From my own experience in a labor camp, I knew something about sugarcane. Besides the actual spreading of fertilizer, and the cane cutting itself, such fields were left untended. It gave me a perhaps illusory but valuable sense of security. We crossed a road, between two cane fields, and I ducked just in time, as a bicycle weaved its way along, almost knocking me down. The cyclist didn't see me. There was a girl on the pillion, hugging him close. They were talking softly, and the girl was giggling and laughing. Here were two people, I thought to myself, who had temporarily escaped from communal life. Almost certainly, they had slipped away from their respective dormitories.

It was nearly dawn again, and we came to a sizeable river. There was no bridge. Perhaps further down there was a ferry, but it was out of the question for us to use it. We looked like ghosts, caked with mud and dirt, scratched and weather-beaten. Longfellow had not warned us about the river, and perhaps he had forgotten about this unexpected hurdle. Ideally, we should retire to our hiding place for the day, for it was already light, but we realized to our horror that we were now in a fairly populated area. We appeared to be close to a village. Across the river, there were several small brick houses, with smoke coming out of their small chimney stacks. Inside, people were already cooking their morning meal. As we watched, a man came out of one of the houses and looked over the river straight at us.

We waited until he had gone indoors; then, barefoot, crawled carefully to the riverbank. In a large plastic bag which we had brought for the long swim on the final stage of our escape we put all our belongings, including my watch. As carefully as possible, we swam across, scrambled up the riverbank on the other side and plunged into the comparative security of a cane field on the other side of the row of houses. We knew that we were making a lot of noise as we plunged into the field in single file, Longfellow leading, but knew, too, that the deeper inside it we got, the safer we would be. We paused and our fears were confirmed. We heard dogs barking, and people shouting. They were probably used to catching escapers, so close to the frontier, and probably got rewards for doing so.

Huddled inside the cane field, we held a brief council of war. Fatty was exhausted, and could hardly speak. "If . . . we're . . . caught," he said, "say . . . we . . . don't . . . know . . . each . . . other." Mok shook him roughly, and he moaned. "I know we'll be caught, I know we'll be caught," he said over and over again.

Longfellow kicked him. "Listen, we've been seen. They may search the cane field. We'd better split up. We have a better chance that way."

Hsu didn't want to contradict Longfellow, but I could see he was unhappy at the idea. "If you want to go your own way," he said, "that's all right with me. Macao's very near. My wife and I will go on alone."

Mok rubbed his injured eye. "I'm a local man. At worst they'll only send me back to my village. I don't mind being caught too much." Then, as before, I was amazed at Mok's passive temperament, which contrasted so much with his physical force and bursts of energy.

They looked at me. I wanted Longfellow to stay with us, but decided to use another argument. Whispering to them, I explained that I had worked in cane fields before. This was not harvest time. There was no reason why anyone should come here during the day. In any case, I said, if the militia found us, we had no chance of escape. We were dog-tired. My advice: to rest up where we were, and trust that, even if they searched the cane field, no one would find us. "We're a needle in a haystack," I said. To my surprise, Longfellow agreed.

We then realized that in our mad scramble to get away from the riverbank, we had left our plastic container behind. If the villagers found it, we were really in trouble. Hsu volunteered to go back and get it. He came back grinning, holding it in both hands. He said that he had found it where we landed, and that the people in the little brick houses were going about their business in a normal, relaxed way. They didn't appear to be taking us very seriously, he said. We sat back in the stinking cane field, on a bed of ooze, chewing sugarcane contentedly.

CHAPTER XVI

ESCAPE (3)

WE DOZED OFF at intervals during the day. Mok was still complaining about his eye, and I bathed it. It looked bad. We brought out our food bundles again, and ate what we had left. Someone simply had to leave our hiding place and buy some more. Fatty said it was out of the question for him to go. His clothes were torn, and besides, he was afraid. Hsu couldn't go either: his uniform was in rags by now, and he had a four-day growth of beard. Even in a remote country area, where army men usually looked scruffy, he would have been an oddity. Longfellow finally said that Mok should go. He was from the area, spoke the local dialect, and looked like a young Kwangtung farmer.

Mok was in one of his energetic moods, and, despite the obvious dangers involved, he was delighted. "Boy, am I hungry," he said. "That sugarcane didn't help a bit." Before he left, we helped him clean up, scraped some mud off his clothes, and I gave him some money. I pulled out the ration cards I had bought on the black market. They were blanks, and Fatty filled in Mok's name, writing in clerkly script with a practiced hand. We reminded Mok of his story, and made him memorize the name of the relatives he would claim to be visiting if he was questioned.

For the next two hours I regretted having sent him on such a dangerous errand. Two hours later he returned carrying a large bag. He was beaming. He poured the contents onto a towel: a large piece of roast pork, apples, pears, some canned goose, cigarettes, cakes, bread, cough lozenges, some herbalist oil, a bottle of Chinese wine. As we ate greedily, Mok told us about his trip. The village was well stocked, he said, and the food stalls did good business. First thing he did was to stop at one of them and eat two bowls of noodles with pork. Then he went to the marketplace, bought some cigarettes and talked to some of the stall owners. He said he wanted to buy gifts for the relatives he was visiting. After buying the food for us, he didn't dare make himself conspicuous, so he did his best to slip away unnoticed. But he had had time to see that even in this tiny, peaceful village, there were political struggles going on, and the Red Guards appeared to be quite active. A man was being screamed at in the village square. From what the crowds were saying, Mok got the impression that he had been caught trying to escape to Macao, and was being given the Black Categories treatment before being handed over to the police.

The meal—our first real one in five days—made us confident, and when night came, we were no longer afraid of being picked up by the villagers. Even the fact that we had to swim across another river seemed of no consequence. We were used to the drill by now, and stored everything in our plastic sheet. Our clothes were wet, but our body heat soon dried them off.

We were in sugarcane country still, and the going was hard. We crossed a ditch, and Mok, full of strength again, carried me across it on his shoulders. Soon after, we came to the main Shihch'i-Macao highway, a sizeable steel bridge over a large river. We hid on the side of the road, for a searchlight, perhaps a mere lighthouse beam, lit up the bridge at regular intervals. It was un-guarded, Longfellow whispered. But one couldn't overlook the possibility of it being watched, from afar, by army outposts in the hills above. We lined up, ready to run across as soon as the beam had passed it. When Longfellow said "go," we clattered across, making an appalling noise. I remember thinking: if they bothered to guard the bridge, no one would ever escape.

Leaving the bridge, we half walked, half ran up a hill on the other side, until we were out of reach of the searchlight. The going was hard, but the hill, though slippery, was not steep. On the other side was a lush, rich valley with streams and terraced fields. We dared not stop here, for the farmers might be out at work very soon—it was getting light again—so we left the valley, and found ourselves walking up a slippery sand dune, with cutting grasses and some scrub. This might be our only place to spend the day, now that the sun was coming up fast. But it was going to be an exposed and dangerous place to rest, as well as terribly hot.

Longfellow found a clump of bushes with some shade, and was building our nest when he gave a sharp cry and pulled his hand away. He showed me his hand. There were two small marks where a snake had bitten him. It was swollen, and he immediately felt weak. He bit into the place where the snakebite was, with his teeth, sucked at the wound and spat. He lay down, ashen-faced under the dirt and grime, and I remember praying to myself that it wasn't serious, for without Longfellow, I knew, we would never make it. Longfellow said he'd be all right. There was nothing to do but rest and wait until the poison had worn off. It was a small snake, Longfellow said, and not a lethal one. I had another look at Mok's eye. He had a big purple bruise all around it, but could see better. It was not as serious as I had thought. At Fatty's request, I mended his trousers.

It was time to eat. We had five small moon cakes left, and the canned goose. Fatty had already opened the can, and was wolfing it down with his fingers. Longfellow stopped him. He handed me the can and told me to divide it. "Share and share alike," he said. With some tree twigs, I improvised a pair of chopsticks. Piece by piece, I fed everyone in turn. I gave Longfellow the best pieces because of his snakebite. I thought, as I shared out the food, that in less than a week I had got to know the four men with me better than anyone I had ever known before. Longfellow I called Uncle. He liked that. Mok was like a younger brother. They had all taken good care of me.

Only Fatty behaved badly. But he was not entirely to blame: he was used to a good life in Canton, and a soft one. "If I'd known it was going to be like this," he said over and over again, "I would have stayed at home."

I was strangely elated, despite the fact that I was often on the verge of collapse. The very fact that we had come this far, I thought, was proof that we were meant to succeed, and my cheerfulness may have affected the rest of the party. I felt embarrassed at the deferential way Longfellow and Mok treated Hsu and me; we were educated city people, and knew the world, they said. I pointed out that without Longfellow, our education would have got us nowhere.

With luck, this could be our last night's trekking, and we were impatient to move off. The thought that this might be our final day in China gave us additional energy. By now we were, if anything, overconfident. Shortly after starting out, for instance, we had to cross a paddy field. In the center of the field, there was a small watchman's hut, with a lit oil lamp at the entrance. It was impossible to avoid going past the hut.

We decided to walk boldly by. The hut, we felt, was too small to house more than one, or at most two, people. If they were old peasants, we might be able to buy some food from them, or at least talk our way out. In an emergency, I could even give them my gold ring as the price of silence. Many peasants, particularly the older ones, hated the party and its constant dragooning, so much that they would even go out of their way to help escapers, sometimes at considerable risk to themselves; I remembered a former fellow prisoner telling me how, in this same area, an old men had helped him on his way. We need not have worried. The hut was empty.

Now we were very near the coast indeed, and the going was mostly across marshes and small sand dunes. It was tiring. Longfellow was still seriously affected by his snakebite, and, giving my own heavier pack to Hsu, I carried his lighter one. For the first time, there was a moon—only a sliver of a crescent, but it reminded us that the escape had taken far longer than we had expected.

Eventually, we left the dunes and the marshland and come to a main road—perhaps the same main Macao highway—and we paused under cover before crossing it. As we waited to see that all was clear, someone grasped Hsu from behind.

"Don't be scared. We're escaping too."

There were three of them, all teen-age students. We couldn't see them very well in the dark, but kept quiet as they whispered their story. They were desperately hungry, they said, having eaten nothing but sweet potatoes they had stolen from the fields for the last two days. I brought out some of the dry cakes we had, and they gave us sweet potatoes in return. They wanted to tell us all about their adventures. Longfellow cut them short. Eight people together was madness, he said. We had to split up. The students agreed. "On the other side of the road," said their leader, "there's a village. Beyond the village, the sea. Tomorrow, we'll all meet in Macao."

The students decided to go first, skirting the village to the north. We would follow, on the south side. To our practiced ears, the students were making a great deal of noise, and we were glad they had left us.

We moved a little closer to the village, squatting beside the wall of a pigsty. Suddenly, from the other end of the village, there was a hideous noise: dogs barking, pigs squealing, people shouting, blowing whistles and running in all directions. There were cries of "There they are!" The students had been caught.

Longfellow didn't waste time. "Over you go," he said, pushing me over the wall. He instinctively knew we had a better chance of making it through the village now that the people there were occupied with the unfortunate students. "Keep running, but don't get lost." We did as he said. As we ran, we blundered into a peasant carrying a huge bundle of bamboos. He didn't show any surprise or yell. We were out of the village and its surrounding fields now. and we realized that the students had been wrong: we were near the coast but not all that near. Between the sea and us there was a smallish, black-looking hill. As we got nearer we saw that all along the base of the hill there was a continuous barbed wire fence, with pickets and thick thorns and brambles. We walked along it for a hundred yards, looking for a gap. There was none. Longfellow said it was not electrified, but that it was probably regularly patrolled.

Without wire cutters, getting through was almost impossible. Hsu went first, using a small knife to cut away as much of the thorns and brambles as he could. It took him at least half an hour to get through. We followed, one by one, almost as slowly, and when we emerged on the other side—having negotiated a concealed ditch —we were scratched and bleeding. We walked away from the wire fence, found a hiding place and, as the sun was coming up, decided to rest to regain our strength.

We were desperately hungry again, and no one could sleep. With a needle, I removed some of the deepest thorns from my palms, and then did so for everyone—Fatty had some deeply embedded in the soles of his feet. We held a small council of war. "We can't go on like this without food," Mok said. "Someone must buy some more." Mok was in one of his bad moods again. "I'm not going shopping again," he said. "If I'd known it was going to be like this," he said, copying Fatty's way of speaking, "I would have stayed at home."

Longfellow said, "I'd go, but I feel awful. Look." He showed me his hand, which was still badly swollen. Hsu wanted to go, but Longfellow wouldn't let him. "Look at you," he said. "They'd pick you up straight away." That left Fatty. For a while no one spoke. Longfellow said softly, "I know where we are now. There's a stone quarry at Tawentsun, about a mile away—with shops and food stalls there for the workers. It's easy enough."

Fatty got up. "Give me the money and the paper and I'll go and get the food." I gave him the last of my money, about twelve Chinese dollars, and all that was left of our ration cards I had bought on the black market. Longfellow gave him detailed directions, and last-minute advice. Fatty left, saying, that he would bring marvelous things back with him, a chicken maybe.

It had been a mistake to send him, I thought, he's just not up to this sort of thing. He'll either get lost, or lose his nerve, or just leave us and return to Canton. I had a strange feeling that we should never see him again.

All day long we waited for Fatty to return. At 5 P.M. we decided to wait another hour and at six we decided to wait till seven. My misgivings persisted. He was exhausted, and, at best, not very good at finding his way alone. He could have gotten lost. He had become increasingly disgruntled with the hardships of the trip. When he couldn't actually see the sea, he blamed Longfellow for getting us all lost; when he did see the sea, he grumbled that he was a bad swimmer, and that we would eventually get him drowned or leave him. For all his skill as a black marketeer, his morale was so low that he could very well have been arrested for not taking the necessary precautions—and there was always the possibility that at the last minute he had decided that the whole expedition was not worth it. Those ration cards were enough—if he sold them—to pay for his trip back to Canton and still have something to spare.

By seven we decided to move on. We had water, but only a few dry cakes that I had hoarded for a final emergency. I was light-headed and dizzy from hunger. The men found some breadfruit growing in a field and munched it. They gave me some, but, hungry as I was, I couldn't stand the bitter taste. It only made me thirstier. I gave my share to Mok, who munched happily.

We staggered up another hill, and I kept slipping and got to the top mostly on my hands and knees. Mok tried to help me but even his strength was gone—he, too, was faint from hunger. I was worrying about what would happen next. We could hear the roar of the sea, and knew we were very near the coast. I felt we would never have the strength to swim any distance at all, let alone the seven miles across the straits to Macao.

Even the sight of Macao's lights from the top of this last hill failed to give us strength. Yet they were now so near that we felt we could almost touch them. Having been to Macao before several times, as a child, I could point out the various landmarks to the rest of the group. "There's the Central Hotel," I told Longfellow, "where the casino is with a dance-hall and several restaurants." (I didn't know that during my stay in China it had stopped being a casino, and had lost much of its former appeal.) "There's the Avenida Almeida Ribeiro," I said. I prayed.

Mok noticed that I was praying. "If I really make it to Macao," he said, "I'll become a Catholic too." Longfellow and Hsu said they would as well. What followed could only be described as a minor miracle. Blundering along on all fours, I suddenly touched something. It was a large plastic bag of stodgy cooked rice, which some smugglers or escapees must have left behind. Looking further, I found a half-full can of condensed milk. We ate some of the rice, and took swigs at the can, rested a little and started our trek downwards towards the sea.

Even the few mouthfuls of stale rice we had eaten had given us badly needed strength and we all felt better. But we found that we had all underestimated the time it would take us to reach the point on the coast where we intended to start swimming towards Macao. For several hours, we cautiously edged our way downwards, over large rocks, avoiding the sheer drop of the cliffs and trying not to make too much noise. Halfway down, it began to get light again. Rather than risk being spotted by coastal guards, we decided to postpone our swim by a day and try to get our strength back. All that day, huddled together on a ledge, we rested and tried to sleep.

That early morning was full of hostile sounds. Dogs barked. I thought I heard footsteps around us, but it could have been stones dislodged by the wind. We could hear singing ("Sailing the seas depends upon the Great Helmsman," over and over again) coming from behind the hill to the west, where there must have been either a fishing village or a rural commune. No point in moving before sunset. Eventually, we found a small cave and sat in the shade, too excited to sleep. We talked about what we would do in Macao: Longfellow said he would continue peddling Tall Bamboo there, if only he could find the necessary ingredients, and would keep Mok with him as his assistant; Hsu and I didn't talk about the future at all. Just the prospect of reaching Macao was so overwhelming that I couldn't think any further.

Those were the longest hours of our whole trip—waiting for the sun to set so we could get down to the water's edge. Finally we set off, but Longfellow warned us to be especially careful, for it was common knowledge, he said, that troops patrolled this area constantly and those commune inhabitants who were sufficiently trusted to be allowed to live so near to Macao got good rewards for turning smugglers and escapers in to the authorities. We walked close to the commune from which we had heard singing emerging that morning. They were at it again, with the same songs. Walking along a narrow path, near the sea, for the pounding of the waves was louder than ever before, we hid from a patrol just in time. They had been making a good deal of noise, and Longfellow, whom we were watching carefully, dived into some bushes. We followed suit and hid. Three minutes later, twenty-three soldiers followed in a single file. Even after they passed, we decided to wait, and I was glad we did: ten minutes later, another patrol, seventeen men this time, clumped by in the opposite direction. The coastal guard was obviously being relieved.

At last, having waited a long, long time, we set off again and a few minutes later we were on the shore. We had spent too much time on the way hiding from the patrol and the new moon was now up. Its light was negligible, but we realized we had only a few minutes to get going again. We shared the rest of the cold rice and hid in the bushes what we decided to throw away. I wrapped my watch in a small plastic bag. From my pack I took out a dark blue cotton pullover. That, and my underwear, was all I wore. The men stripped down to their underpants. We left the rest of our clothes and our packs behind.

We hadn't expected anything like the waves which crashed over the rocks around us. Apprehensively, but keeping my fears to myself, I entered the water.

It was obvious within a few minutes that the tide was edging us, despite our efforts, far over to the right. This in itself was not disastrous, for the coastline ran along to the right, and we could, if exhausted, land at some point along it and then resume our swim. We swam for about an hour, but the going was appallingly hard. The tide was coming in, and almost without consciously changing our direction, we found ourselves, gasping, on a deserted beach. We had made some progress—a mile perhaps—but still had an immense way to go. The lights of Macao looked almost as distant as ever.

For the first time, Longfellow gave serious signs of exhaustion. He gasped for breath. "I don't think . . . I can go on," he whispered. We were on a highly exposed stretch of beach, and in full view of any army patrols that might come our way. I huddled next to him for warmth, and told him not to worry. The tide would turn. We had no clothes by now, of course, except those we were wearing, and Mok, shivering, made the most noise. His teeth chattered incessantly. Hsu, indefatigable, was in and out of the water, watching for a change in the tide. After about two hours, he shouted: "I think it'll be better now. Let's go."

Once more we entered the water and linked ourselves to one another with the plastic clothesline I had bought, it seemed years ago. This time we made good progress, and were soon far out to sea. Mok and Longfellow were surprisingly strong swimmers, and their natural pace was faster than Hsu's. Without saying anything, they untied the clothesline and were soon far ahead. I was angry that they should have left us alone in the water, but couldn't blame them too much. Perhaps they felt that they were dragging us along, and wanted to preserve their own strength. I shouted to them in the water once or twice to stay together, but they didn't hear or deliberately ignored me.

Hsu had not been bragging when he had told Longfellow that I was a strong swimmer. All my meager spare time in Canton, I had spent in the local swimming pool, and I never swam less than thirty or forty lengths at a stretch. For the last year, the official policy, handed down from Mao himself, had been to toughen up all the young people by urging them to go on long swimming expeditions and mountain hikes. I had taken part in some of the group marathon swimming competitions and had done well. I knew that I could keep going for at least seven miles. I had done so before.

But I had reckoned without Hsu. He was, if anything, a better swimmer than I, but an hour after our second takeoff he cried out: he had cramp in one leg. He was now a terrible burden. I had to help haul him along, and desperately urged him to keep going, faster. I was dragging a dead weight and was sobbing with fatigue and frustration, for I could see Macao's yellow lights and now could even make out the trees and lampposts on the main coastal road.

Some fishing junks went by and I stopped swimming. Treading water, I suggested to Hsu that we should yell for help. They would take us aboard and bring us into Macao the easy way. "And what if they're Communist junks?" Hsu said, struggling for breath. "It's too dangerous." I wanted to say that these junks were burning incense and small oil lights on deck, which meant that the people on board were practicing Buddhists and hardly likely to be dedicated Communists, but it was too tiring to argue. We plodded on, agonizingly slowly, and dozens of fishing junks sailed by us. It was now quite light, for we could see the fishermen clearly. No one saw us.

Infinitely slowly, we edged nearer and nearer Macao's waterfront. I had lost all sense of time, but it was now morning. There was traffic on the waterfront road. I could see a long jetty and a large, streamlined motor launch. This, I found out later, was the new Macao-Hongkong hydrofoil, but at the time I thought it might be some kind of navy vessel and swam west of it, to a spot a few hundred yards down where I remembered there had once been a filtered sea water swimming pool where I had often gone as a child. Gasping for breath and utterly worn out, I managed to climb the small iron ladder, rung by rung, which took one up to the swimming pool itself. I lay at the top, dazed and aware only that, at last, our journey was over. So tired was I, I forgot all about Hsu, who clung to the ladder below, and shouted for me to get him. Hauling him out of the water and up the ladder drained all the remaining strength I had. My arms and legs twitched. I lay at the side of the swimming pool, sick with exhaustion and indescribably happy.

Swimming pool attendants found us half an hour later. The owner was himself a former refugee, and his employees treated us like heroes. They gave us dry clothes, warm milk, bread and tea. We sat in deck chairs, being fed. We were too tired to speak. A Portuguese police car came and took us away. After a short drive, we found ourselves in a police headquarters, and there, grinning, were Longfellow and Mok.

All day in a daze we sat in a dark, dingy room being "processed." Our fingerprints were taken, and we were given temporary papers. We waited while the impersonal Portuguese officials went away for a three-hour lunch. Eventually the formalities were over, and we were taken to a refugee center on the outskirts of Macao. It was September 19, a day I shall never forget. None of us talked. I, for one, could not believe that we had succeeded. That night, before falling into a deep sleep, I told myself: we made it.

EDITOR'S NOTE

One of her last thoughts on that day was that now she must start a new life. This is what happened to the group:

Longfellow is back at his old trade—peddling Tall Bamboo in Macao's streets. He hasn't made a fortune, but he says it's a living, and he earns more money than he used to in China.

Mok did not join him. Shortly after escaping, he fell seriously ill, and was treated, for tuberculosis, ironically in Macao's leading Communist-run charity hospital. He is now cured, and has a job in a textile mill in Macao. Out of his small salary he tries to send something to his mother every month.

Hsu is in Macao, giving cello lessons and gradually building up quite a good clientele among Macao's music-conscious middle class. He is working hard, preparing for a concert recital to be held in Macao this year, to be given jointly with another refugee, a pianist. He hopes to get permission, eventually, to settle in Hongkong and marry Lai.

Lai, who was able to prove that she had once been a Hongkong resident, got her new identity card on the eve of Chinese New Year, and joined her family in Hongkong. She has a job painting scenery at a large movie studio, and hopes to resume her painting on a full-time basis.

The fate of Fatty is tragicomic: from letters which he managed to write and post undetected to Longfellow in Macao, we learned that his nerve failed him, and that he had deserted the group at the last minute. He was held by the police for a time on suspicion because he couldn't explain what he was doing so near the frontier, but thanks to his own cunning, and his connections, he was released.

Back in Canton he found himself, as a result of his escapade, under serious surveillance and unable to indulge in his black market activities on anything like his former scale. The last letter Longfellow had from him thanked him for sending some gold paper sheets he had earlier requested. Fatty described how he had turned his talents, temporarily, to satisfy a new demand. He used the sheets, he explained, to emboss carved wooden quotations of Chairman Mao, which he hawked on Canton's streets. There was, he said, a big demand for these and he makes a good living selling Mao quotations. The market was unlimited and his sales were restricted only by his rather small daily output. But how long, he asked, would this craze last?